The Harvard Medical School Guide to Healthy Eating for Kids

EAT, PLAY, AND BE HEALTHY

W. ALLAN WALKER, M.D.

WITH COURTNEY HUMPHRIES

McGraw·Hill

New York   Chicago   San Francisco   Lisbon   London   Madrid   Mexico City
Milan   New Delhi   San Juan   Seoul   Singapore   Sydney   Toronto

Library of Congress Cataloging-in-Publication Data

Walker, W. Allan.
    Eat, play, and be healthy : the Harvard Medical School guide to healthy eating for
kids / by W. Allan Walker ; foreword by Walter C. Willett.
       p.   cm.
    Includes bibliographical references and index.
    ISBN 0-07-144186-7
    1. Children—Nutrition—Popular works.   I. Title.

RJ206.W258   2005
618.92'39—dc22   2005000870

1 2 3 4 5 6 7 8 9 0   DOC/DOC   0 9 8 7 6 5

ISBN 0-07-144186-7

Illustrations on pages 12, 36, 55, 71, 80, and 148 by Patrick Scullin; figure on page 76 by
Raquel Schott.

McGraw-Hill books are available at special quantity discounts to use as premiums and
sales promotions, or for use in corporate training programs. For more information, please
write to the Director of Special Sales, Professional Publishing, McGraw-Hill, Two Penn
Plaza, New York, NY 10121-2298. Or contact your local bookstore.

The information contained in this book is intended to provide helpful and informative
material on the subject addressed. It is not intended to serve as a replacement for
professional medical advice. Any use of the information in this book is at the reader's
discretion. The author, publisher, and the President and Fellows of Harvard College
specifically disclaim any and all liability arising directly or indirectly from the use or
application of any information contained in this book. A health-care professional should
be consulted regarding your specific situation.

This book is printed on acid-free paper.

I dedicate this book to my grandchildren,
Douglas, Lena, and Giselle.

Contents

Foreword

When you become a parent, protecting your child and investing in his or her future becomes second nature. You look for a pediatrician with a great reputation, shop for the safest toys, and scout for the best school system. You probably also know that feeding your child well is important for growth and development. What you might not know is that what children eat today powerfully influences their health as adults.

Most likely when you were a kid, your parents taught you about eating from the four food groups. Treats were just that, treats. School cafeterias didn't offer "fast food." And you probably walked or rode your bike to school and had gym class several times a week. Things are very different today. As a population we eat more food overall, more refined and processed foods, and move less.

Today, nutrition is a science—not just a set of food groups. This book distills decades of research on childhood nutrition and tells you how to use that information to feed your child well. It will also tell you how to get and keep your kid moving. Whether your child has a ravenous appetite or is a finicky eater, whether she is tethered to computer games or he is a soccer fanatic, this book will help you keep your kid healthy—now and in the future.

What kids eat today, and their level of physical activity, is radically different than in the past. Research has shown that many kids are jeopardizing their future health, and usually neither they nor their parents know it. Why is this? What has happened to create this threat, and what can be done about it?

Human beings have been around for about a million years. For nearly all that time, our relationship with food was unchanged. Our ancestors ate what was available, when it was available, and did not wonder whether or not it was healthy. The main thing that they likely recognized as unhealthy was not eating.

With the development of agriculture and farming, human societies began to control the availability of food. As recently as one hundred years ago, most people in the United States raised their own food; nearly 90 percent of the population lived on farms. Meals were taken at the dining room table, or in the fields—not in restaurants, and not (for children) in and near school. Although the study of food was not yet a robust science, people understood what they were eating.

During the twentieth century, in the developed nations, what and where people ate changed dramatically. Increasingly, we bought food from a grocery store or in a restaurant, and much of it had been processed, mixed with synthetic chemicals, or precooked or frozen. A century ago we ate corn off the cob, picked hours before on our own land. Today, we eat corn chips manufactured many weeks before in another state. At the turn of the twentieth century, people also were much more physically active than they are today. Farming was demanding physical work. Even people who lived in cities engaged in physically taxing work. And we walked a whole lot more.

In short, in the twentieth century, what we put on the dining room table, where we ate, and our levels of physical activity changed profoundly. If you think of the million-year history of humankind as being represented by a twenty-four-hour day, then the twentieth century occupied about the last ten seconds of that day. In other words, our species has made radical changes in nutrition and physical activity, very rapidly. That sort of sudden change was likely to have consequences, and it has.

However, until recently, we didn't recognize those consequences. The developments of the twentieth century seemed more good news than bad news. Unlike many of our ancestors, very few of us faced famine. Labor-saving devices, from the car to the washing machine, offered us newfound leisure time. Moreover, the state of our health seemed to be improving. Indeed, in developed nations life expectancy increased remarkably, from about fifty years to about eighty years. It was hard to imagine that we might actually be paying a price for our sudden change in lifestyle.

Over the past fifty years, a growing body of research has shed light on this apparent contradiction. We are living longer because many infectious diseases have been controlled by improved sanitation, immunization, antibiotics, and other drugs.

However, deaths from other diseases—among them heart disease, stroke, many cancers, and diabetes—have increased, largely because of the dramatic changes in our nutrition and physical activity. (See Figure 6.1 on page 88.)

You can't open a newspaper or watch the news without hearing that some foods are good for you, others are not, and that exercise is good for you. But how do you actually start to eat better and become more physically active? In today's fast-paced world we need practical strategies and achievable goals.

That is why I wrote the book *Eat, Drink, and Be Healthy: The Harvard Medical School Guide to Healthy Eating*, first published in 2001. In that book, I tried to summarize what solid scientific research has taught us about a healthy lifestyle—for adults.

In this book, *Eat, Play, and Be Healthy*, my colleague W. Allan Walker, M.D., the first Conrad Taff Professor of Nutrition and Professor of Pediatrics, as well as the director of the Division of Nutrition at Harvard Medical School, undertakes the same task—for kids. Dr. Walker, an internationally renowned expert, summarizes the results of nutritional research in children. Not surprisingly, many of the principles of healthy eating in adults also apply to children—but not all. As pediatricians are fond of saying, children are not simply little adults. They are growing, and that imposes a unique set of nutritional needs.

Their unique nutritional needs do not, however, protect kids from the same nutritional problems that we adults are experiencing. For example, more kids are overweight. The social penalties are great, and the health penalties are perhaps greater. Children are developing what used to be adult diseases, including type 2 diabetes and high cholesterol levels—problems that will dog them well into adulthood.

You can do something about that. Today. Dr. Walker not only describes what we know about healthy eating in young kids, but he presents a practical plan of action for both nutrition and exercise. It is a plan that kids—with their parents' help—can follow. Read this book, and work with your kids to protect their future.

Walter C. Willett, M.D.
Fredrick Stare Professor of Epidemiology and Nutrition and
    Chairman, Department of Nutrition
Harvard School of Public Health

Preface

I chose to train in pediatrics after medical school because I felt that providing the best medical care for infants and children could assure them of a better quality of life as adults. By knowing the early predictors of chronic diseases, I hoped to help prevent children from developing life-threatening diseases later in life. Prevention is one of the guiding principles for pediatricians caring for infants and young children. We now know that establishing healthy nutritional habits early in life can have an enormous impact on the development of cardiovascular disease and other health problems. It is therefore my intent in this book to translate the knowledge gained from clinical studies over the last two decades into a guide that is understandable and provides practical recommendations for nutrition from birth until eight years of life.

This book is a sequel to Dr. Walter Willett's book titled *Eat, Drink, and Be Healthy*, published in 2001 as part of a series of high-quality books about health from Harvard Health Publications. I will comment on how the Healthy Eating Pyramid that Dr. Willett introduced in that book applies to nutrition in infancy and childhood, and where the unique aspects of childhood nutrition differ from recommendations for adults. In addition, we have relied on nutrition policy statements issued by the Committee on Nutrition of the American Academy of Pediatrics, the most influential body for advising pediatricians on appropriate nutrition care for children, and their recently published *Pediatric Nutrition Handbook* to provide the most updated, accurate recommendations for establishing good nutrition in infants and children.

Unfortunately, the kind of epidemiologic data provided by Dr. Willett from the Nurses' Health Study dating back to the early 1970s is not yet available for children, because pediatric research often lags behind adult studies. However, that picture is finally beginning to change. Researchers are now analyzing data obtained more recently from the children of the Nurses' Health Study participants, and we should have important findings to report in the foreseeable future. The National Institute of Child Health and Human Development of the National Institutes of Health is establishing a large-scale database of newborn infants from various ethnic and racial backgrounds to help find predictors of adult-onset disease early in life. Through studies like these, we hope to find answers to questions such as how nutritional habits from birth to adolescence influence weight gain, and how they might predict a person's chance of being obese in adulthood. Until then, pediatric nutrition must rely on the evidence we have so far, and I hope to convey to parents the best and most current available knowledge.

My own interest in pediatric nutrition and the need for establishing healthy eating habits early in life stems from my undergraduate premedical days at a small midwestern liberal arts college, DePauw University. As a participant in a service project in my senior year, I worked with welfare agencies in Indianapolis to help prevent malnutrition and subsequent infection among inner-city children. This happened in the days before the National WIC and School Lunch Nutrition Programs offered federal support to nutritionally needy kids. My interest in childhood nutrition continued when, as a medical student at Washington University School of Medicine in St. Louis, Missouri, I delivered milk to inner-city kids in Chicago. As a resident and chief resident in pediatrics at the University of Minnesota teaching hospital in Minneapolis, Minnesota, I became interested in how the digestive system develops in babies and the role that nutrition plays in keeping them healthy. After my residency, I trained at Massachusetts General Hospital (MGH) in gastroenterology and nutrition and established the first Pediatric Gastroenterology and Nutrition Division at that hospital. In the early 1980s, I was asked to merge the two pediatric gastroenterology and nutrition programs at Harvard (based at the Children's Hospital Boston and the Massachusetts General Hospital for Children) into a combined training program for pediatricians. During the last twenty years, I've helped train many, if not most, of the pediatric nutritionists in academic centers throughout North America and Europe.

My interest in nutrition has also extended into scientific research. As a National Institutes of Health–funded investigator, I studied how nutrition influences the development of intestinal allergies and intestinal immune defenses against infections. As a result of this effort, I successfully competed for an NIH-funded Clinical Nutrition Research Center (one of seven centers funded in the United States), became the recipient of the first Chair in Nutrition at Harvard Medical School (Conrad Taff Professor of Nutrition), and began the Division of Nutrition at Harvard Medical School. This background and the division's commitment to public education has been the basis for writing a book that helps parents establish healthy nutrition habits for their children. It represents the ultimate attempt to bring preventative health care in pediatrics to the public.

We hope you find the guidelines in this book helpful for enabling your kids to eat a healthy diet from infancy on.

Acknowledgments

This book was conceived of as a sequel to the very successful guide to healthy eating titled *Eat, Drink, and Be Healthy*, by Walter Willett with P. J. Skerrett. I am grateful to Walter for recommending this book be written, and for suggesting me with Courtney Humphries as its authors. I am also grateful to Harvard Medical School for establishing a schoolwide Division of Nutrition in 1996 and asking me to be its first director. The intent of establishing this division was to give more visibility to nutrition as an important part of medicine and to organize the large but diffuse resources in nutrition at the medical school and its major teaching hospitals into a single coordinated entity. At the request of numerous graduating classes of the medical school, the Division of Nutrition was charged with bringing practical information about nutrition into the medical curriculum so that physicians would be more knowledgeable in the use of nutrition in medical practice.

In this book, we have carefully considered clinical studies that strongly suggest the recommendations made in the various chapters. Much of the published work comes from position papers written by the Committee on Nutrition of the American Academy of Pediatrics (AAP), the most influential advisory body on nutrition for practicing pediatricians in North America, as well as its recently published *Pediatric Nutrition Handbook*. Dr. Nancy Krebs, the chairman of this committee, has reviewed specific chapters of this book and provides an endorsement of their content and recommendations. I am grateful to Dr. Bill Sears, an expert in communicating medical advice to parents, and Dr. Ronald Kleinman, editor of the AAP nutrition handbook and former chairman of the AAP Committee on Nutrition, for their endorsements as to the importance of this book. They too have read selected chapters and support their message.

As this book was being written, we had several pediatric experts in nutrition and new mothers read the chapters for content and readability. I am grateful to Drs. Carine Lenders and Alison Hoppin, our experts for optimal weight for life programs at Children's Hospital Boston, Boston City Hospital, and the Massachusetts General Hospital for Children, respectively, for providing a review of the factual content of this book. We received input on the content and readability of the text from Dr. Kim Walker, a child psychologist and my daughter; Dr. Helen Delichatsios, an internist; and Dr. Annemarie Broderick, a pediatric gastroenterologist, all of whom are new mothers. Courtney Humphries, a gifted science writer, has helped to translate complex medical terms into a text understandable to parents. Sharon Collier, a well-known pediatric nutritionist who has run the Nutrition Service at Children's Hospital for more than a decade, has contributed to the text by reviewing chapters and providing practical dietary suggestions for the recipes in Chapter 12. This is particularly true of homemade weaning foods, healthy snacks for toddlers, and suggested homemade lunches for school-age children. I also wish to thank Lisa F. O'Gorman, a certified executive chef, for the practical recipes provided to parents wishing to make healthy meals and school lunches for their children. Dr. Chris Duggan also provided valuable advice. Dr. Tony Komaroff of Harvard Health Publications provided important support and encouragement in the development of this book, and Ms. Nancy Ferrari and Ms. Christine Junge assisted in many aspects of its production. I also would like to thank McGraw-Hill and executive editor Judith McCarthy for their help in editing and organizing this book.

As always, I am grateful to my wife, Dr. Ann Sattler, who is also a pediatrician, for her encouragement and support of my many activities in pediatric nutrition and to my children, Kim, Mike, Andy, and Meredith, and grandchildren, Douglas, Lena, and Giselle, for keeping me honest in my suggestions for practical approaches to developing healthy eating habits during childhood.

1

What Kids Eat and Why It Matters So Much

K ids today are growing up in a world of unprecedented variety in food choices.
An astounding array of foods from all over the world fills our supermarket
shelves, restaurants, and food courts. Ingredients that once seemed exotic are now
regular items in stores. New products are often designed to fulfill our desire for foods
that are, or seem, healthier. For instance, most stores now carry soy milk, fat-free
dairy products and desserts, exotic grains and whole-wheat pastas, organic produce,
veggie burgers, and tofu hot dogs—the list goes on and on.

But what is a healthy food, anyway? What makes one food better than another?
And more important, how can different foods be put together into a healthful diet
that is practical and affordable?

Even as health foods enjoy a growing market, it is apparent that many people
are confused about which type of diet is best and how they should be feeding their
children. Today, kids' diets are often overloaded with foods that are high in calories
but low in nutrients that growing bodies need. Overweight and obesity afflict twice
as many children as they did fifteen or twenty years ago. And growing evidence sug-

1

gests that many of the chronic diseases that affect adults, including diabetes, heart disease, and certain cancers, are rooted in lifestyle choices, including a poor diet and lack of exercise. If children today are to avoid the burden of disease from unhealthy lifestyles, parents need to make sure they are growing up with the habits and knowledge to help them make better choices as adults.

In 2001, my colleague at Harvard Walter C. Willett released a book called *Eat, Drink, and Be Healthy: The Harvard Medical School Guide to Healthy Eating*. It argued that current nutritional guidelines, as represented by the United States Department of Agriculture's (USDA) Food Guide Pyramid, were flawed. Willett instead put forth a newly redrawn pyramid based on years of extensive research, including findings from the large-scale Nurses' Health Study and the Health Professionals Follow-Up Study, which he directs. That book showed how current nutritional guidelines offer an overly simplified view of healthy eating. Instead, a healthy diet for adults should emphasize regular exercise and eating the right amount of food to prevent weight gain, eating whole grains and healthy fats from plant oils, limiting foods such as refined carbohydrates and unhealthy fats, eating plenty of fruits and vegetables, drinking alcohol in moderation, and taking a daily multivitamin for nutritional insurance.

The argument caught on. The cover of *Newsweek* questioned whether the USDA pyramid was sound, and countless articles in newspapers and magazines brought the flaws in the pyramid to the public's attention. The assault was so effective that the USDA is now in the process of reevaluating the pyramid. We have yet to see what its newest incarnation will be—whether the pyramid will better reflect decades of research, whether the image of the pyramid itself will be thrown out in favor of some new image or set of guidelines, or whether very little will change at all.

One of the lingering questions that many people had when reading *Eat, Drink, and Be Healthy* was how to apply the latest nutritional knowledge to children's diets. The guidelines that Dr. Willett puts forth are based on studies on adults, and their goal is to move people toward a diet that limits their risk of developing chronic disease. How do these findings translate to children's health and the goals of children's nutrition? What is the current state of knowledge about how children should eat? How should a family that is trying to eat more healthily adapt the family diet for children?

This book will help parents adopt a nutritional strategy that is best for the long-term health of their children. I will bring you up to date on the latest knowledge about how the foods children eat affect their health. Much of the advice in this book will echo the latest recommendations for a healthy adult diet. But I will also point out some important differences unique to kids. The choices you make are important from day one, and I will guide you through the unique nutritional needs of children in their first eight years of life.

In your baby's first months of life, the main choice that most parents make is whether to feed their baby breast milk or formula. And this choice is not a trivial one. I'll explain why an overwhelming consensus indicates that breast milk is best for babies. For parents who do use formula, I'll explain what goes into it and how to choose the best kind.

Once a baby is ready to start solid foods, the more complex choices begin. Which kinds of foods to feed, and how much? I will talk about how to begin children on a diet that meets their nutrient needs and sets good habits from the start.

The second year is a time of transition, when a growing toddler still has important needs but also begins to have more control over eating—and more likes and dislikes. We'll talk about feeding strategies for toddlers and how to establish good eating habits in this transitional stage.

The rest of this book will take a comprehensive look at nutrition for children aged two to eight, including:

- Why the emotional and social context of eating is so important, and how to establish healthy eating habits in children.
- Why physical activity and weight control early in life are necessary for children's long-term health.
- What are major components of food (carbohydrates, fats, and proteins) and how to choose the healthiest sources of them.
- Why kids today need to eat more whole fruits and vegetables, and how to incorporate these into meals and snacks.
- Why dietary supplements aren't a substitute for healthy foods, and when vitamin or mineral supplements are appropriate for particular stages of growth.
- Why beverages play such a big role in how healthy (or unhealthy) children's diets are and how to curb the excess calories that many kids get from drinks.
- How to recognize a healthy (and unhealthy) school lunch program.

Finally, I will provide recipes and meal plans for toddlers and children, as well as tips to help you find and prepare simple, healthy, and delicious foods for the whole family.

Kids Are Not Little Adults

One of the main premises of this book is that good nutrition for infants and children is not simply a scaled-down version of an adult diet. Children's bodies are smaller, of course, but they are also different in other ways. They are growing and developing, undergoing constant change, and they have different requirements from bodies that are already grown. The first priority of nutrition for children is to give kids foods that provide the elements they need to grow properly and thrive. Many of the basic principles for adult nutrition do apply to kids, but when differences arise it is usually because of the unique needs for growth.

Current research in children's nutrition supports many of the principles that now guide adult nutrition. Certain types of foods, for instance, have a positive effect on cardiovascular health, cancer prevention, and a healthy metabolism, no matter what your age. But the special needs for growth and development change the picture; infants and children have special needs for vitamins, minerals, fats, and protein, and these needs may change at different ages. For instance, some of the specific areas where my advice will differ from Dr. Willett's advice for adults are the following:

• *Meat and dairy.* Infants and children have special needs for protein during growth, and animal products are the most efficient sources of protein. I will put a greater emphasis on meat and dairy products for children, while helping you cut down on the harmful saturated fat that is found in these foods. Infants and toddlers younger than two years of age also have a greater need for the fats found in animal products, which is why the first two years are the only time children should consume whole milk instead of skim or low-fat milk.

• *Calcium.* Because children's bones are growing larger and stronger, you're setting a foundation for healthy bones for the rest of their lives. Their needs for calcium are higher, and I will argue that dairy products, for most kids, are a more important part of the diet than for adults.

• *Vitamins, minerals, and dietary supplements.* While many adults choose to take a daily multivitamin, infants and children have more specific needs for certain vitamins and minerals at particular stages of growth. I will talk about when specific supplements are a good idea for kids, but I will also argue that a daily multivitamin is no substitute for all the important nutrients found in a balanced diet.

It's important for parents today to educate themselves on the basics of good nutrition for their children, because most of the nutritional advice circulating in the public sphere is not designed for kids. The most common stories in the news are about weight loss and fad diets. Many people confuse diets that help people lose weight with diets that are best for health, and that can have disastrous consequences for children when parents limit important components of their diets based on an idea proposed by an adult weight-loss plan. And even legitimate books about nutrition and health for adults will not always translate exactly to the needs of children.

Many Kids Today Have a Diet That Is Out of Balance

People today have an enormous desire for information about nutrition. Nutrition news always garners the top headlines, discussion of the latest diet fad tops the list of conversation topics, and magazines and websites devoted to nutrition and health are always popular. But in the midst of all this concern, today's diet is in a crisis, and the effects of that crisis are increasingly seen in children.

Not long ago, the main concern of children's nutrition was making sure that kids had enough food to eat, that they were growing properly. Now, more and more we see the opposite; kids are eating too much, and the health problems they deal with are rooted in poor nutrition. Sadly, even when kids are getting enough or more than enough food, they can still suffer from malnutrition if those foods don't provide all the nutrients they need.

Not only has the amount of food that children eat increased, but the types of foods have shifted. People are buying more processed, ready-made foods and making fewer meals from scratch. A USDA survey that tracked how children's diets changed throughout the 1990s found that kids aged six to eleven are eating fewer traditional foods such as milk, bread, beef, pork, eggs, and vegetables like peas and green beans. And they are consuming more soft drinks, fruit drinks, fried potatoes, grain products like chips and crackers, skim milk, cheese, and candy. In a list of top foods eaten by children and adolescents, the first fruit doesn't appear until number fourteen, as fruit juice, and no vegetable other than potatoes makes the top thirty.

What does this picture tell us? Parents have changed their children's eating habits to reflect recent nutritional guidelines for reducing saturated fat by cutting back on whole milk and limiting meat. But what has replaced these foods? Sugary beverages have taken the place of milk, a trend that has been associated with a higher caloric intake and excessive weight gain in kids. And more of children's diets are filled with snack foods that are low in nutrients. This trend demonstrates some of the confusions surrounding good nutrition. If parents reduce the amount of meat their children eat—and with it an excellent source of protein, iron, zinc, and several vitamins—but don't replace it with something nutritious, they can do more harm than good.

The problem is that our ideas about nutrition are often piecemeal, a guideline here and a guideline there. We get the message that certain foods are "good" while others are "bad." But we miss the more important idea of how different kinds of foods work together to make a healthy diet.

What Children Eat Now Affects Their Health Later

From the day children are born (and even before that, while developing in their mother's womb), nutrition matters. In my upcoming book *Eating Right for Baby* I'll explain how good nutrition in pregnancy can give children a healthy start. Giving children a healthy diet now is important not only for their needs during this time of growth and change, but also for its impact on their later health in a few important ways.

Children's Eating Habits Carry into Adulthood

The focus of adult nutrition is often to convince people to change their eating habits to keep themselves healthier. This is easier said than done! How many of us have wished, at some time or another, that we could cut back on sweets or curb our appetite for rich foods, only to see our good intentions topple in the face of tempting treats? We are creatures of habit. The choices that parents make in feeding infants and young children will help establish tastes, preferences, and habits that will carry into adolescence and adulthood.

You have the chance to set in motion a pattern of healthy eating that will follow your child into later life, to perhaps prevent the difficult task of having to change to a healthy diet once poor eating habits have set in. Throughout this book, I will emphasize the importance of healthy eating habits—from the first foods you feed your infant. Here are some of the important factors parents should consider:

- Exposing children to a wide variety of healthy foods from the start will help them develop broader tastes and a preference for natural flavors, as opposed to overly sweet, salty, processed foods.
- Setting aside regular meal and snack times will help discourage idle snacking that can lead to overeating, and also helps young children learn social aspects of eating.
- Teaching children about food and nutrition will help them gain a personal investment in their own health and positive attitudes toward good foods.
- Paying attention to portion size of foods and beverages and encouraging children to stop when they've had enough are critical strategies for raising healthy children in our current environment, where food is everywhere and overeating is all too easy.

Many Lifestyle Diseases Have Their Roots in Childhood

We never thought of childhood as a time to be concerned about long-term health. You didn't have to start thinking about eating right to stay healthy until you got older, right? Well, that picture is starting to change. Two diseases that are causing increasing health problems in our population—obesity and diabetes—now are surfacing more and more in young kids. And as we track the roots of cardiovascular disease, we see that early warning signs like high cholesterol levels, high blood pressure, and atherosclerosis also begin early in life. It makes sense if you think about it: our bodies are very good at keeping their systems running smoothly, so when something goes awry, like a clogged artery or the loss of sensitivity to insulin that develops in diabetes, it's not just a freak occurrence. Instead, these signs of disease take years to develop, and they are the result of the body gradually losing the ability to maintain its health under abnormal conditions.

Overweight children tend to become overweight adults. And the child whose poor diet leads to clogged arteries, high cholesterol, or resistance to insulin moves into adulthood already burdened with early signs of chronic disease that are very difficult to reverse. It's critical that parents take steps early to make sure these health problems never develop. While some people are more genetically susceptible to certain diseases than others, these problems are often triggered by poor diet and little physical activity. We will talk about how to keep track of children's height and weight to make sure they are not gaining too much weight as they grow. And we will look at ways to get children used to a healthier lifestyle that is active and includes a good diet, as an important step to help prevent disease.

The Life Course Approach to Disease Prevention

The realization that childhood habits have lifelong effects on health demands a new approach to health. Some of my colleagues advocate what they call the "life course" approach to thinking about chronic diseases. According to this view, disease prevention is something we must think about at all stages in life, especially at early stages when the body is developing and individuals begin to adopt patterns of

 How Do We Know What We Know?

Where do we get our knowledge about raising and feeding kids? We may get advice from our parents and other relatives, from friends, from the newspaper or TV, or from books and magazines. We may even have ideas about the "right" way to do things and have no idea where they came from. But how do these ideas fare under the lens of scientific studies?

Building enough scientific evidence to support one way of doing things over another is difficult. It often requires multiple studies and many years of research. This aspect of nutritional science can be frustrating, especially when each study in a slowly accumulating body of evidence is reported in the news as if it were the final word. First we hear that fat is bad for us, and then we find out only certain fats are unhealthy. Or one article might talk about the dangers of caffeine, and a few months later we hear that caffeine might actually help prevent certain diseases. Many people are left feeling that nutrition is a mass of contradictions.

In fact, what's really at odds is the interests of the public and the interests of researchers. Most people would like to know, in very straightforward and simple terms, what's good and what's bad, what's healthy and what's not. Every day we make decisions about what to eat; we don't have time to wait for ten more years of data before making those choices. Researchers, on the other hand, are cautious. They don't want to come to conclusions that may be false, and they are skeptical about claims that have not been carefully scrutinized. The end result is that people's need for answers always outpaces the rate at which answers can be found.

Studying how foods affect health is a tricky business. Only after studying large numbers of people over long periods of time do discernible patterns in nutrition and health emerge.

behavior. In order to better prevent disease, we start at its very roots. That's why this book starts at the beginning of life, before nutritional problems develop.

I don't intend to imply that every wrong move you make as a parent will doom your child to poor health. It's not as extreme as that. Instead, I'm urging parents to take their children's health seriously and to look at this time in their lives as an opportunity to give them a healthy start. Parents often become concerned about their children's health only when they reach adolescence and teen years, when suddenly their kids are eating poorly, becoming overweight or eating too little, or just generally confused about good nutrition. I would argue that paying attention to nutrition in the first eight years of life is a preventive measure for avoiding problems later.

Large-scale studies on adults, like the Nurses' Health Study, the Health Professionals Follow-Up Study, and the Framingham Heart Study, which involve tens of thousands of people over decades of time, have made crucial inroads in our knowledge about adult nutrition and health. Unfortunately, information specific to children's nutrition is even harder to come by, simply because it's harder to do rigorous, well-designed studies using children as subjects. Only recently have large, publicly funded cohorts been developed for studying children's nutrition, and we will have to wait several years before these new studies yield results on par with the information we have on adults.

There are other hurdles to studying children as well. Many studies of nutrition patterns are performed by giving subjects surveys about their food intake. When infants or very young children are the subjects, we often rely on their parents to tell us what they ate. Or researchers develop simplified ways of answering questions, such as pointing to drawings that indicate a food or portion size. Both methods bring a certain level of uncertainty.

Our knowledge about children's nutrition, then, is a work in progress. My goal is to give you, as much as possible, advice about nutrition that is based on the best available evidence. I won't claim to know the final word on every topic, and in fact I'll be frank when research on a particular question is unclear or still being debated. It's beyond the scope of this book to detail every study and every finding that has gone into building our current nutritional guidelines, and sometimes I will simplify these debates to offer you clear advice to put into practice. But I believe it's important to give you a sense of how we know what we know, rather than just a simple list of dos and don'ts.

Parents Can Set the Stage for Better Health

Parenting is a process of slowly losing control. From the first day that children enter day care or school until the day they leave your home to start life on their own, you can only hope that the habits and knowledge you've instilled in them help them stay happy, safe, and healthy as they gain independence. Having seen four children off to college, I know that they may rebel a little but will often return to the habits and values they learned growing up. In fact, my oldest son is now giving the same advice to his younger brother that I once gave to him.

In this book, I give you the basic knowledge you need to understand how to make healthier choices for your children. I realize that feeding kids is never a simple matter of following guidelines. As much as we would like to have complete control over our children's nutrition, their own ideas and opinions intervene. So I will also offer tips and tricks for helping you put those principles into practice, including ways to make healthy foods appealing to children. I will also offer ideas for incorporating more healthy choices into a busy lifestyle.

Parents have an enormous influence over their children's eating habits, perhaps more than they realize. As an illustration, one study conducted several years ago asked about fifty young children to choose a meal from a variety of foods. A second time, the children were told their parents were monitoring their food choices, and finally the parents were present as children made their choices. Having their parents watch them or thinking they were being watched was enough to make children choose more nutritious foods and eat fewer calories.

Of course, you can't always be present when your children eat, especially as they get older. But your influence will be felt. From day one, it's not just a matter of what you feed them; your attitudes about food, your approach to eating, and the lifestyle you follow all make an impression on your children. I believe that, with a little care and effort, starting kids early on a diet filled with healthy foods is within anyone's reach.

2

Nutrition for Young Infants and Babies

In the first few months of your child's life, you don't yet have to worry about choosing the right balance of foods, pleasing a picky eater, or finding snacks that are quick but healthy. Let's face it; nutrition would be easier to figure out if we all ate the same thing day after day like newborns do. But even though babies have only two options—breast milk or formula—the past few decades of research have shown us that this choice is an important one that can affect a baby's health now and later in life.

Conventional wisdom has always focused on *how much* babies get. Are they feeding enough? Are they growing fast enough? While growth is the most obvious sign of health, it's equally important to look at the *quality* of the nutrition babies are getting. In terms of quality, human milk is best for babies.

After sinking to an all-time low in the 1970s, breast-feeding rates are climbing: in 2001, rates of breast-feeding reached their highest levels yet, with nearly 70 percent of mothers initiating breast-feeding, and one-third continuing for six months. Breast-feeding is experiencing a renaissance thanks to a greater awareness of all the benefits of breast milk and efforts to make breast-feeding acceptable and encouraged in the workplace.

Breast-feeding is not an option for everyone. Choosing a feeding strategy for your baby is a complex decision, and I can't tell mothers which choice is right for them. But I can share some of the research that has accumulated lately on the myriad health benefits of breast milk. What we have found is that nature knows best: the more we study breast milk, the more we find that it has remarkable properties that are exquisitely matched to what babies need to grow and thrive. Taken together, these findings show that when mothers are able and willing to breast-feed, they are making a positive impact on the health of their babies.

Breast Milk Is Different from Formula

Companies that make infant formula are always advertising the latest nutrient they have added to make their products more like human milk. It's true that commercial formulas have made vast improvements since they were first introduced at the beginning of the 1900s. But they are based on science less than a century old. If you think of human milk as a formula that has been under development for many thousands of years, it's no surprise that nature still far outpaces science in producing a food precisely tuned to what a baby needs.

Most infant formulas are derived from cow's milk. It may seem like an obvious point, but the needs of human babies are completely different from those of calves. The cow's milk is then carefully modified to be more like human milk—but it is still just an approximation. Formula is often seen as an exact substitute for breast milk: it looks like milk, babies like it, and they grow normally when feeding on it. Both fluids have the same rough composition—water, lipids, carbohydrates, proteins, and some vitamins and minerals. But the similarity begins to fade when we look more closely. While formula and breast milk provide the same basic categories of nutrients, the type of nutrient differs somewhat, and these differences can affect the infant's development and overall health. A quick look at the basic nutritional differences between human milk and formula will help you understand why the details are important.

Different Proteins

Formula, whether based on cow's milk or soy, has a different mix of proteins than human milk, though the overall amount of protein is similar. Remember Little Miss Muffet eating curds and whey? Whey is the watery stuff that separates from clotted milk, and it is also the primary source of protein in human milk. About 70 percent of human milk is in the form of whey, while 30 percent consists of the "curds," a family of proteins called *casein*.

While cow's milk is naturally low in whey, most commercial formulas now come with a ratio of whey to casein that simulates the levels in human milk. However, the whey used in formulas is still derived from cow's milk, so the exact proteins it contains are not the same as in human milk. The whey in human breast milk contains several important proteins that are not found in cow's milk, including lactoferrin and immunoglobulins, which help keep a baby from getting infections. The proteins of human milk are also made of the amino acids that babies specifically need, making it a more efficient delivery system of protein. Formula-fed infants excrete more protein in their urine, which suggests that they are getting too much protein or are not able to use the protein from formula as well.

Different Carbohydrates

You may have heard about the importance of different types of carbohydrates in terms of adult nutrition. Much current research has focused on the way that refined, easily digested carbohydrates can send blood sugar levels spiking faster than carbohydrates that are digested more slowly. The resulting surge in insulin levels can leave you hungrier sooner, and may contribute to insulin resistance—a characteristic of diabetes—over time. The main carbohydrate in most formulas is lactose, a simple, easily digested sugar. Besides lactose, human breast milk also contains a large proportion of carbohydrates called oligosaccharides, which are more complex and slower to digest.

Still, you might wonder whether any of this applies to babies—after all, these are little feeding machines that seem to need all the energy they can get to grow, not adults worried about weight loss and diabetes. Beyond the effect on blood sugar, the type of carbohydrate your baby gets is actually very important for a special reason.

When you digest food, you are not doing the job alone: a whole staff of bacteria in your intestines is doing much of the work for you. In fact, there are more bacteria in the human digestive system than there are cells in the body—a strange thought if you don't usually consider yourself home to an entire community of life. These "good" bacteria are different from the infectious bacteria that sometimes give us gastrointestinal problems. They have developed alongside humans in a mutually beneficial relationship—we give them a place to stay, and they work for us.

The carbohydrates in a baby's digestive system help control which kinds of bacteria eventually take root there. The large oligosaccharides of human milk don't get completely digested in the upper intestine; instead, they end up in the colon, where they provide an attractive home for fermenting bacteria that are beneficial to a baby's health. Slower-digested carbohydrates are also the reason why breast-fed babies often have looser, fuller stools, and why constipation is a common and sometimes chronic problem among formula-fed infants. It's also why parents of breast-fed children are pleasantly surprised when their baby produces nearly odorless stools, and why weaning them onto solid foods can abruptly end this pleasantness.

Different Fats

Fats are the main source of energy for babies, and also play an important physiological role in brain development and building and maintaining cells. Human milk is made of roughly equal portions of unsaturated and saturated fats, though the proportion of different kinds of fats varies according to the types of fats in the mother's own diet. The fat in cow's milk is mostly saturated, so infant formula is reconstituted with unsaturated fats from plant oils to improve the ratio.

Human milk is also naturally high in polyunsaturated fats such as omega-3 fatty acids, as long as the mother eats a diet that includes sources of these fats. They are good for adults, but they are especially important for developing babies, because they are a component of the substance that insulates developing nerve cells, and they also help control inflammation. Formula companies have recently begun adding these kinds of fats to their products to keep in step with human milk. However, just as with proteins, the exact mix of fats is never quite the same. Human milk also comes with an enzyme called *lipase* that actually helps the process of digesting fat—it breaks down fat molecules in the baby's digestive system so they can be more easily absorbed.

Cholesterol levels are surprisingly high in human milk. Naturally, formula companies are reluctant to add cholesterol to their products to mimic breast milk, given that it has been seen as a nutritional pariah for years now. We don't know exactly what the cholesterol in human milk is doing, though it is thought that this early dose in infancy may actually help prepare babies for processing cholesterol later in life. We do know that it has no negative effect on later health—in fact, a recent meta-analysis of studies that looked at infant feeding and blood cholesterol level found that adults who were breast-fed as infants had slightly lower cholesterol levels than those who were formula-fed, even though breast-fed infants have slightly higher cholesterol levels at the time they are feeding.

Breast-Feeding Provides Safe, Economical, Ideal Nutrition

Breast milk is the one example of perfect human nutrition we have, so it's probably a good sign for nutritionists that breast milk contains many of the important elements we have come to recognize are good for overall health: a healthy level of usable protein, slowly digested carbohydrates, and polyunsaturated fats.

Mothers do everything they can to care for their baby's needs. Breast milk is really a biological extension of this maternal care; it is amazingly tuned to the needs of a growing baby. Human milk actually changes its composition over time according to the nutritional demands of the baby—it even varies from hour to hour. Colostrum, milk from the first few days after birth, is rich in protein, including specific proteins that help protect against infection. As the protein needs of the baby lessen in later weeks and months, the protein content of the milk decreases, while levels of fat increase. Formulas are designed to feed the fastest-growing infant in their particular age group, and much of the time babies may be getting more than they need.

Nursing during the first few weeks of a baby's life is especially important because the early milk is loaded with nutrition and ingredients that help the immune system, so mothers who can't nurse for very long are still helping their baby's health. For those who are able to continue nursing, breast milk can usually provide all the energy and nutrients a baby needs for at least the first four months of life. One of the reasons some mothers switch to formula is the worry that their babies aren't getting enough energy—after all, it's hard to imagine that everything a rapidly growing infant needs can be provided by something made by your own body. The marketing of formulas only encourages this idea; many now position themselves as supplemental nutrition for older infants and toddlers. But in this case it's better to trust nature over science; mothers do indeed have everything they need to nurse.

Breast-Feeding Reduces the Risk of Childhood Infections

Breast milk is much more than perfect nutrition for your baby; it can actually reduce the risk of some childhood infections because of special ingredients that help an

What's Good for Baby Is Good for Mom, Too

Did you know that breast-feeding is the healthiest choice for mothers as well as for babies? Nursing is a natural process that helps complete the cycle of pregnancy and birth. Here are a few of the positive effects on a mother's health that come with nursing:

- **Helps you recover faster.** When a baby nurses within an hour of delivery, the suckling stimulates a hormone in the mother that contracts the uterus and reduces bleeding, allowing the uterus to return to its normal size more quickly.

- **Helps you lose weight.** Nursing takes energy—about 500 calories a day, to be exact. When breast-feeding, your body is working overtime and will return to its pre-pregnancy weight more rapidly and without reducing the amount you eat.

- **Helps you feel better.** Nursing releases hormones that stimulate a feeling of well-being in mothers.

- **Costs less.** Buying formula, bottles, and nipples adds up to thousands of dollars per year. As a new parent, you could think of better ways to spend that money.

- **Lowers your cancer risk.** Women who breast-feed have lower incidences of breast, uterine, and ovarian cancers. Lactation lowers estrogen levels in the body, and lifetime exposure to estrogen is a risk factor for these cancers. The longer you nurse, the more the benefit.

- **Lowers your risk of osteoporosis.** Breast-feeding increases bone density, reducing the risk of osteoporosis and fractures in older women who have breast-fed.

infant's immune system. The protective effects of breast milk are more apparent in developing countries where the threat of childhood infection is more serious. But even in regions that have low rates of infectious disease, the overall effects of a healthy immune system are still an important reason to breast-feed.

Babies are not born with fully functioning immune systems. They lack some of the key elements needed to fight off infections. Through laboratory research, we have discovered that breast milk provides a good many of these elements, essentially complementing the areas where the baby is lacking. The content of breast milk changes over time; early milk has a higher concentration of protective factors than mature milk. Human milk even contains active, live white blood cells that can directly attack foreign invaders, which just shows that breast milk is a living substance, not simply food.

The primary immunity booster in breast milk is a molecule called immunoglobulin A (IgA), an antibody that is found in the body's secretions—saliva, tears, mucus, and breast milk—and on surfaces like those that line our respiratory, urinary, genital, and digestive tracts. These surfaces act as gates between the inside of our bodies and the outside world. As such, they are major entry points for infectious bacteria and viruses.

IgA molecules line these walls like palace guards—they keep foreign invaders from attaching to our cells and causing an infection. Infants have very low levels of IgA, leaving them vulnerable to infections. Human milk contains a concentrated amount of IgA, which can help boost the security at the gates of the baby's digestive tract.

In addition to the general protective effects of IgA, human milk contains specific antibodies for foreign invaders that the mother has been exposed to. Immunity is necessarily a product of our environment: it is crucial to our survival that we can adapt the weapons we have to fight the invaders that live around us. By giving the baby specific antibodies from its mother, breast milk helps prepare babies for the invaders that are lurking in the mother's—and therefore baby's—surroundings. It is like a test prep course for all the immune challenges the baby is likely to face.

Though the presence of antibodies in breast milk is well-known, an amazing number of other immunity-boosting proteins and chemicals have been discovered as well, and only some of these have been fully studied. More than just providing passive protection from factors in the mother's immune system, breast milk contains chemical signals that actively encourage the baby's immune system to develop more rapidly.

Breast-Feeding Helps Establish a Healthy Digestive System

In addition to the ingredients in breast milk that directly promote a healthy immune system, specific proteins and carbohydrates in human milk help establish a healthy digestive system that is guarded from gastrointestinal illness and infection. As I mentioned before, one of the critical benefits of breast-feeding is that it encourages good bacteria to thrive in the baby's digestive tract. When babies are born, they move from the sterile world of the womb to a world filled with microorganisms. During and after birth, bacteria quickly settle into this new home.

Which types of bacteria eventually flourish in the digestive tract can have an effect on the baby's overall digestive health. Good bacteria help our digestive systems function properly, and they also compete for territory with bad bacteria, keeping us safe from potentially harmful infections. In addition to encouraging good bacteria to grow, breast milk discourages bad bacteria from setting up camp in a baby's digestive tract, because certain proteins in breast milk can trap the food that these bad bugs feed on.

The main thrust of my research over the past twenty years has been to study the subtle interplay between human infants and the bacteria that live in their digestive tracts. We have been realizing more and more that bacteria play an indispensable role in overall digestive health. I believe the early establishment of a healthy digestive system is one of the most important effects that breast milk has, and it is yet another reason why those early feedings are especially important.

Breast-Feeding Reduces the Risk of Some Allergic Diseases

Allergy is like a security system gone haywire—instead of keeping out dangerous intruders, the body's immune system attacks harmless entrants. That is why everyday particles in the environment such as pollen, certain food proteins, or molds can work some people's immune systems into a tizzy of aggressive responses that include inflammation and congestion or worse. It is estimated that one-third of all people in the United States suffer from some kind of allergy. Asthma is an allergic condition in which the airways become chronically inflamed. Asthma attacks are the most common reason for a hospital visit in the United States, and the prevalence of asthma in the Western world has doubled in the past twenty years.

With all the investigation into the factors of breast milk that help fight infections, many researchers have been looking at its effect on allergy as well. There seems to be a strong genetic basis for allergy—children of allergic parents are more likely to suffer from allergies—so it has been difficult to single out the environmental factors, like breast milk consumption, that may also have a role. There is good evidence that breast milk is protective against some types of allergic disorders including eczema, in which the skin is prone to itchy and painful rashes. Several epidemiological studies suggest that breast-feeding for six to twelve months offers some protection against other allergies, an important benefit for infants who have allergy-prone parents.

Breast milk also helps reduce the risk of food allergies, like the dangerous reactions to wheat gluten that people with celiac disease suffer from. Human milk contains fewer elements that might stimulate allergies than any other food, and it even has ingredients that help reduce allergic reactions. On the other hand, cow's milk, which is the basis of most formulas, is a primary food allergen that many newborns cannot tolerate well.

The flip side of this is that proteins from foods that tend to provoke allergies, like peanuts, do occasionally make their way into breast milk and lead to food allergies in a baby. The effect is more common in mothers who have severe food allergies, so these women should get some advice from their doctors about nursing. Women suffering from acute attacks of asthma or allergies should also consult a doctor before breast-feeding, since inflammatory chemicals from their bodies could potentially make their way into their breast milk.

Breast-Feeding May Reduce the Risk of Obesity in Later Life

Children being overweight has become one of the top concerns of parents and pediatricians; 15 percent of children in the United States are overweight and the rates are increasing (see Chapter 6). Many of these problems stem from a society that makes getting fatter easier than staying thin: watching TV and playing video games have replaced active play, physical education programs are becoming a rarity in schools, and cheap, unhealthy food tempts kids everywhere they look. It is a complex problem with many causes, but evidence in the past few years has suggested that breast-feeding may have an early role in reducing a child's risk of becoming obese.

Several studies have suggested that infants who are formula-fed are more likely to become obese later in life. A study of fifteen thousand children of participants in the Nurses' Health Study II at Harvard found that children who were mostly or exclusively breast-fed for the first six months of life had a lower risk of being overweight than children who were mostly or exclusively fed formula. The risk of overweight was lower among children who had been breast-fed longer.

These findings are far from conclusive, and it will take several studies to tease out the precise role that breast-feeding plays in the chorus of factors that contribute to obesity. However, establishing good feeding habits may be part of the equation, since the process of breast-feeding is quite different from bottle-feeding. An infant who breast-feeds tends to take what it needs and then stop feeding. Studies have shown that babies who feed from a bottle tend to take in more calories, perhaps because parents feel they should finish the whole bottle regardless of hunger. There may also be something about human milk that triggers hormones or other chemical signals in the body that prevent weight gain.

Breast-Feeding Has a Positive Effect on the Brain

A baby's brain doubles in size in the first year of life. But the development of the brain is much more than adding bulk—nerve cells are laying down the circuitry that helps the baby learn and remember all the information about the world that is flooding in and develop the motor skills needed to execute increasingly complex feats of athleticism.

The first study to compare cognitive development in breast-fed babies versus formula-fed babies, conducted in 1929, found that breast-fed infants had slightly higher IQ scores. Since then, several other studies have also found differences in IQ. Many people have been critical of these findings because, on average, mothers who breast-feed have some of the same traits that correlate with higher IQ—such as higher socioeconomic level and better education—and it's hard to rule out these factors even with statistical tricks that adjust for different variables.

However, a 1999 meta-analysis of twenty such studies found an overall increase of 3.16 IQ points in breast-fed infants versus formula-fed infants after adjusting for potential confounding variables. And there was a greater difference in IQ among infants who had been breast-fed for longer periods of time. This offers the best evidence that the cognitive benefits of breast-feeding are real.

However, three points is a small difference, and should in no way suggest that formula-fed babies are not as smart as their breast-fed peers or are developmentally impaired. These findings do suggest that there may be an underlying mechanism at work, something in breast milk that is helping the infant's developing nervous system, just as it boosts the immune system. A lot of research has been done in the past five years on factors in human milk, such as certain polyunsaturated fats, that promote better brain development. However, there may be other simpler reasons why breast-feeding is good for the brain. One important benefit of nursing is the close human interaction a baby gains from breast-feeding, which can be an important factor for behavioral development. The comfort and warmth of breast-feeding provide emotional nurturing that bottle-feeding can't.

Breast Milk Is Insurance for Your Baby's Health

Human milk is like a helping hand from Mom. Some of its beneficial elements can even make up for deficiencies in an infant's health that may not show up immediately. An example of this effect is a deficiency in thyroid hormone. Infants who are unable to produce thyroid hormone develop a kind of mental retardation called cretinism, because the hormone is critical to brain development during this initial period of rapid growth. The problem is greatly lessened in breast-fed babies, because

 Do Better Fats Build Better Brains?

Formulas are constantly adding new substances that have been identified by research to be important components of breast milk—which is great news for parents who formula-feed. The problem is that the resulting press releases and advertisements can give parents the idea that science has finally found the perfect substitute for breast-feeding. The latest ingredient to enter the limelight is a group of fats called long-chain polyunsaturated fatty acids (LCPU-FAs), specifically DHA and AA. DHA is a source of omega-3 fatty acids, and AA is a source of omega-6 fatty acids; both of these substances have generated a lot of interest in the past few years for their role in cognitive function and immune health.

Formulas have recently added LCPUFAs under FDA approval, and there have been some reports that formula-fed infants supplemented with DHA do better on cognitive tests than infants without it. It is certainly a good idea to add these fats to formula to match the levels found in human milk. But we have not yet determined which factors in human milk are responsible for its beneficial effects on brain development; LCPUFAs may play a role, but so may other factors. It's too premature to say that formula with LCPUFAs will do everything that breast milk does for a baby's development.

the circulating thyroid hormone from their mother's milk can correct the imbalance during this vital window of time.

This is a very rare example, but one that illustrates how breast-feeding is great insurance for a baby's health. In many ways, breast milk is like an extension of the umbilical cord—it continues to offer a level of maternal protection to ease the baby's transition into the world.

Choosing the Feeding Strategy That's Right for You

Exclusive breast-feeding—meaning no use of supplementary formulas—is the best choice for a baby's health. In light of all the benefits we have discovered in breast milk, and all the others we may not even know about, doctors agree that mothers should be strongly encouraged to breast-feed if they can. Most professional pediatrics groups and national and international medical organizations have developed guidelines that strongly encourage exclusive breast-feeding for one year.

However, the purpose of these recommendations is not to give mothers unreachable goals that discourage them from nursing at all. If you are a working mother who can't take the time to breast-feed for a whole year, you shouldn't automatically turn to using formula exclusively. Breast-feeding is not an all-or-nothing decision. It's more like insurance: a lot is best, but a little goes a long way. I would urge any mother who is able to breast-feed to give it a try as soon as she gives birth, especially since that early milk is particularly rich in factors that boost a baby's health.

Some women find it difficult or painful to breast-feed. The fact is, not every woman and her baby fit together naturally like an idealized image of mother and child. Successful breast-feeding takes some effort and may require instruction. New mothers who want to breast-feed should inform hospital staff of their decision and ask for help, and they can also consult a lactation specialist to help overcome any problems. It is best to avoid bottle-feeding during the first month to ensure that your baby gets used to nursing from the breast. Working mothers can express milk at work using a breast pump and store it for later feedings. A wealth of information is available for nursing moms, and support groups around the country can help you nurse successfully. See the Selected Resources section for a list of resources on breast-feeding.

Fathers and other family members can make life easier for a breast-feeding mother by offering support, keeping her comfortable while nursing, and helping her find time in a busy schedule to nurse.

Nursing Mothers Need Good Nutrition

Breast-feeding is designed to provide nutrition to your baby without you having to put much thought into it. Nature favors the baby during pregnancy and lactation, and even women whose own health and nourishment are in jeopardy manage to nurse adequately. However, the quality of breast milk does reflect the diet of the mother. We know that some of the ingredients in milk vary according to what the mother eats. When a mother eats a diet high in unsaturated fats, more unsaturated fat will be in her milk; when she eats a diet high in unhealthy trans fats, these will also show up in greater quantities. Levels of some vitamins and minerals are also affected by the mother's diet. In general, it's best for a nursing woman to follow the same basic dietary precautions as when she was pregnant. Caffeine and alcohol should be limited because they do show up in breast milk and have been shown to affect infants' behavior.

Lactating moms are still eating for two, though to a lesser extent than when pregnant. You should plan on eating about 500 extra calories, including 20 extra grams of protein, beyond what you were used to eating before pregnancy—about what you'd get from one cup of plain, low-fat yogurt or a small turkey sandwich. If you are worried about losing weight after your pregnancy, keep in mind that any weight loss should be gradual; you won't have to restrict calories severely because nursing will burn many of them for you.

It's also important to keep calcium and phosphorus levels particularly high—1,200 milligrams per day of each—or else those minerals could be leached from your bones, leading to osteoporosis. Drinking three eight-ounce glasses of low-fat or skim milk a day provides 24 grams of protein, an extra 300 to 400 calories, as well as most of the calcium and phosphorus you need, as does eating three or four servings of dairy products like cheese or yogurt. Phosphorus is also abundant in protein-rich foods like fish, meat, legumes, and nuts. If you don't consume much dairy, calcium becomes a little scarcer, but it can be found in tofu, broccoli, leafy green vegetables, and fish, such as salmon and mackerel. Talk with your doctor to make sure your diet is adequate, and if not, a calcium supplement made from calcium carbonate may also be necessary to make up for a low dairy consumption.

Special Diets

Women on special diets should consult their doctor to make sure they are getting the balanced nutrition they need to breast-feed. Vegetarians are particularly vulnerable to vitamin B_{12} deficiency, because this vitamin is not found in plant sources

Your Diet, Your Baby's Tummy

Occasionally, the foods you eat while nursing might affect your baby's digestive system. Every baby gets gassy, but some may experience gas or intestinal discomfort in response to something their mother eats. Colic, a condition characterized by long crying spells and irritability, can sometimes be eased by cutting back on cow's milk in the mother's diet. It is usually fine to still eat some dairy products, such as yogurt and cheese, especially in small portions. But drinking lactose-free milk won't help, because the proteins in cow's milk can cause sensitivity and allergic reactions, not the lactose. While there are many theories about which foods in a mother's diet may cause gas in nursing babies, there is no evidence that any particular food should be avoided. Some mothers find that cutting back foods that give them gas or discomfort also alleviates the problems in their babies. Try modifying your diet, and if the problem persists, contact your pediatrician for advice.

of protein. In 2001, the Centers for Disease Control and Prevention issued a warning regarding two cases of vitamin B_{12} deficiency in infants who were breast-fed by vegetarian mothers. These babies had serious developmental delays, which could be only partially corrected by later supplementation with vitamin B_{12}. Any nursing mom who is vegetarian or vegan should take a B_{12} supplement, and should review her diet with her doctor to see if she needs to make additional adjustments.

Vitamin D Supplements for Infants

There is always some debate in the medical community about whether breast-fed infants truly get enough vitamins, minerals, and other nutrients from nursing. In most cases, if a mother has a good diet, her milk won't lack anything her baby needs. The exception is vitamin D. Unlike other vitamins that are found in foods, vitamin D is found in very few places in the diet, and is very low in human milk as well. Instead, we make vitamin D in our skin when exposed to sunlight. But many babies don't spend much time directly in the sun, nor should they without adequate skin protection and sunscreen. The American Academy of Pediatrics recently issued a statement recommending that all children, from birth through adolescence, take a vitamin D supplement, at a dosage of 200 international units (IU) per day. For

Foods with Nutrients That Moms Need

The following vitamins and minerals are most frequently in short supply in the diets of breast-feeding mothers. Fortunately, they are available in a variety of great-tasting foods:

NUTRIENT	FOOD SOURCES
Calcium	Milk, cheese, yogurt, and other dairy products; tofu processed with calcium sulfate; bok choy; broccoli; kale; collard, mustard, and turnip greens; and breads made with milk
Zinc	Meat, poultry, seafood, eggs, seeds, legumes, yogurt, some whole grains
Magnesium	Widely found in small amounts in many foods, including nuts, seeds, legumes, whole grains, green vegetables, scallops, and oysters
Vitamin B_6	Bananas, poultry, meat, fish, potatoes, sweet potatoes, spinach, prunes, watermelon, some legumes, fortified cereals, and nuts
Thiamin	Found in many foods, including pork, fish, meats made of organs, whole grains, legumes, corn, peas, seeds, nuts, and fortified cereal grains
Folate	Leafy vegetables, fruit, liver, green beans, fortified and whole-grain cereals, and legumes

breast-fed babies, vitamin D drops are the best method of supplementation. Formula-fed babies can get this level from drinking at least 500 milliliters (17 ounces) per day of formula, if it is fortified with vitamin D. Once they are weaned onto foods and their intake of formula drops below this amount, they should begin getting supplements, too.

A Few Supplements for Mom, to Be Safe

A balanced diet usually provides all the nutrients a lactating mom needs. But there are a few dietary supplements that all breast-feeding mothers should consider taking:

• *Iron.* Iron deficiency anemia is the most common nutritional disease in infants. Human milk is rather low in iron, though breast-fed infants are better able to absorb the iron they do get. All breast-feeding women should take an iron supplement to ensure that their milk does not have below-average levels.

• *Omega-3 fatty acids.* Omega-3 fatty acids found in fish have been shown to aid development of the nervous system, reduce inflammation, and may even help babies sleep. Fish is one of the best sources of omega-3 fatty acids, but women who are pregnant or breast-feeding may not want to eat a lot of fish because of concerns of mercury toxicity in some varieties. An easy, cheap alternative is to take a daily fish oil pill.

A daily multivitamin that includes iron and a fish oil supplement will help complement a balanced diet to make up for any potential vitamin deficiencies.

Can a Woman Take Medications While Breast-Feeding?

In most situations, the answer to that question is yes. Unlike herbal supplements, most prescription drugs and over-the-counter medications that are approved by your doctor have been better tested for potentially harmful effects. While many medications do make their way into breast milk, they are often in such small quantities that it is not harmful to the infant. In most situations, the benefits of the medication to the mother's health and the benefits of breast-feeding for the baby's health outweigh the risks of exposure to medication. However, there are some important exceptions (see Table 2.1) and mothers should review all medications with their doctors, including medicines bought over the counter, vitamins, and dietary supplements.

There are some classes of drugs, such as antidepressants and painkillers, where a safer alternative exists among several options. Keep in mind that the precise effects

Table 2.1 Drugs and Breast-Feeding

DRUG CATEGORY	DRUGS THAT ARE CONTRAINDICATED OR SHOULD BE TAKEN WITH CAUTION	DRUGS OF CHOICE WITHIN CATEGORY
Analgesic drugs or painkillers	Meperidine (Demerol), oxycodone (OxyContin, Percocet, Percodan)	Acetaminophen (Tylenol), ibuprofen (Advil), flurbiprofen, ketorolac (Toradol), mefenamic acid (Ponstel), sumatriptan (Imitrex)
Antiarthritis drugs	Gold salts, methotrexate (Rheumatrex), high-dose aspirin	
Anticoagulant drugs	Phenindione	Warfarin (Coumadin), acenocoumarol, heparin (Hep-Lock)
Antidepressant drugs	Fluoxetine (Prozac), doxepin (Sinequan), lithium (Eskalith)—use with caution	Sertraline (Zoloft), tricyclic antidepressants
Antiepileptic drugs	Phenobarbital (Arco-Lase, Donnatal), ethosuximide (Zarontin), primidone (Myidone, Mysoline)	Carbamazepine (Carbatrol, Tegretol), phenytoin (Dilantin), valproic acid (Depakene)
Antimicrobial drugs	Chloramphenicol (Chloromycetin), tetracycline (Helidac, Sumycin)	Penicillins, cephalosporins, aminoglycosides, macrolides

DRUG CATEGORY	DRUGS THAT ARE CONTRAINDICATED OR SHOULD BE TAKEN WITH CAUTION	DRUGS OF CHOICE WITHIN CATEGORY
Anticancer drugs	All anticancer drugs are considered too potent for breast-feeding women	
Cardiovascular and antihypertension drugs	Acebutolol, amiodarone (Cordarone, Pacerone), atenolol (Tenormin), nadolol (Corgard, Corzide), sotalol (Betapace)—use with caution	Beta-adrenergic antagonists (beta-blockers), propranolol (Inderal), and labetalol (Normodyne) are safe.
Endocrine drugs and hormones	Estrogens (Cenestin, Premarin, Ortho-Est, Estropipate), bromocriptine—may suppress milk production	Propylthiouracil, insulin (Humulin, Novolin, Humalog), levothyroxine (Levothroid, Levoxyl, Synthroid, Unithroid)
Immunosuppressant drugs	Cyclosporine (Gengraf, Neoral, Sandimmune), azathioprine (Imuran)—use with caution	
Respiratory drugs	Theophylline (Uniphyl, Theo-24, Theolair)	
Radioactive compounds	All require temporarily stopping breast-feeding	

The Dangers of Herbal Supplements

Just as in pregnancy, breast-feeding mothers should not take any alternative or herbal treatments that have not been strictly evaluated for potential harmful effects on a breast-feeding baby. Though herbal supplements like Saint-John's-wort, gingko biloba, kava kava, valerian root, and echinacea are often touted as "natural," this in no way means they are harmless. After all, cyanide, hemlock, and poison ivy are also found in nature, yet are toxic to humans. And what may be harmless for you might not be harmless for a developing baby.

Many of these herbal remedies are borrowed from cultures where they have been used medicinally for years. However, taken out of their cultural context, these substances are simply added haphazardly to vitamins, beverages, and snack foods by companies with no expertise in their proper use.

We know very little about how these substances—which are not regulated by the FDA like other drugs—affect adult bodies, much less those of infants and children. The FDA does keep a website that lists herbals that have been found to cause dangerous side effects (cfsan.fda.gov/~dms/ds-warn.html). But keep in mind that these are only the incidents we know of; just because a substance does not appear on the list doesn't mean that it's safe. Your doctor can also be a source of information, but some physicians may not be aware of herbal remedies.

In light of all the unknowns, it's a good idea for pregnant or lactating women to avoid herbal medications entirely. Be wary of any herbal tea, supplement, or snack that promises to treat a medical condition or alter mood. Stick to the basics when choosing a multivitamin—avoid "designer" vitamins that claim to relieve stress, keep you focused, or prevent memory loss. Be label-savvy: many manufacturers list herbal ingredients on their labels in the same format as other nutrients, but if there's no recommended daily allowance from the FDA, it may not be safe.

that many drugs have on breast-feeding babies are not entirely known, so if you're in the habit of using over-the-counter medications often for minor ailments, it may be worthwhile to reevaluate your need for these medicines while nursing.

Not surprisingly, illicit drugs such as amphetamines, cocaine, heroin, and marijuana rank high on the list of substances that should not be taken while breast-feeding. Methadone or buprenorphine, used to treat addiction, are usually safe and a much better option for women struggling with addiction. Women who quit smoking while pregnant should continue not to smoke—for their health as well as the baby's—but those who are unable to quit smoking should still breast-feed, because of the potential protective effects of breast milk against respiratory illnesses in babies.

Sources listed for breast-feeding in the Selected Resources section also offer further information on taking medications while nursing. But ultimately your doctor should be your source for the most up-to-date information about the safety of individual medications.

Table 2.1 lists some of the medications that can potentially harm a breast-feeding baby, as well as safer alternatives in some classes of drugs. Common brand names are listed in parentheses. This list is not an extensive one, and should in no way substitute for advice from your doctor, who should be aware of all medications and supplements that you are taking.

Choosing a Formula

While breast milk is the optimal food for babies, breast-feeding is not possible for every baby and for every family situation. Many women choose not to breast-feed, or limit nursing to a short period of time. Millions of babies have been raised on formula and have grown up to be perfectly healthy and happy adults. Abundant data suggest that formula-fed infants have no detectable developmental impairments. Formulas are getting better and better, and while they still lack many of the added benefits of breast milk, competition between formula companies provides an incentive for them to add anything they can to make their products better.

All formulas have to pass FDA approvals, and mandates about the kinds of nutrients they should have help standardize different formulas. Most formulas are fairly similar, but there are a few things to look for. The whey-to-casein ratio should be similar to human milk (70 percent whey to 30 percent casein). Formulas should also be supplemented with iron. Newer formulas have long-chain polyunsaturated fatty acids like DHA that are present in human milk and are probably beneficial to the baby's immune health and development.

Soy-Based Formulas

A formula based on cow's milk is the best option unless your baby has difficulty digesting lactose. There has been intense debate in the past few years on the potential health risks of soy formulas. With the benefits of soy being trumpeted in the media, it's no wonder that more and more parents are buying soy formulas under the assumption that if it's soy it must be healthy. Manufacturers of soy-based formula and a very powerful soybean industry in the United States have helped boost the use of soy-based formulas to one-quarter of the formula market.

Every mammal is first fed its mother's milk, so it is unusual for an infant to be raised on plant-based protein, which does not contain all the amino acids that mammals need. Most soy-based formulas are supplemented with the protein components they lack, and they provide the same overall nutrition as cow's milk–based formula. But soy has a couple of extra substances that have caused some concern. Soy contains phytates, which keep minerals such as calcium, phosphorus, iron, and zinc from being absorbed in the infant's digestive tract. Soy formulas should contain extra amounts of these minerals to help offset this problem.

Soy also comes with a dose of biologically active substances called *phytoestrogens*, which behave like weaker versions of the hormone estrogen in the human body. The effects of phytoestrogens in adults are still unclear, but there is some evidence that infants may be more sensitive to hormonal changes caused by phytoestrogens. In one study, adolescent girls who were fed soy formulas as infants reported heavier menstrual flow and increased discomfort with menstruation. This is the strongest reason why formulas derived from cow's milk are the best choice until more is known.

Soy milk formulated for adults, and other soy-based shakes and beverages, are not the same as soy-based infant formula. Infants should not be fed soy milk or any other adult beverage as a substitute for formula.

Hypoallergenic Formulas

On rare occasions, a baby will develop a food allergy to breast milk or conventional formulas. Signs of a food allergy include hives, runny nose, intestinal problems, breathing problems, and shock. A breast-feeding mother who suspects her baby may have a food allergy should first try to eliminate common allergens from her own diet: cow's milk, fish, eggs, peanuts, walnuts, pecans, and almonds. If the symptoms persist, hypoallergenic formulas are available that are able to help the vast majority of allergic babies.

The Bottom Line: A Simple Strategy for the First Months

- During this time of rapid growth and development, good nutrition is especially critical for babies. Breast milk is optimal nutrition for babies, especially very young ones. Breast-feeding is a positive step to take for your baby's health.

- Breast-feed during the crucial first weeks and you've already helped boost your baby's immune system and established good digestive health.

- If you can continue breast-feeding, do so. Nurse exclusively for four months before weaning. Continuing to nurse for a full year is optimal for your baby.

- What a mother eats can affect a nursing baby. Eating a balanced diet with a variety of foods should cover most of the nutrients you need. It's a good idea to take a multivitamin that provides extra vitamin D and iron while breast-feeding, and fish oil pills are also good insurance for the baby's development.

- Avoid taking herbal remedies while nursing. Consult your doctor about any medications you are taking.

- Parents who use formula can find a range of well-tested products to meet their baby's nutritional needs. A formula based on cow's milk is safest for most infants.

Human Milk Banks

Another alternative to formula feeding is human milk banks, which collect donor milk from lactating women and distribute it to babies whose mothers can't breast-feed. Banked milk is only available through a doctor's prescription, and usually is recommended for very premature infants, or infants who are allergic to formula or have special nutritional needs. Because of storage problems and concerns about HIV and other viruses being transmitted from donors, banked milk is often pasteurized and frozen, which deprives it of many of its immunological benefits. Because of this, it's probably not worth trying to use banked human milk unless recommended by a doctor.

3

Starting on Solid Foods

Those first few months of seemingly constant feedings are over. Now the real fun—and the real challenge—begins: it's time to introduce your baby to solid foods. Weaning is the name given to the transitional period in which infants are still feeding on liquids—either breast milk or infant formula—but are also being gradually introduced to solid foods, often called *complementary* foods because they complement the baby's liquid nutrition but do not replace it completely until the baby is at least a year old.

The process of weaning is subject to all the unique foibles and successes of any new task that children take on. Some babies will try a bite of infant cereal and get hooked; others will refuse anything but a nipple for weeks. Don't despair if your experience isn't the neat, orderly process you initially envisioned. The purpose of this chapter isn't to give you a foolproof system, but to arm you with the nutritional know-how to choose the right foods during weaning and to make sure your baby is eating and growing properly. We now know that infancy is a critical time for developing tastes and preferences that will last a lifetime. Use this opportunity to make your baby's first exposure to foods a fun and nutritious one.

When to Wean

A lot of research has focused on the timing of weaning. A slew of studies has examined whether early weaning or late weaning results in slower growth, a tendency toward obesity, nutrient deficiencies, or developmental problems. Though you might get a slightly different interpretation from different sources, the chorus of recommendations really matches quite closely and can be boiled down to this: between the ages of four and six months, most babies are ready to gradually accept solid foods into their diets, in addition to breast milk and/or formula.

What is so special about this time period? Most babies are ready to begin eating solids at the four- to six-month mark for a few reasons:

• *Developmental changes.* Newborns have the innate ability to suck and swallow; without this level of muscle coordination, they would not be able to take milk from their mothers. During the period between three and six months, infants' brains gain better control over swallowing, and the muscles in their mouths become more refined and coordinated. Now they are ready to explore the world with their mouths, as many of them do with a singular fascination, and they are developmentally ready to take on the challenge of eating more complex and solid foods.

• *Physical changes.* Babies are not born with the fully functioning organ systems of adults. Before four months, an infant's digestive system and kidneys can't handle the burden of processing different kinds of foods or taking on a heavy load of nutrients. By four months, the kidneys are prepared for a gradual introduction of new foods; by a baby's first birthday, the kidneys have doubled in size and are ready to manage a varied diet.

• *Nutritional need.* After a few months of feeding solely on breast milk or formula, a baby's needs outgrow the energy in these liquids, and growth may lag. But it's not only more calories that babies need—they can also become deficient in iron and zinc, two minerals that are absolutely critical to good health in developing bodies. Before babies are born, their mothers give them a bundle of iron and zinc that gets stored in their bodies. By a few months of age, these internal stores become depleted, and babies need to find these minerals in other foods. This issue is not so critical in infants fed with formulas, which are supplemented with iron and zinc, though these infants will still need to eat foods high in these minerals once weaning begins.

Why Not Feed Solids Before Four Months?

For parents, feeding a baby is not just about providing adequate calories—it's about giving nourishment and love, and seeing their baby develop new skills. Maybe we all want our children to be precocious, or maybe we simply don't trust liquids to provide everything our children need. Whatever the reason, surveys have shown

that a majority of parents in the United States and other countries choose to introduce solid foods earlier than four months, even though health authorities recommend waiting.

Though the precise age of weaning is by no means set in stone, parents shouldn't
feel rushed to push solid foods onto their babies before four months. For one, the
baby may simply not be ready for the challenge of eating nonliquid foods, and can
choke easily on the unfamiliar textures. For another, some evidence suggests that
babies who are fed solids too early may be getting too much food. Though parents
have traditionally viewed rapid growth as a sign of good health, these days we recognize that getting too big can put infants at risk for obesity later in life. Good eating habits should begin early in life, and infants shouldn't get in the habit of
consuming more calories than they need.

The First Feedings

Infant cereals are generally the best choice for the first feedings. They are easy for
babies to take, and are supplemented with iron and zinc, making them a great addition to breast milk or formula. You can first dilute the cereal with some breast milk
or formula to thin it out if needed, and gradually dilute it less and less. Feed solids
with a spoon (or even a fingertip to start), rather than mixing cereal in with formula and feeding with a bottle. The common myth that adding cereal to a baby's
bottle will help her sleep hasn't held up in studies, and the extra food only adds
unneeded calories.

One New Food at a Time

After beginning feedings with infant cereals, a good rule of thumb is to introduce
one new food at a time for a period of three to seven days before adding another.
Each new food should contain only one ingredient. This way, if your baby has an
allergic reaction to any particular food, you will be able to identify the culprit for
the allergy. You may want to wait longer between new foods if your family has a
history of food allergies. Watch for gastrointestinal upset (vomiting, diarrhea,
gas), wheezing, or skin rashes and flushing that appear soon after eating. If you
notice any of these symptoms, refrain from feeding the new food and contact a
pediatrician.

Feeding Solids Safely

Eating solid foods is a big adjustment for babies to make. Some foods are easy to inhale or choke on, especially hard foods and round shapes. The following foods should *not* be fed during a baby's first year, and even well beyond:

- Hot dogs

- Nuts

- Grapes

- Raisins

- Raw carrots

- Popcorn

- Rounded candies

Always mash or puree whole foods in a blender so that they don't have solid lumps that could be inhaled.

Foods can be served cold or warm, though conventional wisdom often argues for serving foods at body temperature (lukewarm) because babies sometimes reject foods that are too hot or cold. Just make sure foods are not so hot they will burn the baby's mouth. If you warm foods in the microwave, make sure you mix the food after it is heated and then test it, since some areas will heat faster than others.

Easy Does It

Don't worry if your baby is reluctant to feed; he may simply not be ready yet. Babies who are ready for the challenge of eating solids usually display an increasing amount of independence and motor control. They are better at holding themselves upright and keeping their heads steady when sitting up with the support of an infant seat. They will begin reaching for food with their hands or putting objects in their mouths. They may also show curiosity at watching you eat, following the spoon with their eyes or opening their mouths to imitate you taking a bite.

Babies who are ready for solids should readily accept a spoonful of food without pushing it out with their tongues. Never try to force a feeding. A baby just learning to accept solid foods won't be eating much at a time—at this point, solids are more of an experience than a significant source of calories. Each feeding only needs to be a spoonful or two at first, since it's not good for an infant to get in the habit of eating more than needed at a sitting.

Over time, infants increasingly gain better motor control and will be able to do more to feed themselves. From seven or eight months of age, babies are able to grasp objects like food with their fingers rather than their palms, gain better hand-eye coordination, and can begin to transfer things from one hand to the other. Parents can help further this development by exposing infants to spoon-feeding, teaching them to drink from a lidded cup with a spout (a "sippy" cup), and helping them feed themselves finger foods that are easily grasped.

Choose Foods with the Right Nutrients

There is no good evidence that specific foods need to be introduced to infants in any particular order. But it's important that the new foods contain nutrients that infants need. Weaning can be a nutritionally vulnerable time period. While breast milk and formula are designed to provide complete nutrition, adding variety to the diet leaves open the possibility that the new foods won't be nutritionally complete.

After cereals, the next important foods for weaning are pureed vegetables and fruits, which are rich in vitamins and minerals. Again, there's no need to try them in any particular order, but make sure you include a balance, rather than just feeding fruits or only one kind of vegetable. If you choose too many fruits over vegetables you may also miss the chance to accustom your child to the subtle flavors in vegetables, rather than quickly developing a taste for sweet foods. Vegetables with deep colors, like the green of broccoli or the rich orange of carrots and sweet potatoes, are always a good choice because they are loaded with vitamins like C and A. Keep adding new foods separately, one at a time, to help identify any food allergies.

Meat is also a great starter food, because it contains iron and zinc, as well as other vitamins and protein. Some parents are leery of meat because they have heeded the message of the health community to limit meat intake in their own diets; others are vegetarians because of religious or moral reasons. While vegetarian diets can be very healthy, those of us in pediatric medicine tend to discourage vegetarianism in infants and young children, simply because meat is such an efficient delivery system of important nutrients. If your baby does not eat meat, choose cereals and other baby foods that have iron and zinc added to them, and use citrus fruits in combination with green vegetables—the vitamin C will help make the iron in green vegetables more easily absorbed. And when in doubt, see your doctor to check for any potential deficiencies and consider using a supplement of iron and zinc, in the form of drops.

Other good sources of protein are cooked dried beans, tofu, eggs, and peanut butter, but with the exception of beans, these foods are common allergens, so use caution when first feeding them. Yogurt is also a great protein-rich starter food—plain or mixed with pureed fruit, but not sweetened. See Table 3.1 for foods that are high in specific nutrients.

Because you are introducing new foods slowly, a baby's diet will be somewhat limited in the first few weeks. But after you have introduced cereals, some vegetables and fruits, and protein-rich foods, and other grains, you will want to start feeding these foods in a balanced way every day. Starting infants on solids is like composing music. You begin with cereal as the bass line; vegetables and fruits enter like a rhythm section; protein sources form the melody. Eventually, all of these components should be playing together in harmony—this is what we call a balanced diet. See Table 3.2 near the end of this chapter for a feeding guide that will help you choose the right quantities and varieties of foods throughout the first year.

Start Good Habits Early

While you should introduce only one food at a time every few days, your ultimate goal is variety, which is not only the spice of life but also the key to good health. Some interesting studies looked at how kids develop tastes for different foods, and many of these indicate that eating habits start very early, in the first two years of life.

Yes, babies do have a taste for sweet things, perhaps because of the naturally sweet flavor of human milk. But with some encouragement, most babies can learn to accept lots of different kinds of food, and this willingness to explore is a great trait to develop for later health. Think of a baby as a captive audience—this may be the only time you feel in complete control of what your child eats. Use this

Table 3.1 Food Sources of Important Nutrients During Weaning

VITAMIN A	VITAMIN C	CALCIUM	IRON	ZINC
Asparagus	Asparagus	Yogurt	Fortified cereals	Fortified cereals
Broccoli	Broccoli	Broccoli	Cooked dried beans	Cooked dried beans
Cantaloupe	Cantaloupe	Herring	Red meats	Red meats
Green peppers	Green peppers	Grapefruit	Poultry, dark meat	Poultry, dark meat
Kale	Kale	Kale	Eggs	Eggs
Spinach	Spinach	Spinach	Dark leafy green vegetables	Yogurt
Tomatoes	Tomatoes	Cheese	Dried fruit	Peanut butter
Carrots	Oranges	Tuna	Liver	
Apricots	Potatoes			
Bananas	Strawberries			
Peaches	Tangerines			
Plums	Brussels sprouts			
Sweet potatoes	Cauliflower			
Winter squash				

opportunity to make fruits and vegetables a big part of the diet, and to develop a sense of adventure and a taste for new things.

Babies learn by modeling adult behavior. If weaning your baby turns out to be a messy or frustrating process, relax and stay patient. Try to keep feedings fun and model a positive attitude by eating new foods with a smile. The old game of the airplane coming in for a landing may seem silly, but these kinds of games not only help get that spoonful in but also send an important message. If feedings become a chore for both of you, your baby might learn to associate food with negative feelings.

Infants Are Not Little Adults

In the late 1970s, my colleagues and I at Children's Hospital in Boston began seeing young infants who had severe diarrhea that wasn't caused by an infection. With some questioning, we discovered that the parents—who were very health-conscious—were feeding their babies a low-fat diet, in the belief that what was good for adults was also good for young infants. This resulted in a diet that was heavy with carbohydrates and dangerously low in fats and proteins. Fat is not simply an inert substance that pads our bellies and thighs; it contains essential fatty acids that are necessary for life, especially for growing infants. There have also been cases of parents mistakenly feeding infants with soy milk, diet drinks, vegan diets low in protein, herbal remedies, and other trendy adult foods, sometimes with dangerous consequences. So when I talk about starting good habits early, I don't mean simply feeding babies and young children according to the latest adult health fad.

A baby's food should also not be prepared to suit an adult's taste. In the past, companies made baby foods that appealed to mothers, usually with added sweetness or flavoring. These days, most baby foods are plain and simple, with no extras, which is much better for infant nutrition. It may seem awfully bland to you, but babies have not yet developed our finicky palates and don't need all those additives for flavor. In fact, this is a great opportunity to get your child accustomed to eating foods in their natural state without all the fat, salt, and sugar we often crave. Whether making your own pureed foods or using special baby foods, choose plain foods with no extra flavors or seasoning, rather than foods made for you. And satisfy a baby's natural taste for sweet things with fruits, rather than the excessive sweetness of sugar.

Should I Make My Own Baby Foods?

We've all heard how eating too many processed foods can be costly for our health. Many health-conscious adults are now seeking natural, whole foods and shunning the high trans fats, salt, and sugar packed into ready-made foods. When these adults have babies, they naturally assume that better nutrition means making their own baby foods—right?

Well, for babies it's not so simple. Infant cereals, as well as some premade baby foods, contain nutrients such as iron and zinc that we know can be deficient in an infant's diet. These additives are actually beneficial, and can take some of the guesswork out of trying to provide all the vitamins and minerals babies need with other foods. And most good baby foods don't come with the added sugar or salt we typically associate with packaged foods.

Everyone should use specially prepared infant cereals, usually made from rice and barley, that are fortified with iron and zinc. However, buying jars of baby food can get expensive, and some parents simply like to prepare pureed foods themselves. If you decide to make your own baby foods, you may want to ask your doctor about giving your baby an iron and zinc supplement, in the form of drops, to replace all those extras that prepared foods carry. Also remember that baby foods are not the same as adult meals run through a blender. Parents who decide to make their own baby foods can have a tendency to serve high-carbohydrate foods that are easy to prepare and include too many of the additives found in adult meals. If you do make your own foods, recognize that it will take a little extra time and effort to prepare separate foods for your baby. Stick to the one-new-food-at-a-time rule, and emphasize protein, fruits, and vegetables rather than just cereals. Fresh or frozen pureed vegetables and fruits are better than canned, which often come with extra sugar and salt. See Chapter 12 for recipe ideas for weaning infants.

Juice in Moderation

Lots of parents like to feed infants juice, simply to keep them busy during the day or to give them something to sip before bedtime. However, even 100 percent juice is loaded with fruit sugars that can lead to tooth decay and cavities—sometimes called *nursing bottle syndrome* in young infants. Drinking lots of juice can overweigh the diet with carbohydrates, and excessive amounts lead to diarrhea. Juice is really a liquid food, just like formula, and parents shouldn't treat it like a substitute for water. Babies should be given juice in moderation or not at all. In fact, babies who are getting breast milk or formula generally don't need extra fluids, even water, even if they live in hot, dry climates.

While 100 percent juice has the advantage of providing vitamin C, babies should get this and other vitamins from pureed whole fruits. Don't feed any juice during the first six months, and for the second six months keep juice intake to four to six ounces a day or less. Use special infant juices or 100 percent juices—not sugar-laden juice drinks—and feed from a cup, not a bottle.

What About Dairy?

I began my medical training in the days when many mothers still fed babies cow's milk as a homemade formula. We would often see babies brought into the hospital with severe anemia from drinking cow's milk, because milk can irritate the lining of an infant's stomach and cause light bleeding, and it also interferes with the absorption of iron from other foods. The lactose in milk can be difficult to digest, and milk also contains too much protein per serving, which can damage an infant's developing kidneys. Nowadays, formulas made from cow's milk are modified so much that the damaging effects of milk on a young digestive system are prevented.

Babies should *never* drink cow's milk during their first year. A better alternative to milk is plain, unsweetened yogurt. The live bacteria in yogurt help digest the lactose in it, making it easier to digest than milk. And because yogurt is not a liq- · uid like milk, babies will eat less of it at a time. The same is true for other dairy products like mild cheeses; it's fine to serve cheese to infants during the weaning period, because they will only be eating small pieces at a time and will not be overwhelmed with lactose and protein the way they would by drinking milk.

Breast-Feeding or Bottle-Feeding During the Weaning Period

The solid foods that we introduce to babies are often called *complementary* foods because they are meant to complement the liquid nutrition that continues to provide the lion's share of calories at first, and then gradually becomes less a part of the diet. Breast-feeding is the best choice for a baby's health, even after weaning. In addition to all the benefits of breast milk we discussed in the previous chapter, a few studies have found that breast-fed infants have a lower risk of becoming overweight the longer they breast-feed.

Ideally, a mom should breast-feed for a full year while gradually introducing solid foods into the diet. But the reality of our society makes it difficult for some working women to continue breast-feeding for this length of time. There are options for moms—some offices have day care, or at least provide breast pumps and lactation rooms that allow you to express milk throughout the day and store it for later. If you are a working mother and want to keep breast-feeding, it's worth exploring these options. After all, the more mothers ask for these services, the better the situation will be.

If You Do Continue to Breast-Feed

If you breast-feed during the entire first year, the complementary foods you give to your baby should be solid foods rather than liquid formulas. During weaning, breast-fed infants will need extra sources of vitamin D (through supplements), and iron and zinc (through foods or supplements).

 Keep Tabs on Diet Outside the Home

One of the biggest struggles parents face is trying to ensure that their children get proper nutrition outside the home. Later in this book, we'll discuss school lunch programs and give you some tips on how to combat some of the unhealthful food choices that bombard kids daily as they get older. The struggle is not as difficult in infancy, but parents who use a day-care service may need to make an additional effort to keep tabs on what their baby eats throughout the day. Investigate what kinds of foods are provided at your day-care service—including how much food at a time—and make arrangements for different options if their choices aren't to your liking. A daily diet for an infant who has already conquered the task of eating solids should include a mix of fortified cereals, protein sources, fruits, and vegetables, plus breast milk or formula. Older infants may get small pieces of adult foods like bread, meats, fruit wedges, and cheese, but not sweets and salty snacks. A caregiver should never overfeed beyond what a baby demands or what is appropriate for her age and individual needs. See Table 3.2 near the end of this chapter for a suggested daily feeding guide with portion sizes.

If You Use an Infant Formula

Mothers who are unable to continue breast-feeding through the entire first year can switch to an infant formula in a bottle or a lidded cup with a spout. As detailed in the previous chapter, infant formulas are fairly standardized in their contents, but it's best to choose one based on cow's milk that contains added iron and zinc. Babies who show signs of allergy to formula or whose parents have a history of food allergies can be put on hypoallergenic formula.

Babies using infant formulas may not have as much need to eat solid foods before six months as breast-feeding infants do. Most infant formulas are supplemented with nutrients including vitamin D, iron, and zinc, and often provide more calories than breast-feeding. You can also continue to use these formulas for a year as well, or until your baby is ready to eat solids alone.

Other Liquids

Breast milk and formula both provide all the hydration a baby needs—no need for extra water or liquids. As mentioned in the previous chapter, cow's milk, soy milk, and other beverages do not substitute for infant formulas. In fact, there have been cases of infants developing severe nutritional problems when their well-educated, well-meaning parents fed them "health" drinks like soy or rice milk.

Supplements During Weaning

As mentioned in the previous chapter, children of all ages are at risk for vitamin D deficiencies, especially if they don't get regular sun exposure or eat a lot of fortified dairy products. The Committee on Nutrition of the American Academy of Pediatrics now recommends supplementing children with vitamin D from birth through adolescence. While your child's needs may vary later in life, infancy is an important time to use a vitamin D supplement, in drop form, since most babies don't see a lot of sun and should not be drinking cow's milk, which is usually fortified with vitamin D. Bottle-fed infants have less need for these supplements, since formulas already have vitamin D added. However, these infants should get supplements as they begin to consume less formula in later months.

Other supplements are not necessary for most infants, as long as they consume enough vitamins and minerals from a combination of breast milk or formula, fortified infant cereals, and a mix of fruits, vegetables, and protein sources as weaning foods. In general, supplements don't make up for a good diet (see Chapter 9 for more information). But if some nutrient is lacking during this crucial time in a child's development, it could have lasting effects on his or her health later in life. Consult your doctor if you have concerns about your baby's diet, and when in doubt, liquid vitamin and mineral supplements can help prevent deficiencies.

Growth Is an Indicator of Good Health

All children are different; they grow and develop at their own unique pace. While there's no need to worry about small variations, consulting a growth chart to see where your infant fits in with the rest of the crowd is a crude but useful indicator of health. For the most part, the height of the parents determines how big an infant is relative to other infants of the same age. But proper nutrition and good health also influence growth. (See Selected Resources section for growth charts.)

Why is proper growth so important? The course of the body's development—from a single cell in the womb to its fully grown adult form—follows a very specific plan that is guided by genes. But all the raw material needed to make the body grow doesn't come from nowhere; it depends on all the nutrients in food to provide the material it needs. Infancy is a time of laying the foundation for the adult body, like the foundation of a building. If something is missing during this critical time—a needed mineral, or an adequate supply of protein, for example—it may have lasting effects, just as a shaky foundation is difficult to fix once a house is complete.

Too little growth has always been an indicator of poor nutrition. Slow growth can impair the immune system, leaving a baby vulnerable to infection. It can also be a sign of zinc deficiency, which can result in cognitive impairments and other irreversible health impacts. Studies now have found that low birth weight and underweight at one year of age may be linked to a greater risk of developing heart disease later in life. Underweight infants may also be predisposed, paradoxically, to developing a greater amount of central fat later in life—a body type sometimes called an *apple* shape that carries a higher risk of diabetes and high blood pressure. The effect is even greater in infants who are born with a low birth weight but then grow very quickly.

Parents have always fretted over babies who don't grow fast enough. But in our society, the real problem is often too much weight, rather than too little. Children today are becoming overweight and obese at ever younger ages. This phenomenon

The Bottom Line: Making a Solid Transition

- Most babies are ready to start trying solid foods at four to six months of age. No need to rush a baby who isn't ready to begin trying more complex foods.

- Feed one new food at a time, starting with infant cereals and adding pureed vegetables, fruits, and protein sources. Continue breast-feeding if possible, or use an infant formula through the first year.

- New foods need to provide good nutrition during this critical period of growth. Infants particularly need iron and zinc through fortified foods, natural food sources, or supplements. Vitamin D supplements are also recommended for infants.

- It's never too early to model good eating habits by making mealtime fun, encouraging infants to develop new eating skills and try novel foods, and never forcing an infant to eat too much.

- Consult a growth chart as an indicator of good health and nutrition. If height and weight are disproportionate, talk to a pediatrician to see if your child's diet needs to be modified.

means that we must adjust what we think of as a healthy baby to include the risks of weighing too much. As anyone who has tried to lose weight knows, being overweight is one of the most intractable problems to change. Even determined adults who are informed about good nutrition and exercise find that losing weight and keeping it off is a superhuman effort; we certainly shouldn't expect obese children to have an easier time slimming down. That's why preventing kids from weighing too much, even as early as infancy, is one of the primary concerns of this book.

Babies have an enormous percentage of fat compared to a healthy person at any other age, and that's normal. But recent research suggests that babies who become too heavy for their height may be saddled with problems like obesity, diabetes, and high blood pressure later in life. A few studies have suggested that a higher body mass index (a ratio of weight to height) during infancy—often associated with formula feeding—may lead to an increased risk of becoming obese and developing diabetes later in life.

Table 3.2   Feeding Guide for Weaning in the First Year

FOODS	4–6 MONTHS	6–8 MONTHS	8–10 MONTHS	10–12 MONTHS
Breast milk or iron-fortified formula	Short, frequent feedings, 4–6 per day, or 30–32 ounces per day	3–5 feedings per day, or 30–32 ounces per day	On demand, or 3–5 feedings per day, or 30–32 ounces per day	On demand, or 3–4 feedings per day, or 24–30 ounces per day
Cereals and breads	Iron-fortified infant cereals, 2–5 tablespoons per day mixed with breast milk or formula	Iron-fortified infant cereals, 3–5 tablespoons per day	Infant cereals or other hot cereals, 5–8 tablespoons per day; small pieces of bagel, toast, or crackers	Hot or cold unsweetened cereals, ¼–½ cup per day; bread, rice, or pasta, ½ cup per day
Fruit juices	None	Infant juice or adult apple juice fortified with vitamin C, 2–4 ounces per day or less	All 100% juices, 2–6 ounces per day or less	All 100% juices, 2–6 ounces per day or less
Vegetables	None	Strained or mashed dark yellow, orange, and green vegetables, ½–1 two- to four-ounce jar, or ½ cup per day	Cooked, mashed fresh or frozen vegetables, ⅓–½ cup per day	Cooked vegetable pieces, ½ cup per day

FOODS	4–6 MONTHS	6–8 MONTHS	8–10 MONTHS	10–12 MONTHS
Fruits	None	Fresh, cooked mashed or strained fruits, ½–1 two- to four-ounce jar, or ⅓–½ cup per day	Peeled, mashed fruit or soft fruit wedges, ⅓–½ cup per day	All fresh fruits, peeled and seeded, ½ cup per day
Protein	None	Plain yogurt (can be mixed with fruit or applesauce), pureed meats, 3–4 tablespoons per day	Lean meat, chicken, fish (strained or in small tender pieces), egg yolk, yogurt, mild cheeses, cooked dried beans, 3–4 tablespoons per day	Small, tender pieces of meat, chicken, or fish; eggs, cheese, yogurt, cooked dried beans, peanut butter, 4–5 tablespoons per day

The best way to make sure your infant's growth is normal is to consult a growth chart, regularly but not obsessively. Don't expect your baby to fall dead center—anywhere between the twenty-fifth percentile and the seventy-fifth percentile is considered normal. But the infant's height and weight should be in proportion to other babies of the same age, and in proportion to each other. For instance, height should not fall in the thirtieth percentile of a growth chart if weight falls in the seventieth percentile. Babies who are small will sometimes gain weight and height unevenly in spurts, resulting in some disproportion between numbers. These fluctuations are normal as long as height and weight eventually come to a balance. If weight continues to outpace growth, you may be feeding beyond your baby's needs. Check with your health-care provider to see if portion sizes, frequency of feedings, and food choices are appropriate.

Another thing to keep in mind when consulting growth charts is that breast-fed and formula-fed infants generally have slightly different growth patterns. Breast-fed babies seem to grow faster for the first two or three months, but afterwards formula-fed infants are, on average, slightly taller and heavier. Standard growth charts used to be based on formula feeding, but several years ago the medical community began to rethink these numbers, under the assumption that breast-feeding should provide the standard against which formula feeding should be compared, rather than the other way around. Current growth charts from the U.S. Centers for Disease Control and Prevention include both breast-fed and formula-fed infants in calculating averages, so the numbers are a little different from what old charts show. Your feeding strategy may account for slightly higher or lower than average numbers.

Nutrition at the First Birthday

By their first birthdays, most infants will be eating a mixed diet with a variety of foods. As outlined in the infant feeding guide in Table 3.2, complementary foods by this time should consist of roughly equal portions of vegetables, fruits, cereals and grains, and protein sources. Maintaining normal growth during the first year is crucial for the baby's health, now and in later life. While there are general guidelines about portion size and feeding frequency, needs vary considerably for each person. Follow your baby's demands for more or less food and also track her growth when deciding how much to feed. The next year will mark a transition from special infant foods to a full-fledged solid diet.

4

Thriving in the Second Year

Weaning isn't just a transition for babies—it's a learning process for parents, too. Starting out, nutrition was blessedly easy: breast milk or formula was a safety net that provided nearly complete nutrition without you having to do a lot of guesswork. By one year, it's time for you to be weaned off your dependence on these liquid foods and onto your new role as nutrition provider. In other words, you'll be working without a net now, and it's up to you to choose the right foods to make your child's diet nutritionally complete.

Taking on the role of a child's nutritionist isn't an easy task—after all, many adults struggle to follow good nutrition in their own diets. As you might expect, the time when breast-feeding ends and solid foods take over is a period in which infants are particularly susceptible to malnutrition and deficiencies of essential vitamins and minerals if their new diets are poor in nutrients. At the same time, dietary deficiencies are potentially more harmful than in adulthood, because an infant's body is still undergoing change and growth.

During their second year, infants become more mobile toddlers, begin speaking, and gain a more active role in the feeding process. With their newfound skills comes a whole new set of challenges for parents. While some women may continue to breast-feed in the second year, in general, children move to a diet based almost entirely on solid foods and begin to join in family meals. Think of this as an important time to create some good habits and dietary patterns that will last a lifetime, in addition to making sure your child is healthy and happy. This chapter will give you some tips and tricks for keeping your child's diet healthy during this time. Later chapters will discuss healthy food choices for children in more detail.

A Matter of Taste

As busy parents, why isn't it enough to keep your toddler fed with whatever foods are easiest to prepare, and then follow up with a supplement or toddler formula that contains vitamins and minerals? Because developing good eating habits and a taste for healthy foods is just as important as making sure the nutrients are all there. Let's be realistic: there is no failsafe way to prevent your child from becoming a picky eater or demanding sweets over salads. However, by setting the stage for a healthy approach to eating, parents can really make a difference in the way their children eat later in life. Infants learn how to eat by watching their parents, so all healthy eating habits begin with the model that parents set.

Why does one person have a sweet tooth while another hankers for salt? Why do some relish a piece of fruit for dessert while others pine for ice cream? Our food preferences are very complex, and result from several influences. While each individual is susceptible to certain preferences because of genetic factors, tastes can also come and go like the latest fashion trend, depending on the environment and even the ideas that a person associates with food. Research has shown that dietary patterns established in infancy and early childhood can affect how people eat later in life, and how they think about food. Parents can teach their kids how to eat well, not just by choosing good foods but by showing them how to explore new tastes and enjoy things that are good for them.

First, Some Responsibilities

As much as we try to make mealtime fun, it also can become a battle between parents and kids. It would be wonderful if kids always wanted to eat what we'd like them to, but the fact is that instilling good eating habits usually means setting some rules and sometimes saying no. As your young toddler becomes increasingly inde-

pendent and vocal, you may feel that the boundless power you enjoyed while he was a baby is starting to slip away.

Because you and your child aren't always going to agree about diet, let's set out some responsibilities for both of you:

- Your child is responsible for deciding how much he needs to eat at any one time and determining when he's full.
- You are responsible for choosing which foods your child eats and determining the environment in which food is eaten.

I'll explain the rationale behind this division of labor. Parents, of course, should have the lion's share of responsibility in this relationship. But it can be difficult to know when young children should be indulged or disciplined. Often, parents focus on how much kids eat, rather than what they eat, but in fact the emphasis should be reversed.

Eating Habits Change After Year One

During the first year of life, your baby's body was undergoing a building boom, just about tripling in weight in a mere twelve months. Now it's time to take a little rest—it will take roughly another full year for birth weight to quadruple. Many parents become concerned when their infant suddenly eats less or loses interest in food in the second year, but this is almost always just a result of needing less fuel for growth. Though the numbers vary from child to child, infants gain roughly fifteen pounds and grow about ten inches in their first year, but only gain about five pounds and four or five inches in their second year.

It can be disconcerting if you've been carefully measuring out the proper portions for every meal and your child suddenly will only eat a few bites at one sitting. This is also normal. Studies have found that, while children may eat more erratically from meal to meal as they reach toddlerhood, they are usually able to self-regulate how much they eat over the course of a day so that the total calories they take in is roughly constant.

A lack of appetite should only concern you if it lasts for several meals or if your child's growth isn't progressing normally. As long as children are still growing, there's no need to force them to finish a meal if they're not hungry. If they pick at lunch, they can simply follow it up with a larger snack later. The exception is when children refuse to eat something that's good for them and want to move on to dessert. Make sure that sweets and treats are a very small part of your child's food intake of any given day, or she will learn to refuse meals.

Young kids have small stomachs that aren't designed for eating large meals. It's better for toddlers to eat several times throughout the day—usually three small meals with a couple of substantial snacks. Because snacks are a critical part of a child's daily nutrition, they shouldn't just consist of the "junk" food we often associate with snacking, like chips or candy. Instead of looking at snacks as a nutritional afterthought, see them as an opportunity to bring in more healthful foods like fruits and vegetables to complement meals.

Many of us grew up with our parents telling us to finish our meals or face punishment. But this traditional form of discipline no longer makes sense and may be detrimental to good eating habits. Toddlers have an innate sense of when they are full and should stop eating, but by the time they are a few years older, many kids have learned to overeat. We will discuss the growing concerns over weight control and childhood obesity later; for now, keep in mind that it's good to encourage young toddlers to follow their instincts about how much food they eat.

Daily Intake and Growth

Young toddlers may seem to eat chaotically, but their intake usually averages out over the course of a day. Table 4.1 provides a rough guideline of the portions of different kinds of foods that an average toddler (if there is such a thing) can be expected to eat in one day.

It's natural for parents to worry about how much their children are eating and whether or not they are growing properly. Today, parents have to be especially concerned about kids who eat too much or aren't active enough to burn the calories they do eat. It's good to get in the habit of consulting a growth chart. (See Selected Resources section.) The chart lists height and weight, and the plotted lines, called *isobars*, tell you in which percentile a child's height and weight fall compared to the average for his age. Never expect a child to fall dead center—differences in size are normal, especially if a child's parents are shorter or taller than average. Parents should pay attention to disproportions in height and weight—for instance, weight that is two isobars more than height could indicate an overweight child. Leaps in isobars are also a cause for concern, if an infant who has always been in a high percentile suddenly drops to a low one, or vice versa. Consult your pediatrician if you notice problems in growth.

Making Food Choices

While children know how much they should eat, it's the parents' job to decide what they eat—and stick to it. Caring for toddlers is not easy, and many parents use food as a bargaining tool to mollify a demanding child or as a bribe in a dispute. This tactic usually results in a child who eats lots of candy, cookies, and soda in place of foods that have nutrients they need.

Table 4.1 Feeding Guidelines for Toddlers Aged One to Two

FOOD GROUP	TOTAL AMOUNT PER DAY	SERVING SIZES AND FOOD SOURCES
Milk and milk substitutes	4 servings (same as 2 cups milk)	• ½ cup whole, low-fat, skim, or chocolate milk, or ½ cup calcium-fortified soy milk • ½ cup yogurt, 1 ounce cheese, ½ cup custard or pudding, 1 slice cheese pizza, or 2 tablespoons powdered milk
Meat, fish, poultry, peanut butter, cooked or dried beans, and other protein foods	2 servings with total 3½ ounces a day	• 1 ounce is 1 egg; 1 slice cheese; ½ cup cooked dried beans, peas, or lentils; 2 tablespoons peanut butter; 1 slice turkey or lean meat; 2 slices luncheon meat; 1 hot dog; 1 slice small cheese pizza; ¼ cup cottage cheese; ¼ cup drained tuna; ½ cup tofu; or 1 soy burger patty • 3 ounces is ½ chicken breast or 1 leg or thigh, or 1 piece meat or fish the size and thickness of a deck of cards
Grains: breads, cereals, rice, pasta, and other starches	4 to 6 servings	• 1 serving is 1 slice bread; ½ bagel; ½ English muffin; 1 small biscuit, roll, or muffin; 6 crackers; ½ hamburger bun; ½ hot dog bun; ½ cup cooked rice or pasta; ½ cup cooked cereal; 1 ounce ready-to-eat cereal • Suggestion: look for cereals with whole grains and whole-wheat versions of pasta and bread products
Fruits	2 servings	• 1 serving is ½ piece fresh fruit, or ¼ to ½ cup canned fruit • Suggestions: oranges, berries, melons, apricots, nectarines, peaches, tangerines, banana slices
Vegetables	3 servings	• 1 serving is ½ cup fresh or canned vegetables • Suggestions: tomatoes, peppers, cabbage, spinach, carrots, peas, beans, squash, sweet potatoes, broccoli

Handling the Joys and Jags of Toddlerhood

As babies become toddlers, many will experience food "jags" in which they suddenly favor one food exclusively over another. Parents often become alarmed, especially if they have been striving to provide a varied diet and now struggle to get their child to eat more than three or four favorite foods.

This is one of the mysterious and absolutely normal quirks of toddlerhood, and shouldn't worry you too much. Keep up some gentle pressure to add other foods to your child's diet; strike a deal that he can have his favorites as long as he eats a few bites of other foods that you choose. Or try to find a compromise food that might have similar appeal but offer better nutrition. Encourage your child to try a few bites of a new food by putting just a spoonful or so on the tray.

Eventually, most toddlers lose these obsessions and relent to trying new things again. Children who persist in picky eating may need to get a vitamin and mineral supplement if the foods they eat don't cover all their nutritional bases. For instance, if meat is not among the select favorites, your child could be at risk for an iron and zinc deficiency—consider a daily supplement at an age-appropriate dose. Breakfast cereals that are fortified with vitamins and minerals are also good—and usually acceptable—food choices for picky eaters.

It's no wonder that many kids learn to love sweets and other junk food and to do whatever they can to get more of them. They may also learn to associate junk foods with a feeling of independence and power over their parents, and feel they are being punished when they eat healthful things. Kids can't be expected to make good choices for themselves; parents have the responsibility to determine which foods are appropriate and which aren't, even in the face of some heavy opposition.

As toddlers increasingly assert their independence, it may help to offer some limited choices so that the mealtime decisions seem a little more democratic. Offering children a choice between two different healthful foods can be more productive than simply staking arguments over healthful foods versus junk foods.

In planning meals and choosing snacks, strive for variety, just as you did with weaning foods. Offer a sampling of lots of different kinds of foods, but not just the leftovers from adult meals—make it a point to serve the kinds of foods you'd like to become part of your child's regular diet. Take advantage of this window of time to make your child's taste experiences an adventure rather than a rut.

Obviously, as kids get older it becomes harder to control all the decisions about what they eat. But for now, your role is to give your child the best nutrition possible, even if that means standing firm in the face of opposition. It also may mean taking an active role in determining what your child is served at any day-care services you use. Find out what kinds of foods they give to kids, and if it's not acceptable, consider preparing your own foods or ask that changes be made.

Push the Fruits and Veggies

While choosing good sources of protein, carbohydrates, and fat is important for a healthful diet, the type of food that is really missing in the diet of most Americans—especially kids—is fruits and vegetables. If we all made an effort to include more produce in our diet, we could lower our risk of disease and increase our chances of living longer and healthier lives.

If you do one thing for your child's nutrition in the chaotic time of toddlerhood, it should be to make vegetables and fresh fruit a big part of her diet. Not only will this help establish good eating habits, but will also provide some much-needed vitamins and minerals.

Make the effort to use fresh, frozen, or canned vegetables in their whole form to accustom your child to the taste, rather than simply serving processed foods that

 If at First You Don't Succeed . . .

You've tried serving broccoli to your toddler, and she has turned up her nose or thrown a fit. Don't give up yet. Very few adults liked coffee the first time they tried it, yet many of us are now addicted to the stuff. Many tastes are acquired, and people often need five to ten exposures to a flavor to get used to it. Parents often make the mistake of giving up at the first sign of resistance, but it may simply take a little extra effort to get used to a new food. You may lose one battle but win the war, with some persistence.

Try the broccoli again the next day, and again with some melted cheddar cheese or mixed with pasta. Try it lightly cooked with yogurt dip, hummus, or ranch dressing (or raw if your child has the hang of eating firm, solid foods already).

contain a few bits of unrecognizable veggies. And fruit doesn't just mean juice—again, whole fruits are best, and unsweetened canned fruit, applesauce, or dried fruit are better snacks than processed fruit roll-ups or candies sweetened with fruit juice.

Be creative in serving vegetables and fruits. If your toddler isn't keen on eating an entire helping of veggies, try adding them to his favorite foods, like macaroni and cheese with broccoli or peas. Add vegetables to a tortilla with melted cheese. Serve carrots and apples with peanut butter as snacks. At mealtime, instead of serving potatoes, try acorn squash, butternut squash, or sweet potatoes, all of which are richer in nutrients like beta-carotene than spuds.

If a particular vegetable is daunting piled on a plate, try it in another form—add finely diced or grated vegetables to rice, pasta, or mashed potatoes. Employ sauces and dips—but avoid ones that are loaded with sugar and salt. Instead, try serving fruits and veggies with yogurt, tomato sauce, cheese, applesauce, peanut butter, bean dip, or hummus.

While sweets should be limited as much as possible, when you do serve them you can make fruits a part of every treat or dessert, like peaches with a small scoop of frozen yogurt, or strawberries with pudding. Fruit can be added to nearly every breakfast food, like applesauce on whole-grain pancakes, or dates and apple chunks with oatmeal. Look for opportunities to include a few bites of vegetables or fruit in nearly every meal or snack. See Chapter 8 for more information on fruits and vegetables in the diet.

Start Early on Whole Grains

For some reason, parents often have the idea that hearty, whole-grain foods are for adults only, while sweets and snacks made of refined flour—often with an extra helping of sugar and unhealthful fats—are the only foods that kids should eat. Maybe it's because every food that is marketed for kids is generally lacking in any whole grains, while cereals, crackers, and bread with lots of whole grains and fiber are touted as "adult" foods.

In fact, it's never too early to feed infants and young children whole grains. Some great whole-grain foods for one-to-two-year-olds are hot cereals like oatmeal and cream of wheat, cold cereals made with whole grains, grits or polenta, whole-wheat bread and bagels, whole-wheat crackers, brown rice, whole-wheat pastas, soup with barley, and corn tortillas.

When shopping for whole-wheat products, make sure you see the word *whole* up front on the ingredient list, not just *wheat flour*. Another way to check to see if a food uses whole grains is to look at grams of fiber; foods made from whole grains should have at least a few grams of fiber per serving. Grocery stores increasingly offer health-food aisles that have a more robust selection of whole-grain snacks and cereals. But beware of falling in the health food trap; some of these foods are more expensive but not necessarily more healthful. For instance, they may carry cookies and sweetened cereals that are all-natural or organic, but organic sugar is still sugar, and the body processes it in the same way.

Add a Helping of Protein and Fat

Even as their growth slows, toddlers continue to need protein to fuel their developing bodies. With the proteins from breast milk or formula no longer part of the diet, serving protein-rich foods every day becomes even more important than during the weaning process.

Parents can start letting their children drink cow's milk in their second year, but should be on the lookout for any allergic reaction or gastrointestinal upset that might indicate a child is lactose intolerant. Yogurt is a great food for infants and toddlers, just be aware that many flavored varieties contain lots of added sugar— an alternative is to add fresh or canned fruits or applesauce to plain yogurt. Toddlers should continue to eat meats for their iron and zinc content, as well as eggs and dairy products like cheese, which is easier on the stomach than cow's milk. You can also bring in more diverse sources of protein, like cooked soybeans, tofu, beans, lentils, peanut butter and other nut butters, and hummus. These foods will help add vitamins and minerals to your child's diet, as well as introducing her to some healthful sources of protein to continue eating in later years.

The first two years of your child's life are not a time to limit fat. While studies have been examining the safety of limiting fat intake in young kids, nutrition experts agree that fat should not be a concern with infants and young toddlers. During the first two years, children should usually eat full-fat dairy products made from whole milk. We'll talk later about trimming the fat from these protein sources in later years.

Fat is an essential nutrient that is used to provide the body with energy and to construct many of the body's tissues and chemical components. This can be a confusing point for parents, since we have been talking about the importance of weight control and not overeating at all ages, including infancy, and many people equate too much body fat with too much fat in the diet. Severely limiting fat during infancy can hinder growth and cause sickness. But fat is a concentrated substance, and a little goes a long way. Most kids get fat hand-in-hand with protein sources—it's plentiful in eggs, milk, cheese, yogurt, meats, and nuts. There's no need to seek out additional sources of fat by feeding your child highly fatty substances like butter or oils.

Keep the Brakes on Sugar and Salt

As I mentioned in the last chapter, prepared baby foods were once made to suit adult tastes, with added sugar and salt. While those foods have changed, it's still a common mistake for parents to feel that they couldn't possibly give their infants and young toddlers food that doesn't taste good to adult tongues. They try a bite of some strangely colored mush in a jar and wonder if it's criminal to make a person eat this stuff.

Our taste for salt and sugar has led to a diet of largely processed foods that increase our risk of chronic disease and crowd out the foods that keep us healthy, like whole grains, fruits, and vegetables. For many of us, eating heavily salted or sugary foods has become a habit that's difficult to break. As a parent, you have the opportunity to nip this habit in the bud—or at the very least postpone it for a while—by keeping excess salt and sugar in your toddler's foods to a minimum.

To encourage a taste for the more subtle flavors of naturally sweet foods, try serving fresh fruits like strawberries, apples, oranges, bananas, mangoes, watermelon, pineapple, kiwifruit, or dried unsweetened dates, raisins, and apricots. Including unsweetened canned or dried fruits with desserts after meals is also a great way to introduce naturally sweet foods over ones full of refined sugars.

Choose fruit juices that are 100 percent juice rather than juice drinks sweetened with corn syrup or sugar. Juice also isn't a substitute for whole fruits, which also contain lots of fiber. While jelly and fruit snacks that are sweetened with fruit juice may be a better alternative to similar sugar-sweetened foods, they are also not a substitute for real fruits. Remember, the key here is taste: foods that have added sweeteners, whether they are natural or artificial, still mimic the sweetness of sugar, and help develop a taste for unnaturally sweet foods. And processed foods, even if they are made of fruit, won't help develop a taste for the real thing.

Cooking your own foods is the best way to limit salt intake, since the level of sodium in many processed foods is invariably higher than what we would add to

Quick and Easy Snacks for Toddlers

Since young children tend to eat numerous times throughout the day, snacks are an important part of their daily nutrition. Too often, snack foods become chips and cookies, which have very little nutritional value and take the place of better foods packed with vitamins, minerals, and fiber. Instead of letting your toddler reach for empty calories as snacks, try stocking your shelves with these easy foods.

- Cheese slices

- Fruit wedges

- Yogurt with fresh strawberries or peaches

- Peanut butter on whole-wheat crackers or apple slices

- Whole-wheat pita bread with hummus

- Hard-boiled eggs

- Carrot pieces with ranch dressing (cook carrots for a short time in the microwave to soften them for younger toddlers)

- Whole-wheat bagel slices with cream cheese or tomato sauce

- Corn tortilla slices with refried beans and melted cheese

- Unsweetened applesauce

our own meals. Unfortunately, many parents don't have a lot of time to do their own cooking and are forced to rely on the convenience of ready-made foods. For now, try to emphasize simple, whole foods that are easy to prepare instead of processed adult foods. Chapter 12 offers some recipe ideas for inspiration.

Creating a Healthy Eating Environment

Parents are responsible for choosing the environment in which their children eat. For infants and young toddlers, setting up some structure in which they can learn good eating habits is important. As we will discuss in later chapters, there is growing evidence that distracted, disorganized eating patterns can be detriments to good nutrition and contributing factors in being overweight.

Parents can initiate good eating habits by setting fixed times and locations for meals and snacks, instead of letting their young toddlers munch distractedly while sitting in the car or in front of the TV. Let eating be an activity that holds your child's full attention. Of course, a child's attention is never held for very long—setting aside about fifteen to twenty minutes for mealtime is about as much as you can expect from a toddler.

Infants and young toddlers should always be supervised, since they are still new to eating solids and can choke or gag on pieces of food. When it's time to eat, place your child in a high chair that is free of other distractions like toys or TV and spread foods out on a tray. Children should drink juice from a cup instead of a bottle once they learn how, usually around fifteen months in age.

Eating is an interactive process for toddlers, who are figuring out how to grab utensils, scoop and move food around, and eventually feed themselves. At this age, they are learning all about causes and effects: what happens to food when they drop it or squish it, which actions make their parents pleased or angry, how foods of different color and texture taste. The unavoidable messes of mealtimes can be frustrating, and parents have to walk a fine line between teaching appropriate behavior and letting their child have fun with food. Toddlers are messy, and it's best if parents and other family members expect some spills and stains and take some preventive measures. For instance, place a drop cloth under a toddler's high chair, so that messes can be easily whisked away without the stress of cleaning carpets.

Encourage exploration and a growing independence, but let your toddler know what is expected of her to help her learn the social aspects of eating. These early meals and snacks can also be a great opportunity for some interactive learning. Allow toddlers to handle a fork or spoon, even if they are unable to use utensils properly. Say the names of the foods you are serving, point out the colors of different fruits and vegetables, and talk about their shape and texture. When meals are a learning experience instead of a mindless chore, kids develop a positive, inquisitive attitude about food and nutrition.

5

Healthy Kids Aged Two Through Eight

After two years of age, children have developed the ability to eat a large variety of foods. They can begin to take part in meals that the rest of the family eats, though some foods will still require special preparation to prevent choking. But while they are capable of eating a more adult diet, young children have special needs separate from the grown-ups in the family. These special needs may not be completely obvious to a parent, but it's important to keep in mind one of the central themes of this book, that children are not simply little adults, and so adult eating habits may not always fit their needs.

The primary difference between the needs of children and adults is that children's bodies are still growing, so it is particularly important for them to eat a diet rich in nutrients. All that new tissue needed to construct a growing body doesn't come from nowhere: their diet must provide the raw materials to make it. Protein, for instance, is used to fashion new cells and to perform critical tasks within the body. And children's demand for calcium is higher, because the mineral is required to sculpt ever-expanding bones. Other vitamins and minerals are also more critical for kids than for adults, because a deficiency could interfere with an important process during development and cause long-term harm. Fortunately, little kids aren't as susceptible to these problems as they were in their first two years, since the fast-paced growth of infancy has slowed to a more even clip. But providing young children with a diet rich in nutrients will ultimately help ensure that they grow into healthier adults.

Another difference is simply that children need less food than adults, and sometimes even less than parents might think. As we discussed in the previous chapter, toddlers and young children have the ability to know when they are hungry and how much they need to eat. Parents often assume otherwise, and try to bribe and cajole kids to eat more in the belief that they aren't consuming enough. Children who are able to eat when hungry and whose food is not restricted will almost always consume enough calories to grow to their potential. Parents should trust in the body's ability to regulate its own intake, and encourage children to stop eating when they are full.

Parents can also be overly worried about their child's eating habits. One recent study in Finland compared the eating habits of a group of five-year-olds whose parents considered them "poor eaters" to the eating habits of a control group of so-called "normal" eaters. The researchers found that the poor eaters received fewer calories from hot meals and more from snacks. But in the end, there was no real difference in nutrition between the two groups.

Though they eat less at a time, children may also need to eat more frequently, usually three small meals with several snacks throughout the day. Since snacks will make up a big part of a child's daily intake, they can be considered "mini meals" and deserve the same attention to good nutrition that you would pay to a meal. In other words, a snack isn't just something to keep your child full until dinner. It's an opportunity to add some fruits, vegetables, protein sources, and other components of a balanced diet.

A Good Diet Is More than Eating the Right Foods

While good nutrition is important for children, many of the health problems that kids encounter stem from poor dietary habits, an unhealthy attitude toward food, and a lifestyle that is increasingly sedentary. In other words, sometimes the social and behavioral aspects of nutrition can be just as critical as the actual foods that children eat.

As I mentioned before, the rise in "lifestyle" diseases shows how clearly our choices and behavior can affect our health. By the time we are adults and start to worry about our health and our risk of disease, we are already creatures of habit. We know which foods we like and dislike. We know what times of the day we like to eat and how much we will eat at a sitting. Of course, we can still make changes, but doing so can be a painful process, like learning a new language. How much better to help children live healthier lives from the start, rather than letting them face the rude awakening of a drastic lifestyle change in adulthood.

Most parents quickly realize that providing a nutritious diet involves more than just knowledge about food, though that is a primary concern of this book. If eating right was just a matter of knowing which foods to choose, we would have far fewer problems with nutrition today. In fact, there is a deep psychological component to eating, and simple education about what's healthful or not doesn't always translate into healthy habits and perfect eating behaviors.

For parents, these other tasks can be trickier, because they involve dealing with behavior, ideas about food, and the social and environmental context of nutrition today. Here are only a few of the challenges parents face in promoting good nutrition in their kids—we will keep these challenges in mind when we look at how to turn your nutritional knowledge into a practical diet that works for your child.

Pleasing a Picky Eater

Young children between two and five years of age become notoriously reluctant to try new foods, though this is an important time to bring variety to their diets. Variety matters for two reasons. First of all, with a diet that includes lots of different foods, children are more likely to take in a complete range of vitamins and minerals and a balance of nutrients than if they only eat a few foods. Second, by exposing children to different foods, parents can help them overcome their reluctance to try new tastes and help them be adventurous eaters later in life.

As I mentioned in the previous chapter, it can take up to ten exposures to a new food to get kids used to eating it, but many parents give up long before that. Persistence and some creativity can often help you win over a picky eater. Just be careful not to overdo it: forcing children to eat healthful foods like vegetables can just turn them off, signaling to them that healthful foods are punishments or inherently unpleasant. Instead, offer the food multiple times, and ask your child to try it, even if that means eating just a few small bites. Serve it as part of a favorite dish or mixed with another favorite food or sauce. Remember that kids may be wary of trying new things, so putting the new food in a familiar context can help to reassure them.

Putting the Ritual Back into Eating

In every culture, food plays a part in society's rituals, and ritual plays a part in the way we eat. We have established fixed times to eat throughout the day, created special rooms and furniture specifically for eating, and developed a repertoire of rules for mealtime, from the order in which the dishes are served to how far it's acceptable to reach for a salt shaker.

There is no inherent reason why eating must be such a ritualized process—and in fact, that fixed structure is now on the wane in our society. In America, it is now very common to "graze" on food throughout the day, to eat dinner in front of the TV, to munch on a breakfast bar during the morning commute or ride to school. Sitting down to meals can be a rarity for some families.

Families today are diverse and varied. Some are single-parent households, some designate one parent to stay at home with the children, others have two parents working full-time, and still others manage through a mixture of part-time work, shared responsibilities, and day care. The demands of work and child care can leave little time for life's rituals, like cooking meals from scratch and sitting down to every meal as a family.

However, there is some evidence that our fast-paced lifestyle causes health and nutrition to suffer. Eating breakfast, for instance, has been associated with better performance in school and a higher intake of vitamins and minerals in children. Breakfast cereals are often fortified with extra vitamins and minerals, and children tend to consume more milk, fruit or whole fruit juice, and whole grains at breakfast, all of which contribute needed nutrients. A study of about six hundred children aged four to twelve found that kids who regularly ate breakfast cereal weighed less for their height, consumed more vitamins and minerals, and ate less fat than kids who ate little or no cereal. Yet young children tend to skip breakfast more often than any other meal of the day. Try to ensure your child has time to sit down for a few minutes in the morning to eat breakfast, and if your schedule doesn't always permit this little ritual, make the effort to provide a quick, nutritious substitute.

As young as two and three years of age, children are starting to learn the social norms of eating and what's expected of them. They learn when and where it is

appropriate to eat, as well as the type of food that fits every occasion—sweets after dinner, for instance, and cereal only in the morning. Providing structure during this time helps them learn these habits and may be beneficial to children's health. For instance, one survey found that children in families that eat while watching TV have a poorer diet, consume more calories, and are more likely to be overweight. Many people tend to snack in front of the TV without paying as much attention to how much they are eating as they would if the food were put before them at the dinner table.

One way to encourage a more thoughtful, structured eating style is to only allow eating at the table at set meal and snack times, rather than allowing children to take snacks into their rooms or eat while doing another activity. Young children don't have the attention span of adults, and often would rather go off to play than sit down at the dinner table. You can have your child sit with the family for at least ten or fifteen minutes at mealtime, whether he eats or not.

Finding Time for Home-Cooked Meals

The average family in the United States now spends one-third of its food dollars on foods and beverages consumed outside the home. But these foods also tend to be higher in calories, fat, salt, and sugar than foods cooked at home. And some restaurant entrees contain as many calories as an adult should consume in an entire day. Beverages are another growing part of our diet: those eight-ounce bottles of Coke from my youth have now swelled to enormous twenty-four- to thirty-six-ounce cups, and restaurants regularly offer free refills of high-calorie soda. Researchers are now taking a look at portion size as a factor in the exploding rates of overweight and obesity in this country, even among children.

A national survey of more than six thousand children and adolescents found that, on any given day, 30 percent of children reported eating fast food. Those who ate fast food consumed more total calories, more fat, more carbohydrates, more added sugars, more sugar-sweetened beverages, less milk, and fewer fruits and non-starchy vegetables than kids who did not eat fast food.

Preparing the majority of your own meals is the best way to make sure the quality and quantity of foods your family eats are what they should be. Meals cooked at home don't have to be elaborate. Cooking every day isn't necessary: you can prepare a large main dish during the weekend and serve it throughout the week with a salad or quickly cooked vegetable. You can cook many quick, delicious meals without resorting to prepackaged convenience foods. This book will give you a few ideas to get you started.

Paying Attention to the Emotional Context of Eating

One of the biggest challenges parents face is to be aware not just of the nutrition in their children's food but of the emotional messages that food carries. Parents will often use sweets as bribes in order to get their children to eat more healthily. But these kinds of psychological games can give children the impression that healthy foods are punishments to be avoided, and that unhealthy foods are rewards to be earned.

As much as I advocate the healthiest foods for kids, I also recognize that parents can go too far if they are overly strict about food. Ruling out any kind of sweet, for instance, can backfire if it sends the message that sweets are exciting and forbidden. A child who grows up this way might end up seeking out these forbidden foods as a way of asserting her independence. Not only do these tactics backfire in the long run, but I believe they also underestimate the ability of children to develop positive feelings about health. Throughout this book, I emphasize using positive emotions to teach children about nutrition and expose them to healthy foods.

Parents can also go too far in discouraging a picky eater. All of us have likes and dislikes when it comes to food, and that's perfectly normal. You wouldn't expect to be ridiculed for not wanting to eat a particular food, and children also have the right to develop their own personal preferences in the context of a good diet. Your job as a parent is to expose your children to the best foods and encourage good habits, not to force foods on them or expect them to like everything.

Combating Outside Messages

Unfortunately, sweets are often the currency adults use to control children, whether it is a reward for obeying or a bribe to behave. Even if you avoid using treats this way, you may find it hard to stop others, such as teachers and other caretakers, from doing so. Sweets are everywhere. And most children are exposed daily to messages about food from advertisements on TV and other media. Billions of dollars are spent every year marketing food to children, and most of these foods are not the ones you'd like your child to be eating. Fast-food restaurants and food companies use cartoon characters and toys as lures to capture children's attention, leading them to demand foods that aren't in their best interests. Parents sometimes need to withstand a few tantrums in order to avoid feeding their children these high-calorie, low-nutrient foods. Beyond simply standing your ground when children demand foods they see advertised, one of the best weapons you can use is education: teach your children how marketing works and teach them to talk back to ads.

Getting Kids Involved with Food

Toddlers and young children are like learning machines—everything is new to them and every situation is an opportunity to learn, including concepts about food and nutrition. Parents often think that simply giving their kids the right foods is enough. But you can also teach them about what they are eating, and in doing so ensure that they will carry knowledge, rather than just habits, with them into adolescence and adulthood.

Think of it: if a child ate a diet of mostly prepackaged frozen foods and restaurant meals, he might have no idea what the ingredients of those foods look like in their original form, where they come from, or how they are grown. He might not even realize that all of those foods come from living plants and animals. Because eating is second nature to us, parents can often miss opportunities to turn the daily act of cooking and eating into an educational experience.

One way to overcome resistance to a healthy diet in young children is to get them involved in learning about and preparing food. A study at the University of California at Davis found that a group of children who were involved in planting and growing a garden for one year had a greater nutritional knowledge and a higher preference for certain vegetables at the end of the program. Gardening, even if it consists of planting a small indoor herb garden or growing a tomato plant on the porch, is a great way to educate children about how plants grow and where food comes from. And children gain a sense of accomplishment when their hard work contributes to a family meal.

But you don't have to grow vegetables and fruits to learn about them. A stroll through the produce section of the supermarket can offer an excellent education. You can tell your child where each food comes from and how it grows. One fun activity is to choose a new kind of fruit or vegetable at each shopping trip, look up where it grows, what part of the plant it comes from, and what kinds of dishes it is found in. Then prepare it together as you talk about it. Cooking a meal from another culture is also a great opportunity to learn more about that culture, to connect eating with other places and people. And a visit to a local farmer's market can help reinforce a knowledge about how food is grown and how it gets from farms to the dinner table.

You can also enlist children to help in the kitchen. Knowing they had a hand in preparing dinner can help them accept new foods and enjoy eating meals. Even children as young as two years old can help wash and prepare salads and vegetables, and older children can help measure and mix foods, peel fruits, and arrange foods on a dish or tray. Taking them from start to finish through a recipe can help them appreciate the process of making food, rather than only experiencing the end product. You can encourage their creativity by offering them a few ingredients and asking them to create a snack. It takes a little patience to let children struggle with a new task, but it is worth the effort.

Finding Out What Children Eat Outside the Home

When kids enter a day-care service or school, they will be eating at least a third of their meals outside the home, as well as snacks during the day. No book on children's nutrition would be complete without addressing school lunch programs and other sources of food outside the home. This is also the part of children's diets over which parents have the least control, but there are steps you can take to find out what kinds of foods are available to your child and try to make changes if needed.

The foods provided by day-care services may be very different from the foods you would choose to serve. In particular, they may choose convenience and price over quality, loading up on cheaper foods that are easiest to prepare, like low-fiber breads and sugary beverages such as lemonade, while skimping on fruits and vegetables and foods high in protein. And they may also treat food differently than you do—offering unhealthy snacks as treats, for example—which could potentially undo some of those habits you've been trying to instill.

With day-care programs, the best course of action is to find out what they serve, as well as how often and how much children eat. If you can take the time, spend some time observing a typical mealtime (this is also a great way to find out about other aspects of the service's quality before you allow your child to spend time there). If something bothers you, tell the day-care provider politely what the problem is, why you don't like it, and what you think an alternative would be. Keep in mind, day-care providers are working with a limited budget and serving a variety of children's needs. If they are unable to make changes, you can also prepare homemade meals or snacks for your child and leave special instructions with the staff.

Lunches served in public schools and some private schools are governed by the federal school lunch program, but there are still ways parents can get involved and make changes, and we will talk about some of these in Chapter 11. There is a growing concern these days about the kinds of foods available in schools. The federal school lunch program was developed to ensure that children all over the country received meals that followed certain nutritional guidelines. But in many cases, this admirable idea has failed in practice to provide children with food that is both nutritious and tastes good.

Now, parents are often finding that vending machines hawking candy, chips, and soda are readily available in many schools. This junk food offers kids a tempting alternative to school lunches that frankly taste awful at times. And vending machines aren't the only sources of unhealthy foods: many school groups try to raise money by tempting kids with treats throughout the day. We'll talk about some of the reforms being made nationally to address this problem in Chapter 11.

Figure 5.1   The Healthy Eating Pyramid for kids aged two through eight.

Food Guide Pyramids and the Nutritional Needs of Young Children

In the United States, the primary tool for educating children and parents about food and nutrition is the USDA Food Guide Pyramid for Young Children (see Selected Resources) as well as the Food Guide Pyramid for adults. The pyramid for young children is not much different than the standard pyramid, and in fact both can be used as references for children's diets. The main difference is in how the information in the pyramid is presented: the drawings are kid-focused and include foods that kids typically eat, and drawings around the pyramid depict children involved in activities to emphasize the importance of exercise. The names of categories and the recommended servings have been simplified to make them easier for children to learn—for instance, the group that includes "meat, poultry, fish, dry beans, eggs, and nuts" in the adult pyramid is now just called the "meat group."

After years of existing quietly as an authority in nutrition, the pyramid has recently been under attack, led primarily by my colleague at Harvard, Walter C. Willett. In his book *Eat, Drink, and Be Healthy,* Willett voiced concerns that some aspects of the USDA pyramid for adults are based more on political interests and compromise than on science. The problem stems from a fundamental contradiction in the purpose of the USDA. The department is charged with providing nutritional advice to Americans, but its primary role is to promote the agricultural industry in this country. The result is that the recommendations of its nutrition consultants may run counter to the desires of farmers and ranchers to promote their products. Instead of weighing in with a critical voice on certain foods, it adopts an all-inclusive approach to eating. The end result is only vague information about which foods are healthier than others.

Dr. Willett introduced a new Healthy Eating Pyramid for adults (see Selected Resources) based on current research. The new pyramid emphasized eating more plant oils, whole-grain foods, fruits and vegetables, and nuts and legumes. It downplayed the role of meats, dairy products, and refined grains and starches. And all of this is set atop a base of daily exercise and weight control. The purpose of this pyramid is to help adults achieve a diet that limits their likelihood of developing heart disease, cancer, diabetes, and obesity. The message has caught on, and in response to this pressure the USDA is now in the process of rethinking the content of its pyramid.

In this book, we offer parents a new pyramid for children (see Figure 5.1). The USDA pyramid—and its future forms, whatever they may be—are regular components of children's education about nutrition, and my aim is not to confuse them but to provide a simple reminder of the principles in this book. You'll notice that the specific needs of children align more closely with the USDA's pyramid than adults' needs do:

- Calcium is more important for children, so dairy should play a greater role in their diets.
- Children have a greater need for high-quality protein, and most kids should eat some meat, instead of relying on plant sources of protein.

Because of these differences, the children's pyramid does not need to be so radically redrawn. What most concerns me about the USDA pyramid is not how the different groups are placed and ranked in the hierarchy of a healthy diet. Instead, I'm concerned about the information that is *missing* from the pyramid about how to choose the healthiest foods in each food group. It's not enough to know how many servings of grains or meat to serve kids a day. Which sources of grains? What kind of meat? These are not trivial questions, but ones that have a real bearing on health. How do we choose the healthiest foods in each category? With all the choices we face today, I think it's important for parents to have specific information that they can use when faced with dozens of options in the grocery store.

In the subsequent chapters, we will use the USDA Food Guide Pyramid for Young Children as a departure point for talking about a balanced diet. But we will also look at some of the misunderstandings and inadequacies in the pyramid and give you the information you need to make better food choices. I will show you how to choose better sources of carbohydrates, fats, and protein, and I'll offer tips on bringing better foods into a child's diet. I will also discuss the often overlooked role that beverages play in potentially throwing a good diet out of balance. And I'll address some current concerns of parents, such as the need for kids today to maintain a healthy weight and engage in lots of physical activity; the relative merits and disadvantages of dietary supplements; and finally, what every parent should know about the school lunch program and how to make it better.

Today's Kids Have a Diet Out of Balance

The USDA pyramid replaced the old image of the four food groups as a tool for explaining the importance of a balanced diet. You've probably heard that term *balanced diet* many times, so much so that you may take it for granted. But while balance is a concept we've all heard, it's also an art that few of us put into practice. In general, a balanced diet is one that includes a variety of foods with a mix of the three basic macronutrients: carbohydrates, fats, and proteins. It includes a healthy portion of plant foods like fruits, vegetables, grains, and legumes, which provide vitamins, minerals, and fiber. In a balanced diet, no particular food is eaten in excess or at the exclusion of other foods.

Despite the fact that balance is the foundation of good nutrition, even health-conscious people don't always follow a balanced diet. There are a few reasons why this might be. For one, we all prefer some foods to others and we tend to overload our diet with our favorites, whether that means carbohydrate-rich pastas and baked goods or foods high in fat and protein like eggs, cheese, and beef.

The concept of balance is also a tough sell in marketing terms. Take a look at any health magazine or the health section of a newspaper, and you'll find articles touting the medicinal qualities of specific foods, whether they hold the key to stalling the aging process, giving us energy, preventing disease, or some other specific function—as if loading up on the right fruit or vegetable will improve our lives dramatically. When these articles do address the diet as a whole, it's almost always in terms of weight loss. That means that the only information most people read about how to build their diet as a whole is in terms of weight-loss plans that often greatly skew the balance of the diet (as in very high-protein or very low-fat diets) to help people eat fewer calories and lose weight. In these sorts of articles, the unusual diets hoard the headlines, while the old standby, moderation, gets pushed into the margins.

Another reason balance gets left by the wayside may be our short attention spans. Following a balanced diet requires thinking about what you eat throughout the day and throughout the week. It's easier for people to live meal to meal, and looking for specific foods that they identify as healthy at each meal, rather than taking a hard look at whether all those individual meals add up to anything resembling a well-balanced diet. They may reach for a "health food" like a vitamin-fortified energy bar or a protein shake, without ever thinking about whether they really need extra protein or vitamins and minerals in their diet.

The same problem extends to children. Despite the fact that education about a balanced diet has been around for years, the diets of most children in the United States are actually very lopsided. According to a national health survey, the top ten foods contributing to the caloric intake of children aged two to eighteen in the United States are as follows:

1. Milk
2. Bread
3. Cakes, cookies, quick breads, and doughnuts
4. Beef
5. Ready-to-eat cereal
6. Soft drinks
7. Cheese
8. Potato chips, corn chips, and popcorn
9. Sugar, syrup, and jam
10. Poultry

Not all of these foods are "bad." For instance, milk is a great source of protein and calcium for children, beef is also an excellent source of protein, and breads and cereals provide vitamins and minerals as well as the energy children need to get through the day. What I want to draw your attention to is not the individual foods but how they all add up to a whole diet. I've included a drawing of what the pyramid for a typical American child might be based on this list, an Out-of-Balance

Figure 5.2   The Out-of-Balance Food Pyramid of today's kids.

Food Pyramid (see Figure 5.2). As you can see, this pyramid is built on a hefty dose of fats and sweets, as well as carbohydrates, and includes protein from dairy products and meat, but few vegetables. You may also notice that the pyramid looks like it's bursting at the seams. That's because many kids today are eating larger portions and consuming more calories than they need, contributing to a rise in childhood overweight and obesity. And instead of engaging in active play, as children do in the USDA Food Guide Pyramid for Young Children, these kids are sitting around playing a video game, reflecting a growing trend toward a sedentary lifestyle.

The USDA food pyramid is designed to emphasize some of the food groups that are often overlooked in children's diets, like fruits and vegetables, and deemphasize the added fats and sugar that constitute many of the snack foods kids eat. It also emphasizes variety, because choosing several servings of each group every

What's in a Serving?

Another important confusion that often arises when people consult the USDA pyramid is the concept of servings and portion size. You may have encountered this in your own life, when you ate a bag of chips or cooked a box of pasta and happened to glance at the nutrition label. Not too bad, you may have thought, adding up the number of calories. But then perhaps something drew your eyes to the line reading "Servings per container." Turns out that little bag of chips or that helping of pasta really counts as two or three servings, and you had eaten many more calories than you originally thought.

The same problem occurs when people follow the food pyramid. While we may be happy to learn that a small bit of vegetables counts as a serving, foods in other groups, particularly the grain group, are usually eaten as more than one "serving" per portion in a typical meal. When the children's pyramid mentions a serving of grains, it is a small serving. For example, a serving from the grain group is a slice of bread or an ounce of cereal. So a whole sandwich counts as two servings from the grain group, and a small individual-sized box of breakfast cereal weighing 1.5 ounces counts as one and one-half servings.

day means that children won't simply eat the same few foods over and over, a habit that could put them in danger of a deficiency in certain nutrients. Materials from the USDA (available at usda.gov) can help educate parents in how to use the pyramid to plan meals and snacks for their children from each of the groups of the pyramid, and provide some tips on teaching children about nutrition.

The USDA pyramid is largely silent on one critical issue: which foods are better than others? While the pyramid does an excellent job of capturing the concept of balancing different kinds of foods, it reveals very little about which foods in each category are healthy and which are harmful. The only foods it discourages eating at all are fats and sweets. But within the other basic food groupings in the pyramid, some foods should have a more prominent role in a healthy diet than others.

In essence, the primary piece missing from the USDA Food Guide Pyramid for Young Children is information about *choices*. As I mentioned at the beginning of this chapter, we are inundated every day with choices. With so many food options available to us these days, parents need to be aware of the incredible differences in nutrition between different foods that they see in the supermarket.

A Nutrition Strategy for Healthy Kids

The following chapters will provide you with updated knowledge about the role of nutrition in a healthy lifestyle for children. The new pyramid that I've provided is intended to update the USDA pyramid with information about making smarter food choices and following a healthy lifestyle. Here are some of the key points in building a healthy diet for children aged two to eight, all of which will be detailed in later chapters:

Weight Control and Physical Activity Are the Foundation of Good Health

The pyramid for children shows images of activity, play, and exercise to reinforce the idea that exercise is a part of good health. I would argue that weight control and physical activity are at the foundation of good nutrition, because staying at a healthy weight and keeping active are so important for health. This doesn't mean worrying about body image or thinness at a young age. It means encouraging kids to use their bodies rather than letting them gather dust sitting around the house. It means developing eating habits that help children resist the many temptations of cheap, high-calorie foods. And it means developing a lifestyle early in life that helps prevent disease, rather than waiting for a health problem to emerge before making changes. Chapter 6 addresses these issues.

Better Carbohydrates for Better Health: The Form That Grains Take Makes a Big Difference for Health

The grain group is a prime example of the lack of information about choices in the current pyramid. The group includes carbohydrate-rich foods like bread, hot and cold cereals, pasta, rice, and baked goods like cookies and pastries. It includes everything from oatmeal to cupcakes, melba toast to Cheetos. Within this group are foods that have little nutritive value, and others that are wonderfully healthy and packed with vitamins, minerals, and dietary fiber.

The majority of the grain products we find on supermarket shelves are refined and processed to the point where they no longer are very nutritious at all. Refined grains, as well as starchy foods like potatoes, contain carbohydrates that are so simple they behave in the body similarly to sugar. So the fact that sugary sweets and refined carbohydrates appear at opposite ends of the pyramid is a bit of a paradox. To resolve the problem, parents need to know about how to choose better sources of carbohydrates such as whole-grain foods. The larger, more complex carbohydrates found in whole grains provide more nutrients and have a better effect on the body's digestion and metabolism.

A Place for Fats in a Healthy Diet

The USDA pyramid includes fats and sweets at the top, with the order to "use sparingly." This is undoubtedly a move designed to bring the typical diet of kids into balance, since it is currently sitting on a base of fat and sugar. It does make sense to limit excess amounts of fat in children's diets, because fat packs a lot of calories into a small space, so eating too many fatty foods might potentially contribute to overweight. However, banishing all fats to the top of the pyramid overlooks the place of healthy fats in a child's diet. Fat, along with carbohydrates and proteins, is an essential nutrient without which we couldn't survive. It is not simply an evil lurking in many of our foods that we should cut out entirely. Instead, parents should try to choose healthier forms of fat. But unfortunately, the pyramid tells you nothing about which fats are better than others.

Choosing Better Protein Sources

Foods in the meat and dairy groups are the primary sources of protein in children's diets (the USDA pyramid includes plant sources of protein, like nuts, seeds, and beans, in the meat group). While all of these foods are great sources of protein, animal sources provide a higher quality of protein than plant sources, meaning that they more closely match the needs of growing bodies. The downside is that meat and dairy products have unhealthier fats than plant foods, and the type of fat in foods is important for health. In order to strike a balance between high-quality protein and good fats, kids should eat low-fat, fat-free, or lean versions of dairy products and meats, and their diets should include a variety of plant and animal proteins. Chapter 7 explains how to choose the best sources of carbohydrates, fats, and proteins.

Making the Most out of Fruits and Vegetables

Just about every child in the United States could benefit from eating more fruits and vegetables every day. In the other food groups, I've emphasized that some foods are better than others, and the unhealthiest foods should be restricted. But in this group the main message is more, more, more! Still, choices are important in this category, too. While any fruit or vegetable is a great addition to the diet, even these are certainly not all the same and provide different amounts of needed vitamins, minerals, and fiber. And more important, some fruits and vegetables may be processed or prepared in a form that makes them less nutritious than others. Finally, some vegetables such as potatoes function more like a refined grain in the body, and including them in this group is misleading. In Chapter 8, I will tell you how to make the most out of the fruits and vegetables you serve.

Avoid Sugar and Excess Fat

There is a certain logic to the groups in the lower part of the pyramid, because most of the foods we encounter every day can be assigned to one or more of these categories fairly easily. Milk belongs to the milk group, apples belong to the fruit group, and a turkey sandwich belongs to both the grain and meat groups (and vegetable group if you add tomato and lettuce). But lumping sweets and fats together at the top of the pyramid can create confusion about which foods we should avoid.

Sugar and excess fat may come in concentrated form in some foods like butter or candy (which the pyramid depicts in that section), but they are also distributed throughout foods in the other groups, like the milk, meat, and grain groups. That means that you could avoid any foods that you would specifically identify as a "fat" or a "sweet," but still overload on fat and sugar. It's all a matter of choices: do you choose, for example, sweetened or unsweetened breakfast cereal, whole or skim milk, sugar-sweetened yogurt or plain yogurt, canned fruit packed in syrup or fresh fruit, low-fat string cheese or cheddar slices?

In other words, the kinds of foods you choose from the lower groups often determine how much fat and sugar you consume. And in many cases the sugar and fat in foods is hidden. Let's say you make a peanut butter and jelly sandwich, and choose a whole-fruit spread instead of jelly, believing it will have less sugar. But while sugar isn't in the ingredient list, the "fruit concentrates" in the spread are

Healthy Kids Aged Two Through Eight: The Bottom Line

Children are not just little adults: they have special dietary needs and may have slightly different eating habits.

- Developing healthy eating habits in children requires more than just serving the right food: it means dealing with all the behavioral, social, and environmental factors that influence eating. Parents should seek out opportunities to help children learn about food and get involved in their own nutrition.

- Kids today have diets that are out of balance, providing too many calories with too few nutrients. The USDA Food Guide Pyramid for Young Children is a useful tool for bringing the major components of the diet into balance, but lacks some critical information about how to choose the healthiest foods.

- Knowing what to look for when choosing foods from each group in the pyramid is critical to building a nutritious diet. We will provide you that information.

simply a different form of sugar—the total sugars will still be high. And did you realize that most brands of peanut butter have sugar added, too? Then there is the sweetener in the bread, adding a few more grams of sugar to the total. In other words, children don't need to eat foods we would identify as sweets to get plenty of sugar in their diets. Throughout the following chapters, I'll bring attention to the added sweeteners and fats in foods and beverages and give you tips on cutting them out of meals and snacks.

Supplements Are Not a Substitute for a Good Diet

Many parents wonder whether children need dietary supplements to ensure they have enough vitamins and minerals in their diet. While supplements can provide "insurance" to prevent any deficiencies in the diet, they are not a substitute for eating nutrient-rich foods. In Chapter 9, I'll give you some strategies for building a multivitamin, multimineral diet the natural way.

Beverages Are Foods, Too

Kids today are drinking more and more soft drinks and other sweetened beverages, and beverages are a large source of excess calories and added sugar in many children's diets. I will argue in Chapter 10 that beverages are every bit as important in the diet as solid foods, and that parents need to apply the same limits on beverages as they would to other foods: keeping portion sizes reasonable and choosing healthier drinks like plain water, milk, and juice.

The following chapters will help you understand the major components of food and why some foods should have a more prominent place in children's diets than others. Much of this information will apply to the whole family, but I will also point out special dietary needs of children that differ from adults. In addition, in Chapter 12, I will offer some tips and recipes to help you turn that knowledge into practice, a healthy approach to eating that fits your family's lifestyle.

Finally, while I offer information about what kids *should* eat, now that your child is walking, talking, becoming more assertive, and spending more time outside the home, it may become more difficult to put those "shoulds" into practice. I have included tips to help you make good nutrition acceptable and even fun. Don't expect every child to willingly follow a healthy diet. But despite the challenges, I believe that providing a child with good nutrition is within the reach of any parent willing to take up the task.

6

Weight Control and Physical Activity

Imagine an infection that could slowly diminish children's health; shorten their adult lives; predispose them to diseases of the cardiovascular, respiratory, and hormonal systems; and impair their mental health and self-esteem. Imagine that the number of children hit by this infection, which is very difficult to treat, had doubled in the past two decades. Wouldn't parents be concerned? This scenario describes a growing health problem that, though not an infection, has all the alarming traits of an epidemic. That problem is childhood overweight.

The infectious diseases that once loomed as a constant danger to health are now extremely uncommon in developed countries. Instead, chronic diseases including diabetes, heart disease, and now being overweight or obese have bloomed in their place, posing the greatest threat to health. In Figure 6.1, you can see how the sharp plummet in infectious diseases is a reverse of the rise in obesity in recent years. Unlike a quick infection, these chronic diseases creep in over years and decades, often in response to our behaviors and environment. As the incidence of infectious disease drops and the incidence of chronic disease climbs, it is more critical that we prevent the disease process early in life.

Figure 6.1   The changing health landscape: infectious disease rates are dropping while obesity and other chronic diseases are on the rise.

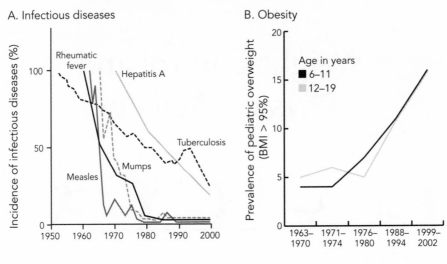

A. Infectious diseases

B. Obesity

1963–70 Pregnancy status not available
1963–65 only data on 6–11 years
1966–67 only data on 12–17 years

If you regularly read a newspaper or watch the news on TV, chances are you've heard something about the obesity epidemic in America. And if you haven't, you will soon. The prevalence of obesity has exploded in the past decade, rising 61 percent from 1991 to 2000. By 2001, 20.9 percent of adults in the United States were obese, an alarming trend that is now being mirrored in children. If no steps are taken to curb this epidemic, this generation of children may face unprecedented health problems from being overweight.

It may seem strange to hear something we often think of as a cosmetic problem referred to in the language of a disease. A few years ago, people in the medical community didn't even talk about obesity as a major public health problem, much less as an epidemic. Of course, physicians have always known about the ailments and health risks that come with being very obese, but being overweight was not always seen as a health concern in itself.

Over the past few years, however, this view of obesity has begun to change. We have realized that being severely overweight is so intrinsically linked to chronic disease and health problems that it truly is a state of poor health, not just a shape of

Overweight Versus Obese

Overweight and *obese* both refer to a disproportion of body weight to height. The U.S. Centers for Disease Control and Prevention have defined these terms for adults based on their body mass index (BMI), a ratio of height to weight. Overweight adults have BMIs of 25 or higher, and obese adults have BMIs of 31 or higher. Both conditions are associated with long-term health problems, but they differ in severity.

Children's bodies are growing and changing, so it's more difficult to set an absolute number on these terms. Instead, epidemiologists use a BMI growth chart for children that compares a child's weight-to-height ratio with typical children of the same age. A child who falls in the 95th percentile or higher for his age is considered overweight, while a child who falls between 85th and 95th percentile is considered at risk of being overweight. The CDC avoids applying the term *obesity* to young children, but other health professionals may use the terms *obese* and *overweight* for the two categories. In reality, individuals fall along a spectrum of weight and health. The definitions are used for tracking health trends, but don't capture differences between individuals with different health habits and body types.

the body. And the rapid spread of this condition across our population over the past decade truly warrants the description "epidemic." It has raised an alarm in the public health community akin to an emerging infectious disease, such as HIV infection and AIDS in the early to mid-1980s.

The costs of health problems related to overweight now rival those of smoking, our greatest public health problem that is linked to behavior, and dealing with our expanding bodies is going to be a major burden on the health-care system. Unfortunately, turning a blind eye to obesity is a habit many find hard to break. Nearly half of physicians still fail to counsel their patients about the health risks of weighing too much.

Being Overweight Is Not Just an Adult Problem

Perhaps the most alarming aspect of the obesity epidemic is how it has infiltrated the lives of children. In the 1970s, only about 5 percent of children were over-

Obesity in Numbers

Not convinced that obesity is a big problem? In public health, numbers talk. Take a look at these:

Percentage of adults in the U.S. who were obese in 2001	20.9%
Percentage of children aged 6–11 in the U.S. who were overweight	15.3%
Percentage of children aged 12–19 in the U.S. who were overweight	15.5%
Estimated amount of money spent annually on medical bills related to overweight and obesity in the United States	$93 billion
Increase in the rate of obesity among African-American and Hispanic children 1986–1998	120%
Percentage of overweight adolescents who become overweight adults	80%
Number of children under five years of age who are overweight in the world	22 million

weight; nowadays, at least 15 percent of kids are overweight, and the numbers seem to be growing. This is no longer a problem of a few kids with weight problems; a significant portion of today's children weigh too much and need to take steps to reduce their weight or face serious health consequences.

Not only are there more children these days who are overweight or at risk of overweight; but kids are also getting heavier earlier in life—that 15 percent prevalence rate holds for kids aged six to eleven as well as adolescents. Because it usually takes an adult several years to become obese, this rapid onset of obesity in children can pose some serious problems for their developing bodies. The growing number of overweight kids means that parents need to be thinking about weight control and physical activity for their children well before they probably think it should be an issue.

Weight Gain in Childhood Can Be Difficult to Outgrow

Anyone who has tried to lose weight knows that gaining weight is a lot like running down a hill: getting back to where you started from takes a lot more effort than getting to the bottom of the hill did. That's why we as a nation spend an estimated $33 billion per year on weight-loss products, yet keep putting on the pounds. Well, losing weight isn't easy for kids either, and in reality those who do become overweight or obese often enter a struggle with weight that will last a lifetime.

In fact, the connection between overweight in childhood and overweight in adulthood is so strong that we can now predict a child's likelihood of being an overweight adult based on current body mass index (BMI). By the calculations of one study, an eight-year-old girl whose BMI is in the 95th percentile for her age group has a 76 percent chance of being overweight and a 46 percent chance of being obese at age thirty-five. For an eight-year-old boy in the 95th percentile, the chances are 72 percent for becoming overweight and 22 percent for becoming obese. And having a parent who is obese can double a child's chances of also becoming obese.

These are just calculations for a hypothetical child; they don't predict what will happen to any particular individual. And they are also not inevitable. These probabilities hold for our current habits and policies, but if we as a society take steps to intervene when children gain weight, we can bring these numbers down. The numbers do, however, illustrate the point that the pounds children gain may stay with them for life if nothing is done to change their situation.

The best chance we have to remedy this situation is to prevent kids from becoming overweight in the first place. While many people successfully manage to lose weight and keep it off, most people who lose weight gain it back eventually. It is very difficult to maintain the diet and exercise patterns that allowed them to lose weight, because old habits are so hard to break. Since it's so hard to undo what's been done, parents have the opportunity and responsibility to keep the problem from ever occurring. If kids develop habits of eating well and exercising while young, they may have an easier time staying healthy later in life.

Being Overweight Is an Energy Imbalance

Let's go back to physics class. As many of us learned in school, the first law of thermodynamics states that the total amount of energy in a system remains constant. In other words, when you put energy into a system, it doesn't just disappear—it must be either expended or stored for later use. This law holds true for the body as well. We take in energy as food, and we use the calories in that food to do work. Some energy is expended simply keeping our bodies alive, and even more is expended when our bodies are more active.

When we don't expend the calories we take in, they get stored in the body—it's that simple. A calorie is simply a measure of the potential energy in food. When we take in more calories than our bodies use, much of that energy gets stored as fat. Some people have the mistaken belief that the fat in your body relates to the fat in the food you eat. Don't confuse the two—fat cells are simply the storage container of choice for extra energy. Whether that energy originally came from fat or carbohydrates or protein doesn't matter—it's all energy, and anything extra is eventually stored as fat.

The body is very good at keeping a balance between how much it takes in and how much it expends. Contrary to popular belief, overweight people usually have a faster metabolism than people who are not overweight, because their bodies actually expend more energy all the time to support the extra weight. For reasons we don't entirely understand, some people's bodies seem particularly gifted at keeping intake and expenditure in balance. These are the people who always order dessert after a big dinner and never seem to gain a pound. The law of thermodynamics tells us that the energy in that dessert can't simply disappear—

Researchers are also starting to realize that it's never too early to think about preventing weight gain for better health. Breast-feeding has been associated in some studies with lower rates of overweight and obesity, as has good maternal nutrition during pregnancy. Another period when children are particularly vulnerable to becoming overweight is the time around five years of age when a child's body mass index begins to grow and the body begins to deposit more fat tissue. Disease prevention is a critical part of keeping children healthy: just think of the immunizations for various infections that are standard practice for every child. The steps you take to encourage healthy eating now can be thought of as a preventive vaccine for obesity and the array of health problems that follow it.

their bodies are simply more efficient at expending energy, whether they seem to be active or not.

For most people, the body can't get rid of many extra calories through metabolism alone. Gaining weight doesn't take a lot of overeating or sitting around; in fact, it takes just a small imbalance in intake over expenditure to tip the scale toward weight gain. Eating about 50 excess calories a day—less than half a can of soda—would eventually add up to a weight gain of five pounds every year. The average weight gain for adults after their twenties is usually less than that, under a pound a year, or ten extra calories a day. It doesn't seem like a lot, but the pounds creep up on you: many people are surprised when they reach their fifties and are suddenly twenty pounds overweight. Contrary to the stereotype of the obese person eating constantly, many people become overweight by taking in just a little more than they expend every day.

It's useful to keep in mind the importance of energy balance when thinking about weight and weight control. Many people become confused by the plethora of weight-loss plans that argue that you can lose weight by eating more of some foods and less of others. In reality, there is no magic or mystery to weight gain or loss. To lose weight you must either reduce the number of calories you eat or be more active, or ideally both. But because cutting back on calories can be so difficult once a person is used to overeating, weight-loss plans offer ways to trick the body into thinking it is getting more calories than it truly is. This is all they do: any diet that allows a person to lose weight is almost certainly doing so by lowering the number of calories the person eats, nothing more, nothing less.

Being Overweight Is Not Just a Matter of Looks

We're all familiar with the social and psychological difficulties that come with being overweight. Kids are especially sensitive to how their peers view and treat them, and extra weight can draw teasing and ostracism. In fact, a recent survey asked obese kids to rank their quality of life and found that they were as likely to rank their quality of life as low as children undergoing chemotherapy for cancer. That's a lot of suffering for these kids to endure.

But being overweight carries serious health consequences beyond the psychological harm. Adult obesity is associated with a higher incidence of diabetes, high blood pressure, clogged arteries, heart disease and heart attacks, stroke, arthritis, certain cancers, infertility, asthma, and sleep disorders like sleep apnea. Because overweight children are more likely to become obese adults, their weight in childhood can be setting them up for a greater risk of adult disease and a shortened life. And they don't necessarily need to wait that long to feel the effects; overweight children have measurable differences in blood pressure and cholesterol levels compared to children of normal weight. The Bogalusa Heart Study, which has tracked fourteen thousand children in Louisiana since 1972, found that about 60 percent of children aged five to ten who were overweight already carried at least one of the risk factors for developing heart disease, such as high blood pressure and abnormally high levels of insulin in the blood. The study has helped to show that a growing number of obese children will likely become adults with higher rates of heart disease, already the leading cause of death in our country.

Obesity, Diabetes, and the Metabolic Syndrome

Diabetes is the most common and serious disease linked to obesity in children. It comes in two major forms. The first, type 1, occurs when the body destroys the cells that produce insulin, the hormone that regulates the amount of glucose in the blood. Type 1 diabetes affects individuals early in life and can be severe and life-threatening if not managed properly with regular insulin injections. This type of diabetes is not associated with being obese. The second kind, type 2 diabetes, accounts for more than 90 percent of diabetes cases, and begins when the body's tissues begin to lose their sensitivity to insulin signaling.

Glucose is a simple sugar that is absorbed from foods into the bloodstream, where it can then be taken up by cells and used by the body for energy. A rise in glucose levels in the blood prompts special cells in the pancreas to release insulin, which acts as a messenger that delivers the glucose in the blood to various tissues, causing blood sugar levels to drop. When cells become unresponsive to insulin's message—a condition called *insulin resistance*—blood sugar levels stay high and the body works overtime to produce more insulin to get the message across. While insulin resistance doesn't always lead to diabetes, it is a prediabetic condition that can progress to full-fledged diabetes if left unchecked. Complications of diabetes may include kidney failure, nerve damage, blindness, heart disease, and stroke. The risk of having a stroke or dying of heart disease is two to four times higher in adults with diabetes.

We used to call the two major types of diabetes "early-onset," and "adult-onset," because type 2 diabetes rarely occurred in anyone younger than forty. But the names have changed with the times because the old monikers have tragically become outdated. While the problem is too new to put a national number on, we are now seeing children acquire "adult-onset" diabetes, and many clinics now report that type 2 diabetes accounts for one-third to one-half of all the cases of childhood diabetes they see.

The exact causes of the rise in childhood diabetes are not known, but it is almost certainly linked to the growing number of kids who are overweight and/or very inactive. In the United States, children of African, Hispanic, Native American, and some Asian/Pacific Islander backgrounds are at greater risk, as are those who have a family history of type 2 diabetes.

Insulin resistance doesn't have to lead to full-blown diabetes to cause health problems. Epidemiologists have noted that many common metabolic disorders don't arrive as solitary visitors—they are often associated with one another and occur simultaneously in the same person. We now call this condition the *metabolic syndrome* or *syndrome X*, and it includes obesity, insulin resistance or diabetes, high cholesterol, and high blood pressure. People with the metabolic syndrome are at increased risk of dying of heart disease, stroke, or kidney failure.

Overweight is a central component of this complex cluster of bodily malfunctions that can eventually lead to disease. At least one in five overweight people is affected by the metabolic syndrome. Overweight people have twice the risk of developing diabetes as lean people. And they are at a higher risk for developing high blood pressure, high cholesterol, and triglycerides (a type of fat) in the blood, which in turn are risk factors for stroke and heart disease. And having excess fat that concentrates on the abdomen rather than the hips and thighs—often called an apple shape—is also associated with a higher risk of heart disease.

The good news is that this progression to type 2 diabetes and other conditions of the metabolic syndrome can often be slowed or reversed by paying special attention to diet and physical activity. People who are overweight can begin to reduce their risk of disease through slow, gradual weight loss—often losing just five to ten percent of their body mass can make a difference. For kids, an even better and more effective strategy is available: prevention. By providing kids with a healthy diet and opportunities for physical activity, parents can make sure their kids never embark on this dangerous journey that often leads to compounding health problems.

When Do I Start Worrying About My Child's Weight?

We've all seen chubby babies and chubby kids lose their "baby fat." Maybe that's why many parents seem oblivious when their children gradually become overweight, eventually putting their health at risk. It's true that chubbiness in early childhood isn't always a sign of impending obesity, especially in infancy and toddlerhood. But in general, parents should probably learn to pick up on the signals sooner, rather than depending on baby fat melting away.

If your child is active and has regular periods of active play outside or in an organized activity or sport, a little extra weight may be part of the growing process and shouldn't concern you too much. What should concern you is a child who continues to be overweight even after growing in height, or engages in little physical activity.

To find a more objective indicator of healthy weight, use a growth chart to keep track of your child's weight and height. (See Selected Resources section.) This chart plots height and weight according to the average values for that age group—the curved lines on the chart, called *isobars*, mark the height and weight for several percentiles, from the 5th to the 95th. A good way to picture this is to imagine lining up one hundred children of the same age according to how tall they are, from shortest to tallest. Any child who is shorter than the fifth child in this row is considered below the 5th percentile for the age group. You can do the same for weight. The only difference is that the growth charts were developed using a large number of children, so they give you a sense of where a child fits in the general population.

The chart does *not* imply that a child must fall near the 50th percentile to be considered normal. Like adults, kids have a natural variety in body size and some are shorter or taller—or weigh more or less—than others. But the child's height and weight should fall on the same or conjoining isobars. In other words, tall children should generally weigh more than short

Why Are Kids Gaining Weight?

There are several theories why our children are rapidly becoming overweight. Obesity is a very complex phenomenon, and anyone who tries to explain it with one or two reasons probably isn't doing the problem justice. Remember, obesity is an energy imbalance, so we can find reasons for becoming obese at both ends of the equation.

children. If weight is more than two isobars higher than height, it signals that the two are out of proportion. The Centers for Disease Control and Prevention (CDC) have defined childhood overweight according to percentiles. Any child over three years old whose weight falls between the 85th to 95th percentiles is considered at risk for being overweight and may be a candidate for change in diet or activity level. And any child whose weight falls at or above the 95th percentile is considered overweight and needs to lose weight to avoid health problems. But keep in mind that these definitions are generalizations, and miss the individual nuances of body size and health.

A child's body is constantly growing and changing, and it has different needs than an adult body. An adult approach to weight loss or weight control is not appropriate for kids, especially young ones. Adults can experiment with unusual diets or limited calories, but children still need a balanced diet to grow and thrive. Parents should never impose fad diets on their children or deny them food when they are hungry. If you have concerns about your child's weight, seek advice from a pediatrician about making gradual, reasonable changes in your child's diet and activity.

When embarking on a weight-control or weight-loss plan, children should understand that these changes are for the sake of their health, rather than just their physical appearance. Weight is never an easy subject to talk about, no matter what your age, and the topic should be handled with sensitivity. Parents shouldn't use guilt or shame as a motivating factor in a child's weight loss, or draw too much attention to body image. Young children who become obese often have underlying emotional and psychological problems that may lead them to eat too much. It's futile for parents to try to fix their children's eating habits without first addressing these issues. In these cases, counseling may be the best first step as part of a path to better health.

- *Too much food.* Food has never been more abundant and available than it is now. With three or four dollars and in as many minutes, a child or adolescent can enter a fast-food restaurant and purchase a meal that provides his entire recommended intake of calories for the day. For busy parents, these meals provide a blessedly convenient mealtime option—they save the time and effort of cooking, as well as the price of going to the grocery store and purchasing more healthful produce or higher-quality grains and protein sources. In many ways, obesity is a natural response to our current environment.

The TV-Overweight Connection

One behavior that has been consistently linked to childhood obesity is television viewing. The Centers for Disease Control and Prevention's (CDC) National Health and Nutrition Examination Survey (NHANES), a large-scale survey conducted every few years, has found that kids who watch more TV are more likely to be overweight and less likely to engage in physical activity.

While watching TV in itself won't make you fat, there are several reasons why TV can encourage kids to gain weight. The first goes back to our simple energy equation. Watching TV takes very little energy, and it steals away time that could be spent moving. Indeed, studies have found that kids who watch more TV spend less time involved in physical activity. However, TV may have other ways of encouraging weight gain in kids.

Take a look at any television programming for kids. Chances are you will see many fast-paced, colorful commercials that all have one thing in common—food. The food industry is a trillion-dollar business, and your child represents an important market force; a recent market research report estimates that kids aged five to fourteen control about ten billion dollars in food spending per year.

Many parents underestimate the impact of this constant exposure to advertising. But studies have shown that kids are able to recognize brand names when they are just a few years old, leading companies to more aggressively market to babies and toddlers—what marketing types call the *drool factor*. And the marketing approaches used by these companies are becoming more sophisticated than simply showing ads. SpongeBob SquarePants, one of the most popular cartoon characters on TV today, is now also hawking macaroni and cheese, crackers, and fast food, as well as other products. And a new approach dubbed

- *Less expensive and easier to prepare processed foods.* Once associated with wealth and excess, overweight and obesity now disproportionately afflict the poor, as well as minority populations. More than 30 percent of blacks and 24 percent of Hispanics are obese, as compared to just under 20 percent of whites. Rates are also higher for people with less education and less money to spend on healthy foods. Healthful eating can be an investment these days, and that's a shame. Processed foods are very cheap to produce and purchase but they are usually overloaded with salt, sugar, and unhealthful fats. It's not just the obvious culprits of Big Macs and

advergaming offers kids free online games that promote a product like candy or chips. (To be fair, this type of advertising is not limited to TV and the Internet—cereal manufacturers now use picture books to hawk their products, ensuring that kids see the brand names early and often.)

Even more disturbing for parents is that advertisers no longer see adults as the important factor in promoting products to kids; instead, they increasingly see parents as obstacles to overcome. Marketers now refer to the *nag factor*, the ability of kids to persuade harried parents to buy products that appeal directly to them. So instead of trying to convince parents that a food is good for their kids, companies reach out directly to children with food that is colorful, tasty, and often very unhealthful, and let the nagging do its work. This kind of strategy pits parents directly against their kids in making food choices, and since no parent wants to trigger a tantrum in a busy supermarket aisle, many will back down and buy the coveted food.

When TV takes center stage in a household, it can lead to poor eating habits. One survey found that kids who watch more TV during meals eat more pizza, salty snacks, soda, and caffeine, and eat fewer fruits, vegetables, and juices than kids in families with low television use. Kids who don't regularly have structured family meals also are more likely to be overweight. Snacking in front of the TV makes eating a mindless task, almost as if taking in calories were just another way to keep your hands busy. This kind of idle snacking can set up some unhealthy habits and lead to overeating.

The American Academy of Pediatrics recently recommended that parents limit the time their children spend viewing TV and video media to a maximum of two hours per day. This should also include time spent on the Internet that isn't directly educational.

fries—many restaurant dishes and prepared frozen foods can be just as bad. The cost of fresh produce—as well as the effort it takes to prepare it—leaves many parents reaching for something quick, cheap, and easy.

• *Larger serving sizes.* Portion size is another culprit in our growing waistlines. Because food is so cheap these days, restaurants can offer more of it without it costing them much more, which gives us a feeling of getting value for our money. Portion size no longer has anything to do with an appropriate amount of food or drink.

In the 1950s, sodas came in eight-ounce bottles, but now sixteen- and twenty-ounce bottles are common. Extra-large sodas may provide 500 calories of pure sugar, much more than anyone should be consuming as a beverage. Most people don't count those calories as the equivalent of a meal, but drink them as they would water.

• *Societal changes.* In most families today, both parents work, which means that infants and young children spend more time in day care and less time under the direct influence of their parents. The food served in day care and school isn't always the kind of food you would choose if you had the chance. And with school lunches often unappealing and unpalatable, many kids choose to buy junk food from vending machines, which are increasingly common on school grounds. Thousands of schools now have fast-food outlets in cafeterias, because of the money they can reap from such arrangements. Unless parents argue for a healthier environment, good food and active play will increasingly become an optional part of school.

On the other side of the energy equation, kids today are spending less time in active play and more time watching TV, playing video games, surfing the Internet, and other sedentary pursuits. These activities can have a double influence on weight gain; not only do they take time away from active play, but they also expose kids to sophisticated advertisements about food and in many cases encourage idle snacking (see sidebar).

Physical activity is also harder to come by for kids whose schools no longer offer physical education programs, and are even cutting lunch and recess time to fit other requirements. People who live in cities but can't afford access to special clubs and classes may feel that there are few safe places for their kids to play outside.

In addition to the complex social changes that may be predisposing us to gain weight, certain individuals may have genetic factors that make them more likely to become overweight than others. But in most cases, genes don't necessarily equal destiny; instead, weight gain may be a complex interaction between genetic factors and lifestyle. An example of this is in certain populations in Micronesia, where an influx of cheap processed foods from the United States has led to alarming rates of obesity, diabetes, and heart disease. It appears that some groups of people have a genetic susceptibility to becoming overweight, but it takes an environmental change, such as exposure to Western-style food, to unleash it.

What Are the Solutions to Childhood Weight Problems?

The solutions to the problem of children being overweight are probably as diverse as its root causes. Changes need to be made in how children eat if we are to avoid burdening children with countless health problems in the future. Undoubtedly, some large-scale changes must be made in how kids access food, whether it means limiting how food is marketed to kids or improving the state of nutrition in our schools. We also should make physical activity a priority for kids, by providing inexpensive and safe opportunities for them to get out and get moving.

Whatever the changes, parents must take a lead role in making children healthier. My hope is that parents will become more aware of the basic principles of nutrition, as well as understand the need to take control of the energy balance to prevent weight gain. Parental involvement can make a big difference in the lifestyle that kids follow. Prevention means not waiting around for a problem to emerge, but taking action to establish good habits early on.

To take some preventive action to keep your child from becoming overweight and unhealthy, you can address both sides of the energy equation, through better diet, portion control, and activity.

Energy In: Eating Appropriate Amounts of Calories

To target the energy-in side of the equation, you can start paying closer attention to where your child's calories are coming from and how appropriate the total amount is. Some kids, especially those who are active, can seem to inhale food and stay thin and healthy. But other kids are either sedentary or have a tendency to gain weight even if they do stay fairly active. For the latter group, it's often necessary to make some restrictions in their diet.

The following chapters will explore what's in foods and what are the most healthful food choices for kids. One of the best ways to both improve health and limit excess calories is to choose foods that actually do something for the body rather than just provide calories. Foods like fruits and vegetables contain needed vitamins and minerals, but they are also full of water and fiber and are relatively low in calories. In contrast, sugary sodas and juice drinks, candy, and chips are basically just cheap and easy calories, with little else the body needs—that's why these foods truly are "empty calories." By limiting the amount of these ingredients their children eat, parents can help limit extra calories and make the most out of the foods kids do eat.

Of course, while good food choices can help, our energy equation shows us that how much you eat is the bottom line. One of the biggest concerns is portion size, or how much of a food we typically eat at one sitting. Few of us are immune to the lures of a heaping portion of a food we enjoy. Several studies have found that portion size is directly related to intake; in other words, when more food is offered, people tend to eat more, whether they are lean or overweight. A recent study from Penn State tested whether feeding children an extra-large portion of a certain dish would affect how much they ate. Children were first served lunches consisting of portions appropriate to their ages, but at a later occasion were given a meal with one of the entrees in the lunch, macaroni and cheese, at double the recommended portion size. The study found that children responded to the large portion by eating larger bites of the pasta—they ate an average of 25 percent more of the pasta and 15 percent more calories in the total meal. So putting more food on the plate can really change how much your child eats. It's always a better option to serve smaller portions and go get seconds if needed.

Some evidence also suggests that eating more than our fill is a skill we acquire, for better or worse. In another study from Penn State, children aged three and a half were offered lunches at different portion sizes and ate about the same number of calories regardless of how much was given to them. In contrast, children aged five ate a greater amount of calories when served a larger portion. This would suggest that infants and toddlers have an innate ability to regulate caloric intake that is gradually lost as kids get older.

Parents are largely responsible for providing their children cues about how to eat, especially when kids are very young. While most parents aren't worried about their kids eating too much when they are only five or six years old, this is actually a perfect time to start developing a sense of appropriate portion size, rather than waiting until kids reach adolescence and their habits are more fixed. Here are a few ways parents can start addressing the intake end of the energy equation:

• From those first feedings of solid foods during infancy, make eating a task that is given your child's full attention. Set aside a space in the high chair or at the dinner table with no distractions like TV. In the mornings before school, make sure your child sits down to breakfast instead of eating food on the go.

• Encourage children to stop eating when they feel satisfied or nearly full. This is a hard habit for parents to learn, since many adults grew up with their parents scolding them for not cleaning their plate. Nowadays those tactics are no longer helpful for most kids. Parents should instead discourage eating beyond the point of fullness, from infancy on.

• Keep an eye on your child's portion sizes to make sure servings aren't too big. Instead of eating from heaping plates at meals, your family can start with small portions and go for seconds if someone is still hungry after waiting a few minutes. At restaurants, you can order from a children's menu if it offers healthy options. But beware: many children's menus offer cheap foods that are easy for kids to accept, and are loaded with hot dogs, french fries, and other less healthy foods. It might be better to order a small appetizer or meal from the adult menu, and encourage your child to leave some on the plate or take part of it home for later. Getting in the doggie-bag habit is one of the best things you can do for your whole family to combat big restaurant portions.

• Make sure as many calories as possible are useful ones. The majority of a child's calories should come from vegetables, fruits, nutritious grains and protein sources, and some healthful fats. Foods that contain added sugar, or are dense with calories from too much fat, should not take the place of more nutritious sources of calories.

• Limit calories from drinks. Sweetened beverages and juices are a primary source of excess calories in many children's diet (see Chapter 10), because people often drink sugar-laden beverages as if they were water, not food. A better idea is to just drink water throughout the day, and low-fat or skim milk with meals. If your child wants something with more flavor than water, try artificially sweetened waters, sodas, or powdered drink mixes.

• Remember that eating is influenced by social and emotional forces, and parents have a big influence on how their children feel about food. By overly restricting certain foods or using them as bribes, you could be sending the message that food is a reward, and may encourage an unhealthy attitude toward eating.

- Don't be afraid to set limits when your child's health is at stake. By giving in to supermarket tantrums, you play right into the hands of advertisers. Instead, treat junk food as you would any item that is off-limits to children, and avoid taking a tired, hungry child to the store.

Putting It into Practice: A Simple Weight Control Plan for Your Family

These simple first steps can go a long way toward helping your family lose weight or stay at a healthy weight:

- Cut back on sugary beverages.

- Eat your breakfast. As I mentioned in the last chapter, people who eat breakfast generally weigh less and eat fewer calories throughout the day.

- Never eat in front of the TV, and limit TV or video time to a maximum of two hours per day.

- Eat meals together as a family as often as you can.

- Plan simple meals that emphasize fresh foods over processed ones. Try some of the recipe ideas in this book, and save time by chopping vegetables or setting aside ingredients ahead of time so they are ready to cook when you need them.

- Include fiber-rich foods at every meal, like fruits, vegetables, whole grains, and legumes. They will keep you fuller longer.

- Make your life a little more inconvenient. Take stairs regularly instead of escalators. Walk or ride your bike to a nearby destination instead of driving. Studies have shown that lifestyle changes such as these can be more effective for weight loss than scheduled exercise, and they are easier to maintain in the long term.

- To step up your activity level, schedule time for a simple daily activity, like walking the dog or riding bikes in the neighborhood. If your neighborhood is not safe for outdoor play, help your child find an indoor activity she can do every day, even for ten or fifteen minutes. It can be as simple as dancing in her bedroom to a favorite CD. Or you can purchase a bicycle stand to turn her bike into an inexpensive home gym—she can even peddle during her TV time.

Energy Out: Staying Active

Little kids love to play, and often seem full of a boundless energy that adults wish we still had. By the time they reach adolescence, however, many kids have grown out of their active play, and unless they participate in sports or another organized activity, they can start to settle into a sedentary lifestyle. Unfortunately, this trend is growing, since kids today have endless distractions that involve no physical activity, from video games to TV to the Internet. And you are in a lucky minority if your child's school still has a physical education program to get kids moving throughout the day.

The period of time from ages two to eight is an opportunity for parents to encourage the natural energy their young children have and start setting up habits to keep them more active as they get older. One of the best ways for everyone in the family to stay active is to build movement into your daily routine as much as possible. By taking stairs instead of elevators, walking to nearby stores or parking at the far end of the parking lot and walking a little more, and making more time for active chores in the house or yard, you can really increase the amount of energy you use every day.

So many parents these days focus on educational games for their children; equally important are games that get kids moving around. As play becomes less of a sport in itself, kids also benefit from structured, organized activities to keep them moving while still having fun. Parents can help their children find organized sports teams or classes in dance, gymnastics, martial arts, skating, rock climbing, skiing, or another activity. Remember, the goal here is to find an activity your child can enjoy for the long term in order to stay healthy—competition may be a motivating factor, but not the ultimate goal. Too much pressure and competitiveness can ultimately make a child lose interest in a sport or stop having fun.

If the price tag of lessons and classes is too steep, there are also many inexpensive or free programs in most cities and towns that are equally as fun and worthwhile. Take a look at your local parks and recreation department, YMCA, Boy Scouts or Girl Scouts, and local club teams.

There is only so much time in a day. Part of encouraging kids to stay active is limiting the time they spend in sedentary behaviors like watching TV, which in health terms is an "empty activity," just like some foods are empty calories. Set specific rules about when kids can watch TV or play video games. Just like junk food, don't make TV time into a reward or bribe—kids will get the message and want more.

Weight Control and Physical Activity: The Bottom Line

- More and more kids are becoming overweight, which predisposes them to several metabolic disorders and health problems, and raises their risk of developing diabetes and heart disease.

- Kids who weigh too much are likely to become adults who weigh too much. It's important for parents to prevent kids from gaining weight in the first place.

- Being overweight is an energy imbalance, and can be prevented by targeting both caloric intake (through better eating habits and appropriate portion sizes) and energy expenditure (through an active lifestyle). On both ends of the equation, parents can limit certain forms of "empty calories" and "empty activities" that are especially detrimental to health.

- Parents should model healthy attitudes toward eating and activity for their kids. A weight-loss or maintenance plan should focus on feeling good and staying healthy rather than drawing attention to body image.

Like Parent, Like Child: Modeling Good Behavior

Your attitudes about diet and physical activity have an enormous impact on your child. Modeling a behavior can be much more effective than telling children to do something you'd like them to do. Even when you are not consciously modeling a behavior, your child is learning from your example.

Kids pick up on their parents' anxieties about weight gain and loss, potentially getting some confusing messages about body image and health. You are probably not even aware of all the subtle messages you are sending your child throughout the day related to eating and exercise. Instead of letting these slip by, pay attention to how you, your partner, and your whole family relate to food as well as physical activity. What kind of messages does your behavior send your child? Some examples of ways to model good behavior:

• Are you trying to discourage your child from overeating? Next time you are served one of those insanely large portions at a restaurant, instead of eating as much as you can and then complaining that it will all go to your thighs, stop eating when you are halfway done and save the rest to take home. Say that you are satisfied and don't like the way your stomach feels when you're too full—and boast about the great deal you're getting, two meals for the price of one.

- When you head to the gym, do you act as if it's something you "have" to do to stay thin? Try talking about how nice it is to move around after a day of inactivity, about the positive feelings you get from a long walk or a workout. Emphasize that activity is important for keeping you healthy and strong, instead of focusing on how it affects your looks.

- Want to encourage your child to eat better foods instead of junk? When you are grocery shopping together, don't talk about buying ice cream as a treat for yourself. Instead, wander through the produce section and pick out your favorite fruit, or splurge for something exotic. Mention how good it looks—the smell, the color—and how much you'll enjoy eating it. Your child will learn that healthy foods can be treats, too.

- Worried about the influence of advertising and TV on your kids? Start talking back to the TV when you are watching it together. Point out the marketing strategies that are being used. Show your child that you won't be fooled, and offer counterarguments to what the ads are saying. Part of the strategy of marketing to kids is to get them to think the food companies are on their side. Don't indulge this fantasy—let your child know that ads are really out to get people to spend money, nothing more.

- Does your child shy away from team sports? Try to find an activity you can do together, even if it's just walking the dog or throwing a Frisbee at the park. Schedule it for a time that would normally be spent in front of the TV, like early evening. Set goals for both of you to keep the momentum going. Your enthusiasm will rub off, and it will provide a great way to spend time together.

7

Choosing Better Sources of Carbohydrates, Fats, and Proteins

M ost of what you eat is made of some combination of carbohydrates, fats, and proteins. These components are called *macronutrients* because they make up the bulk of the diet and provide the body energy and the materials needed for growing and maintaining cells and tissues. Vitamins and minerals, on the other hand, are called *micronutrients*; they are equally critical but are only needed in very small quantities and are not used for energy.

A balanced diet for children means a mix of foods that provides all the macronutrients, roughly in the ratio of 50 percent of total calories from carbohydrate, 30 percent from fat, and 20 percent from protein. It sounds simple, but macronutrients seem to cause endless confusion, and they are currently the subject of bitter debates in adult nutrition. For more than a decade, we were all inundated with messages about the benefits of low-fat diets. In the past few years, the trend has swung the other way, and low-carb or high-protein diets are now all the rage. The same people who once regarded beef as an artery-clogging evil now insist on ordering their burgers without the bun. Many people have the mistaken impression that healthy eating means choosing one macronutrient at the expense of another, as if protein, fat, and carbohydrates are in some kind of tug-of-war in the diet. I believe that any attempt to pit one macronutrient against another is misguided and leaves a lot of people confused and mistrustful of information about nutrition.

First, many people have come to believe that too much of one kind of macronutrient will make them fat. Well, the reality is much simpler: eating too much of *any* kind of food, over a long period of time, would result in an energy imbalance and cause you to gain weight. Many researchers are actively investigating whether a certain balance of macronutrients can help people to lose more weight than others. So far, however, the evidence seems to show that it's not *what* you eat, but *how much*.

Second, many people get confused about what works for weight loss and what's good for health. All of the emphasis on fad diets takes people away from the real issue: which sources of protein, fat, and carbohydrates are healthiest, and where can they be found in foods? I would like to bring a voice of reason to parents who might be confused about all these conflicting messages and wondering how some of these issues affect their kids. The main goal of this chapter is to help you understand:

- What macronutrients are
- What role they play in a healthy diet
- Why it is important to provide children with a balance of all three
- The differences between various sources of protein, fat, and carbohydrates, and which foods are healthiest

Choosing the best sources of macronutrients is a skill that few people learn, yet it can have a big impact on health. As I mentioned in Chapter 5, eating right involves more than just eating a balance of different kinds of foods in the food pyramid, it involves making the healthiest choices within those groups. Putting children's diets in balance is the first step. Providing them with the healthiest foods means learning to be label-savvy and knowing your ingredients.

Carbohydrates

Carbohydrates are the body's primary fuel source, and provide more than half the calories in the average American's diet. They are a quickly and easily digested form of energy, and most civilizations have based their diets on one or more energy-rich carbohydrate source, like rice, corn, or potatoes. But after long enjoying a place of honor in the diet, carbohydrates are currently falling out of favor in the public eye. Many adults in the United States are taking up low-carb diets, and companies are eager to develop and advertise foods that are low in carbohydrates—even low-carb bread!

Being a kid takes a lot of energy. No matter what the latest trends are, carbohydrates are an important source of energy for children. Most children eat a lot of carbohydrates, because they are easy to find and prepare and often have tastes that kids like. But foods that contain a lot of carbohydrates can include everything from whole-wheat bread and oatmeal to candy and soda; they include foods that are highly nutritious and others that provide calories but little else. Kids often get too much of their calories from carbohydrates, because of all the sugar they eat.

What Are Carbohydrates?

You can think of carbohydrates like Tinker Toys or Legos—they consist of chain-like molecules made of smaller units joined together. The smallest unit of a carbohydrate is a simple sugar. The three kinds of simple sugars are glucose, fructose, and galactose. Sometimes these simple units travel solo, but they can be joined together to form larger carbohydrates. Sometimes they pair up. *Sucrose* (table sugar) forms when glucose and fructose link up and is found in cane and beet sugar, maple syrup, molasses, sorghum, pineapple, and carrots. *Lactose*, the sugar found in milk, is formed from glucose and galactose; and *maltose*, the sugar in malted milk, is the pairing of two units of glucose.

When sugars really start to gang up in groups of ten or more, they are called *polysaccharides*. Many of the whole plant and animal foods we eat contain polysaccharides, because they are stored inside the cells of plants (in the form of starch) and animals (in the form of glycogen) as a reservoir of energy for the body. No matter which form a carbohydrate comes in, the body eventually breaks it down to smaller units and converts it to glucose to use it for fuel.

Dietary fiber is a kind of polysaccharide found in plants that cannot be digested by humans. Soluble fiber, which is found in beans, fruits, and oats, dissolves in water and can be partially digested by bacteria that grow naturally in the human colon. Insoluble fiber, found in whole grains and vegetables, does not dissolve and passes through the digestive system largely untouched. While fiber may not be important for providing energy to the body, it has several health benefits, described in the next section.

The Good and Bad of Carbohydrates

I've just told you that all carbohydrates, with the exception of those we are unable to digest, essentially get broken down by the body into the same basic elements. If that's true, why are some carbohydrates healthier than others? Part of it is in the process.

When you eat carbohydrates, the resulting molecules of glucose are absorbed into the bloodstream to be carried throughout the body. The body tries to keep blood sugar, or the amount of glucose in the blood, at a more or less even level. This process is regulated by a hormone called *insulin*. When glucose rushes into the bloodstream, it triggers the release of insulin, which helps deliver the glucose to cells of the body to use for fuel. As the glucose is taken out of the bloodstream by cells, insulin levels also fall. When blood sugar is critically low, the liver releases stores of glucose to keep the levels in balance.

The smaller and simpler a carbohydrate, the more quickly it is processed. Consuming a lot of easily digested carbohydrates, such as simple sugars, can trigger a spike in insulin that forces glucose out of the bloodstream quickly, leaving the blood sugar level lower than before. This insulin roller coaster can leave you feeling hungrier sooner, because the body believes that glucose needs to be replenished. And over time it can contribute to a phenomenon known as *insulin resistance*, in which the body's tissues no longer respond to insulin's signals. Insulin resistance is one of the hallmarks of diabetes, a disease that is increasingly afflicting children. The longer it takes to digest carbohydrates, the more even the insulin response. Larger, more complex carbohydrates take longer to break down into glucose.

The way a carbohydrate is packaged can also influence how quickly it's digested. For instance, the fructose in a piece of fruit is locked inside the cells of the plant, which takes time to digest, whereas pure fructose added as a sweetener to a processed food is freely available. Some starches, such as those in potatoes, are easily digested because they are loosely packed, while others, such as those in grains and many vegetables, are denser and require more effort to digest; cooking starches makes them more digestible because it causes starch-containing cells to soften and break apart, sometimes making a goopy texture.

Will Sugar Make My Child "Hyper"?

We've all heard the theory that eating too much sugar makes kids hyperactive. Is there any truth to the legend? Many studies have attempted to resolve this question, but to little avail. For instance, in six separate studies examining the effect of giving sucrose (table sugar) to children, two reported no effects on behavior, two reported negative effects of sugar, and two found what could be considered positive effects of giving children sugar, and none of these results was strongly convincing. Other studies have examined whether sugar can exacerbate symptoms in children who have already been diagnosed with attention deficit disorder (ADD) or hyperactivity, and they have failed to show that sugar causes hyperactive behavior. Furthermore, there is evidence that the ingrained ideas that teachers and parents have about the effects of sugar can cloud their perception of a child's behavior. In one telling study, parents who were told their children had been given sugar rated their children as behaving more hyperactively than parents who were told their children had received a placebo, even though all the children had in fact been given a placebo. It is possible that the effects of sugar on the body's insulin response could make cycles of fullness and hunger more erratic, which could in turn affect a child's attention, mood, and school performance. But any direct effect of sugar on behavior is probably minimal or nonexistent.

The most resilient carbohydrate is dietary fiber. It comes in such a tough package that it doesn't even get digested, but it affects the digestion of the other food eaten with it. Eat a meal with soluble fiber and you lengthen the time it takes for that food to pass through your digestive system. When soluble fiber meets water, it forms a goopy gel, which can stick to other components of food and slow them down. The stickiness of fiber helps smooth out the ups and downs of the body's insulin response after a meal and delays the time it takes to feel hungry again, keeping you fuller longer.

Eating dietary fiber may also help prevent heart disease. Several large epidemiologic studies have shown that people who consume a lot of fiber, especially fiber from whole grains, have a lower incidence of heart disease. This may be partly because people who eat a lot of fiber-rich fruits, vegetables, legumes, and grains tend to eat fewer foods that are known to contribute to heart disease, such as those high in saturated fat. Fiber is also thought to have a direct effect on lowering cholesterol levels in the blood. Soluble fiber also traps cholesterol-rich bile salts, preventing the body from absorbing the cholesterol into the bloodstream. High blood cholesterol levels are a risk factor for heart disease, a relationship we'll discuss in more detail in the section on fat in this chapter.

Finally, fiber in the diet, especially insoluble fiber, improves the regularity of bowel movements by absorbing water and adding bulk to feces. Constipation is one of the top medical conditions that bring children to a doctor, and regularly eating foods rich in fiber can help to alleviate this problem.

The Greatness of Whole Grains

The foods that our ancestors made from grains were loaded with vitamins, fiber, protein, and large carbohydrates. But since ancient times, people have sought to refine their grains to give them a more pleasing, smoother texture and taste. The Romans used milling techniques to create finer wheat flours for the upper classes, and by the twentieth century, manufacturing improvements made refined white flour accessible to all. White flour is made only from a part of the wheat kernel called the *endosperm*, which contains mostly carbohydrates. Whole-wheat flour, on the other hand, contains B vitamins, some minerals, and dietary fiber. Rice is the primary grain for more than half the world, and it, too, is usually eaten in its least nutritious form. The outer coating of the rice kernel, called the bran, contains healthy plant oils, fiber, minerals, and B vitamins. But this seeming treasure is usually cast off, leaving white rice, which is mostly carbohydrate with few remaining nutrients.

In fact, eating solely refined rice or wheat has been the cause of nutritional diseases like beriberi and pellagra, which result from a lack of B vitamins. To make up for the deficiencies of these "better" products, manufacturers have had to put back in some of the good things that were taken out, in the form of vitamins and minerals. These "enriched" products still lack the fiber of their less refined forms. The manufactured foods we eat today are mostly made from white flour and other refined grains. Many also contain added sugars like glucose and fructose. The amount of fructose in the American diet has been on the rise since the late 1960s, when high fructose corn syrup was introduced. Soft drinks and fruit-flavored drinks are the primary contributors of extra fructose—and soft drinks are the leading contributors of added sugar intake in the American diet.

Paradoxically, as people are realizing how much healthier the less-refined foods are, the whole-grain foods that were once reserved for the lower classes are now

Artificial Sweeteners

More and more products, such as soft drinks, yogurt, and fruit preserves, now contain artificial sweeteners, such as saccharine and aspartame, instead of sugars. They are not absorbed by the body and so do not provide calories. The appeal of these products is that they have fewer calories, far less sugar, but still have the sweet taste of the regular food—naturally they present an attractive alternative for parents trying to limit their children's sugar intake. Can children have their (artificially sweetened) cake and eat it too?

As tempting as artificial sweeteners are, I would caution against relying on them, for a couple of reasons. First of all, eating a lot of artificially sweetened foods gets kids accustomed to the taste of sugar. Artificial sweeteners often taste even sweeter than sugar. One of the main points I've made throughout this book is that establishing tastes and good eating habits is a crucial component of good nutrition for children. Consuming sweet foods and beverages all the time does not benefit children's health, whether the sweetness is providing calories or not.

Artificially sweetened foods fool the body in a way that can undermine good eating habits. The message they give to the body is that it's okay to eat very sweet foods in large quantities, because sweetness is just added to foods for flavor and it doesn't add calories. When confronted with foods that do contain a lot of sugar and a lot of calories, the body has already learned that it's fine to eat more. In other words, these sweeteners are potentially training kids to develop a taste for sweets and for overeating. It's better to rely on naturally sweet foods, such as fruit and sweet spices like cinnamon and vanilla, and only offer sugary foods and beverages as an occasional treat.

more and more in demand. Whole-grain products are now sold as health-food specialties, often at a higher price. It is frustrating that whole-wheat pasta, a delicious and healthier alternative to plain pasta, is also more expensive, as are some other products like whole-grain breads and crackers. But as more and more of these products come on the market, parents who are willing to invest a little extra money and time can often find whole-grain alternatives to their children's favorite foods. Some whole grains are very easy to get kids to eat, such as oatmeal and other hot cereals, granola, brown rice, and whole-wheat bread. And if you start your child eating these more nutritious foods from the start, it will be easier than trying to switch foods once a child's tastes have already been established.

Making the Most Out of Carbohydrates

Carbohydrates will make up at least half of the calories that most children eat. They provide ready fuel to the body, but they can do much more if you choose the right

 Desperately Seeking Fiber

In 2002, the Food Nutrition Board of the Institute of Medicine created guidelines for fiber intake based on current research about the benefits of dietary fiber. Children should get about 14 grams of fiber for every 1,000 calories they eat a day, which works out to 19 to 25 grams of fiber (younger or less active children will be on the lower end, older and more active children on the higher end). Many parents are unaware of the fiber content in their children's diets. Here's a look at how much dietary fiber is in some commonly eaten foods:

FOOD	DIETARY FIBER CONTENT (IN GRAMS)
1 apple	3.3
½ cup black beans	7.5
1 piece of cornbread	1.5
1 slice white bread	0.6
1 slice whole-wheat bread	2
1 raw carrot	2
1 cup Raisin Bran cereal	5
1 packet instant oatmeal	2.8
1 fig bar	0.7
4 whole-wheat crackers	1.7
1 cup orange juice	0.5
1 orange	3
1 baked potato, with skin	4.4
1 cup cooked white rice	0.6
1 cup cooked brown rice	3.5
½ cup cooked broccoli	2.7
½ cup canned chickpeas	5

This information is from the USDA's Nutrient Data Laboratory, nal.usda.gov/fnic/foodcomp, 6/1/2004.

ones. Some of the top-ten sources of calories in American children's diets include cakes, cookies, soft drinks, potato chips, syrups, and jam. All of those foods provide fuel in the form of easily digested sugars and simple carbohydrates. But they represent a missed opportunity to add some fiber, vitamins, and slowly digested carbohydrates that will promote a healthier insulin response. The advice for carbohydrates in children's diets closely parallels the advice that Walter Willett and many other nutrition experts have given to adults; all of the following recommendations apply to the whole family's diet.

• *Limit processed foods.* In general, the more processing a food undergoes, the simpler its carbohydrates tend to be. Potato chips and fries, for instance, use only the starchy part of the potato and not the more nutritious skin. Fruit juice drinks and spreads don't have the fiber of whole fruit, leaving only simple fruit sugars (and many fruit products, like jams, jellies, fruit-flavored yogurt, and chewy fruit snacks also contain a hefty dose of added sugar). When possible, try to choose foods in their least processed form.

• *How whole are your grains?* A lot of the cookies, crackers, chips, pasta, and baked goods you see in stores are made with white flour. It's usually possible to find some whole-grain alternatives, but you need to be label-savvy. Many crackers and breads will say they are made of "wheat," but remember that even the most refined white flour is made from wheat. The magic word to look for is *whole* wheat. Try to find products that list whole-wheat flour, whole oats, or other whole grains at the top of the ingredient list. It does take some searching at the beginning, but once you identify a few good brands, it will be easy to locate them when shopping.

• *Forget the fries.* A potato contains several grams of fiber, plus vitamins and minerals—but the vast majority of these nutrients are in the skin. The flesh of a potato is mostly starch, and you can think of it like a big ball of white bread—very simple, easily digested carbohydrates—but potatoes even lack those "extra" vitamins and minerals that are added to enriched bread. With the exception of baked potatoes or snacks made from potato wedges or skins, most foods made from potatoes are digested like a refined carbohydrate, and are not the most ideal foods for children.

• *Where's the fiber?* Another way to look for whole grains is to check the fiber content of foods—those with intact grains and fruit will contain at least some fiber.

Reading the Fine Print

Here are some of the claims about carbohydrates you may see on food packaging and what they mean:

"Sugar free"	Contains less than 0.5 grams sugar per serving
"Reduced sugar" or "less sugar"	At least 25 percent less sugar than the traditional food
"No added sugar," "without added sugar," or "no sugar added"	No sugars added during processing or packaging, including ingredients that contain sugars, such as juice or dried fruit
"High fiber"	Contains 5 grams fiber per serving (and must meet the definition for low-fat, or include level of fat next to the high-fiber claim)
"Good source of fiber"	Contains 2.5 to 4.9 grams fiber per serving
"More fiber" or "added fiber"	At least 2.5 grams more or added fiber per serving, compared to the traditional food

From *AAP Pediatric Nutrition Handbook*, p. 818.

- *Sugar: what's the bottom line?* Many of the carbohydrates in children's diets come from added sugars. Even foods you might not necessarily think of as sweet, like peanut butter, often have sugar added to make the flavor more appealing. Breakfast cereals are perhaps the worst offenders; many of them have high sugar content and very refined grains. These cereals make a big deal about all the vitamins and minerals they provide, but remember that many of these are simply nutrients that were taken out of the grains to begin with. It can be difficult to tell how much sugar has been added by reading the ingredient list. Check the bottom line: when buying cereal or snack foods, get in the habit of checking the total sugar content on the nutrition label. The FDA provides an online source for help in reading labels at http://vm.cfsan.fda.gov/~dms/foodlab. By looking for products with the least amount of sugar, with a little fiber, and the words *whole wheat* or other whole grains, you stand the best chance of providing healthier forms of carbohydrates.

Fat

Over the past couple of decades, many adults have tried to cut down the amount of fat in their diets and have come to see fat as something bad to be eliminated. The USDA food pyramid encourages this attitude by including fats with sweets at the top of the pyramid with the instruction to limit them, as if fat should be banished to a remote tower and never seen again. This message is misleading because, in fact, fat should make up about 30 percent or so of the calories in an average child's diet. Fat is not only an important source of energy, but also provides some nutrients that are needed by developing bodies.

While fat is essential to any child's diet, the *type* of fat does make a difference. An enormous amount of research has looked into the role of fat in health, and while choosing better fats is more critical for adults who need to worry about chronic diseases, making a healthy start with the best fats is also important for children. The developing bodies of children have different fat requirements than adults, because fats are used in constructing new tissues. At the same time, establishing good habits by avoiding excess fat (especially saturated and trans fats) is important for a child's future health. While infants and young toddlers need more fat in their diet, children over two or three years of age should start eating the kinds of healthy fats that were recommended for adults in *Eat, Drink, and Be Healthy*.

What Is Fat?

We all know fat makes foods taste great. But is it only a guilty pleasure? In fact, fat contains some nutrients that are vital to the growing bodies of children. Some vitamins are fat-soluble, meaning they are dissolved in the fats that we eat. Without fat, children might have difficulty obtaining enough vitamins A, D, E, and K. Some types of fat are also necessary to the body and need to be obtained from food.

Fat is an umbrella term for substances made of fatty acids, characterized by their structure and chemical composition. The four major types of fatty acids found in food are:

- Saturated fatty acids
- Monounsaturated fatty acids
- Polyunsaturated fatty acids
- Trans-fatty acids

All fatty acids are made of the same basic elements: hydrogen, oxygen, and carbon. These elements are present in different numbers and arrangements, and as in many cases in nutrition, the packaging counts. Different kinds of fats have different effects on the body, especially over the long term.

Cholesterol, Fat, and Health

Most of the concerns about high-fat diets and health stem from their effect on cholesterol levels in the body. Cholesterol is a waxy substance that actually plays several critical roles: it is used to make hormones such as estrogen and testosterone, helps form the membranes of cells in the body, and performs other functions in cells. Cholesterol is found in animal products such as meat, fish, egg yolks, and whole milk. However, our bodies are also capable of producing their own cholesterol, and there seems to be little need for cholesterol in the diet.

While cholesterol is essential in the body, too much cholesterol circulating in the blood is a risk factor for heart disease. Cholesterol requires special proteins to chauffeur it through the bloodstream. Low-density lipoprotein (LDL) carries cholesterol from the liver, where it is produced, to the rest of the body, while high-density lipoprotein (HDL) takes cholesterol from sites in the body to the liver to be excreted. Cholesterol that is attached to LDL is often called "bad" cholesterol because too much of it being delivered to the body causes cholesterol to build up in arteries and form traffic jams called *plaques*. Clogged arteries, or atherosclerosis, can lead to heart attacks and strokes when blood clots form at the plaque site. Cholesterol that hitches a ride on HDL is often called "good" cholesterol because the HDL is removing cholesterol from the body, so it keeps the substance from building up in the bloodstream.

You are probably familiar with the maxim of lowering cholesterol and limiting saturated fat for better health. But most parents aren't concerned with their five-year-old's arteries. What does all of this have to do with children? Though atherosclerosis and heart disease may not appear until later in adulthood, these diseases represent the end stages of a long process that unfolds over the course of a person's entire life. In fact, streaks of fat develop in arteries during childhood; though this is quite normal, it is thought that these fatty deposits can eventually thicken and encourage the buildup of plaques over many years. Studies have found that children's cholesterol levels tend to track from childhood into adulthood. For instance, in the large-scale Bogalusa Heart Study, 70 percent of children who were ranked in the top fifth for blood cholesterol fell in the top two-fifths twelve years later, and 70 percent of those in the bottom fifth remained in the bottom two-fifths. This finding suggests that the health patterns established in childhood have a tendency to carry into later life.

Now here's the catch: eating foods that are high in cholesterol is not the primary way that cholesterol levels start to build up in the blood. Epidemiologic studies show a correlation between a high-cholesterol diet and high blood cholesterol, but it is a weak one. Eggs, which contain quite a bit of cholesterol, are fine for children to eat in moderation. Instead, fats seem to have a greater role in determining a person's blood cholesterol levels. There is a well-established link between high-fat diets and the development of heart disease. But not all fats are the same; like actors in a play, each one has a different role in determining the outcome of a person's health. To make the healthiest choices you need to be familiar with the entire cast of characters:

The Villains

Saturated fats and trans fats are the two primary villains in the development of high cholesterol levels and heart disease.

Saturated Fats

Found in meat, dairy products, and in a few plant oils including palm and coconut oil, saturated fatty acids are in the shape of a straight, relatively stiff chain, and this form gives them the ability to form solids at room temperature. Over the past few decades, evidence has steadily built that implicates saturated fat in heart disease, which is the number-one cause of death in developed countries. Heart disease rates are highest in countries that have the most saturated fat in the diet, and epidemiological studies have found that people with diets high in saturated fat have higher rates of atherosclerosis and heart disease. Saturated fats raise the level of cholesterol in the blood more strongly than consuming dietary cholesterol does, and they tend to raise both "good" and "bad" cholesterol.

Trans Fats

Trans fats are even worse villains when it comes to heart health, because they not only raise bad LDL cholesterol but actively lower HDL cholesterol. Trans fats don't occur naturally in foods but are a human invention, created as a way of giving unsaturated vegetable oils a property of saturated fat: the ability to form solids at room temperature. Think of margarine—it's made of vegetable oils but looks and feels like butter. The trick that makes it solid is a process of heating the oils in the presence of hydrogen, called hydrogenation. Hydrogenated oils are used in many manufactured baked goods and most margarines, as well as many fried fast foods.

Current regulations on food labeling do not require manufacturers to list the amount of trans fats in their products, but the FDA has taken steps to require labeling of trans fats by 2006. Until then, you have to look through the ingredient list. Any mention of "hydrogenated" or "partially hydrogenated" oils means trans fat. Now that news on the dangers of trans fats has spread, many companies are taking steps to reduce or eliminate trans fats in their products. A few margarines are available that contain little or no trans fat. And some manufactured products like baked goods are now being made without trans fats (for instance, Frito-Lay has taken the step of eliminating trans fats from many of its chips and snack foods). Often these products will list "no trans fats" on their packaging or nutrition labels to advertise their healthfulness. Once manufacturers are forced to show the amount of trans fat in their food, this trend toward modifying products to eliminate hydrogenated oils should take off.

The Heroes

Monounsaturated fats and polyunsaturated fats are the heroes fighting high cholesterol levels and other threats to heart health.

Monounsaturated Fats

Fats that are unsaturated have a bent shape that keeps them liquid at room temperature in the form of oils, and they are usually found in plants. Contrary to popular wisdom about fat, unsaturated fats actually benefit the heart. They lower levels of bad LDL cholesterol, and at the same time raise levels of good HDL. Many plant oils contain a mix of monounsaturated and polyunsaturated fats. Foods particularly high in monounsaturated fats include canola, peanut, and olive oils.

Polyunsaturated Fats

Polyunsaturated fats are the most important for health. Two kinds of polyunsaturated fats are most important—omega-3 fatty acids and omega-6 fatty acids (also called n-3 and n-6 fatty acids, respectively). These are called *essential* fatty acids because they cannot be made by the body and so must be obtained from food.

They are used in chemical signaling in the body and to maintain the structure and proper growth of cells. Infants get these two critical fats from breast milk or formula, but once they start eating solids, children need to find these fats in foods. Polyunsaturated fats are found in corn and soybean oils, fatty fish like tuna and salmon, seeds, and whole grains.

Fat and Weight Control

Does eating fat make kids fat? The public has developed some misunderstandings about the relationship between fat and weight, often because well-intentioned messages from health authorities get oversimplified in the media. As I outlined in Chapter 6, maintaining a healthy weight is a balance between the amount of energy coming into the body and the amount of energy used by the body. So, an excess in calories—by any food source—will, over time, result in weight gain.

Fat is the most energy-dense of all the macronutrients; a small amount of fat packs a lot more calories than a similar portion of carbohydrates or protein. So, eating a lot of high-fat foods at the same portion sizes as lower-fat foods would result in more calories and potential weight gain. Furthermore, excess fat is treated differently from other macronutrients. Carbohydrates and proteins cannot be stored very well in the body. Instead, when you eat extra carbohydrates and proteins, your body reacts like a bicyclist peddling faster, trying to use more of these nutrients to compensate for the excess. Fat, however, can be stored abundantly in fatty tissue so there's no need to make use of it. When you eat extra fat, the body doesn't pedal faster, it just coasts. The end result is that extra fat is stored rather than used for energy.

Setting limits on high-fat foods will help keep children from eating more than their share of calories. A child who is in danger of being overweight may need to eat a little less fat to trim the amount of calories coming in. But it would be dangerous to eliminate fat completely from any child's diet, and it might even backfire in cutting back calories if it results in eating low-fat but high-calorie snacks loaded with sugar.

The key is to be aware of the relationship between the calorie content of a food and the portion size. For example, instead of eating a lot of low-fat cheese (which I find a little bland and unsatisfying), I like to use a small amount of a flavorful full-fat cheese like sharp cheddar in my foods. Nuts are a great, satisfying snack and contain a lot of healthy fats. But they are also much higher in calories than carrot sticks or fruit, so a small handful of nuts is enough for a between-meal snack.

Fat: Reading the Fine Print

Here are some common claims about fat in food labels and what they mean:

"Fat free"	Contains less than 0.5 gram fat per serving
"Low fat"	Contains less than 3 grams fat per serving
"Reduced fat" or "less fat"	Contains at least 25 percent less fat than the traditional food
"Light" or "lite"	Contains one-third fewer calories or 50 percent less fat than the traditional food
"Saturated fat free"	Contains less than 0.5 gram saturated fat per serving
"Low saturated fat"	Contains not more than 1 gram saturated fat per serving with no more than 15 percent of calories from saturated fat
"Reduced saturated fat" or "less saturated fat"	At least 25 percent less saturated fat than the traditional food
"Cholesterol free"	Contains less than 2 milligrams cholesterol and 2 grams fat per serving
"Low cholesterol"	Contains not more than 20 milligrams cholesterol and less than 2 grams saturated fat per serving
"Reduced cholesterol" or "less cholesterol"	At least 25 percent less cholesterol than the traditional food and less than 2 grams saturated fat per serving
"Lean" (on meat, poultry, seafood, and game meats)	Less than 10 grams fat, 4.5 grams saturated fat, and 95 milligrams cholesterol per serving
"Extra lean" (on meat, poultry, seafood, and game meats)	Less than 5 grams fat, 2 grams saturated fat, and 95 milligrams cholesterol per serving

In other words, you don't have to limit yourself to low-fat foods, only be aware that portion sizes need to be adjusted—especially in the case of prepared foods and snacks that often come in unreasonably large portions.

Also be aware that low-fat foods are not necessarily low-calorie or nutritious. Many low-fat baked goods and snacks are little more than refined flour and sugar. Where possible, compare the calorie and sugar content of a low-fat food with its higher-fat alternative when choosing which one to buy. See the FDA's guide to reading food labels at http://cfsan.fda.gov/~dms/foodlab.html

Protein

Protein is found abundantly in meats, other animal products, and plant foods such as legumes, nuts, and grains. Protein is not used primarily for fuel at all but rather provides the raw materials needed to construct the body and help it function. Ensuring enough protein in the diet has always been a concern in children's nutrition. Just as a house under construction needs adequate supplies of wood, cement, bricks, pipes, and other materials, a developing body needs new proteins to grow properly. Because protein is so important for growth, the quantity and quality of protein in the diet is more critical for children than adults. My recommendations for protein in the diets of children are different from the current guidelines for adults that Walter Willett advocates.

What Is Protein?

Protein is a major structural material of the body, and proteins are needed for nearly every activity or chemical reaction in cells—they are the body's movers and shakers. Proteins are made of smaller units called *amino acids*. When protein in food is digested, it is broken down to these building blocks, which can then be used to construct whatever specific proteins are needed in the body.

Infants and children not only need a certain quantity of protein, but they also need a steady supply. In growing bodies, unlike adult bodies, when amino acids are delivered from food, it's like a work bell going off at a construction site, signaling tissues to start making new proteins. So, eating protein actually helps stimulate growth. And, because the body cannot store proteins for later use, a steady stream of protein in the diet is the best way to ensure that construction never halts. In a baby's first month, nearly two-thirds of protein taken in is directed toward growth; by a few years of age, nearly 90 percent is used just to maintain the body.

While protein is necessary for children's growth, this does not mean that feeding children extra protein will help them grow taller, or that a high-protein diet will help them thrive. Bodies simply don't work that way. Instead, parents just need to ensure that children eat enough protein to allow their bodies to grow to their full potential, about 20 percent of total calories. Children should not consume protein at the expense of other macronutrients and certainly shouldn't follow the high-protein fad diets that are popular with many adults. In fact, doing so can be dangerous. Excess protein is excreted by the kidneys in the form of urea, and too high a load of protein can stress the developing kidneys of infants and young children.

Children Need High-Quality Protein

As I mentioned, proteins are made of basic building blocks called amino acids. Some amino acids can be manufactured by the body, while others cannot; these are called *essential* amino acids and must be found in foods. Different sources of protein contain different combinations of amino acids. Some sources provide all the essential amino acids that humans need—these are often called *complete proteins*. Incomplete proteins lack at least one essential amino acid. Infants and children up to about six years of age have a higher need for essential amino acids, which play a prominent role in growth, while nonessential amino acids are used more for body maintenance. So, the type of protein is especially critical in the diets of younger children.

We can classify protein sources according to their quality. The protein in foods varies in how well it is digested and absorbed and how well its amino acid content matches the needs of children. An ideal food would have protein that is nearly completely absorbed and contains all the essential amino acids in the right amounts. It turns out that animal sources of protein, such as eggs, milk, meat, and fish, are more digestible (at least 95 percent of what is eaten is usually absorbed) and have an amino acid composition that closely fits human requirements. Plant sources of protein, like nuts, grains, beans, and soy, are less digestible and often lack adequate amounts of certain amino acids. Mixing different sources of plant proteins can help overcome the inadequacies of these proteins, but in general it is more difficult to provide children with complete protein without relying on animal sources, including dairy products and eggs.

As you may have noticed, though, the best sources of protein are often foods that are high in saturated fat, something I've just argued should be limited in children's diets. How do we resolve this conflict? Nutritional advice for adults has moved toward advocating more plant sources of protein like soy, beans, and nuts, over meat and dairy. This makes sense for adult bodies that have long stopped growing, and for which the risks of heart disease outweigh the need for efficient sources of protein. But for children, I believe the need for high-quality protein is more important.

Choosing Healthier Sources of Protein

However, there are plenty of ways that parents can cut down on the saturated fat in their children's diets without eliminating meats and dairy. After the first two or three years, switch to low-fat or nonfat milk (as mentioned in Chapter 3, infants and young toddlers should drink whole milk once they have been weaned from breast milk or formula until they are two years old). Low-fat dairy products such as yogurt and cheese are also good options for children, or smaller portions of products that are higher in fat. You can choose the leanest cuts of meat and avoid those meats that are very high in saturated fat, like bacon. When possible, cook foods in an oil that is high in polyunsaturated fat, like canola or olive oil, and skip the butter and lard. Aim for a variety of foods that offer a balance of the best fats and the highest quality protein. Table 7.1 lists the protein and fat content of some common foods.

Chicken and fish both offer high-quality protein with much less saturated fat than beef and most pork products. Most adults should eat very little red meat. Choosing chicken and fish over red meat is also good for children's diets, but there's a caveat: red meat is much richer in iron and zinc, two minerals that are especially important during the rapid growth of infants and toddlers under three. For more information on how to find iron and zinc in foods, see Chapter 9.

Fish is a great food for children and adults because it pairs protein with healthy unsaturated fats, particularly omega-3 fatty acids, which not only promote cardiovascular health but are necessary for proper development of the brain and visual system. However, the mercury content of some fish has increasingly become a health concern in recent years. Mercury is a toxin that can accumulate in the bodies of fish, especially large ones. For most people, the levels of mercury in fish are not harmful, but unborn fetuses, infants, and young children are more susceptible. The FDA and EPA are advising women who may become pregnant, pregnant women, nursing mothers, and young children to avoid shark, tilefish, king mackerel, and swordfish. Canned tuna is an inexpensive way to bring fish into children's

Table 7.1   Protein and Fat Content of Common Foods (in grams)

FOOD	PROTEIN	SATURATED FAT	MONOUNSATURATED FAT	POLYUNSATURATED FAT
3 ounces 85% lean ground beef	22	5	5.6	0.4
½ cup canned baked beans	6	1.5	0	0.2
½ cup low-fat (1% milk fat) cottage cheese	14	0.7	0.6	0
1 ounce cheddar cheese	7	6	2.7	0.3
½ chicken breast	30	1	1	0.7
1 egg	6	1.5	2	0.7
3 ounces cooked salmon	17	1.5	4.5	2
2 slices extra-lean ham	11	1	1.3	0.3
1 cup low-fat (1%) milk	8	1.5	0.7	0.1
1 tablespoon peanut butter	4	1.5	4	4.3
½ cup frozen green peas	4	0	0	0.3
1 baked potato, with skin	5	0	0	0.1
½ cup refried beans	7	0.5	0.7	0.2
½ cup tropical trail mix	4	6	1.7	3.6
¼ of 3- to 4-ounce block firm tofu	6.5	0.5	0.8	2
8 ounces plain low-fat yogurt	12	2	1	0.1

Source: USDA's Nutrient Data Laboratory, nal.usda.gov/fnic/foodcomp, 6/1/2004.

Go Vegetarian?

More and more people are adopting vegetarian lifestyles, and parents who are vegetarian or vegan (consuming no dairy or eggs) may wonder if it's safe to raise their children with the same eating restrictions.

I believe that eating some meat, eggs, and dairy products is ideal for young children, because their growing bodies need high-quality protein. Furthermore, infants and very young children often eat very small amounts of food. Animal products are denser in calories and protein than plant foods, so it can be more difficult for infants and children who only eat plant foods to eat as much as they need. I strongly encourage parents not to put children on vegetarian diets in the first few years of life, and afterwards only with a sound knowledge of protein in foods.

Many children worldwide have been raised following different degrees of vegetarianism without a negative impact on their health. However, cultures that are traditionally vegetarian also have traditional eating patterns that emphasize a wide variety of legumes, grains, and vegetables rich in protein. Following a typical American kid's diet without meat and dairy could lead to some serious protein deficiencies. Parents who still wish to provide their children with a vegetarian diet should take extra care to make sure their children are eating well:

• **Do dairy.** I would recommend at least giving children dairy products and eggs, which are high in good-quality protein, even if they do not eat meat.

• **Mix it up.** For children who get most or all of their protein from plant sources, variety is critical; if they eat a wide range of beans, nuts, grains, and vegetables, they are less likely to miss out on essential amino acids.

• **Don't depend on soy.** Many meat and dairy substitutes are sold nowadays that are made of soy, but though they may look like burgers and hot dogs, their proteins do not. It's best not to rely solely on soy, or any one plant food, for all of a child's protein. Furthermore, soy contains chemicals called *phytoestrogens* that weakly mimic the actions of the hormone estrogen in the body. Though eating soy up to a few times a week is not harmful, and it may have some health benefits for adults, not enough is known about the effects of eating large amounts of phytoestrogens, especially in children.

• **An extra dose of protein.** Diets that limit meat and dairy will need a higher proportion of protein-rich foods to obtain enough of the amino acids they need. Parents of vegetarian and vegan children should try to include at least one protein source at every meal and snack.

diets, but if you buy tuna, be aware that white albacore tuna is higher in mercury than light tuna. The FDA recommends that infants and young children eat no more than six ounces of white tuna per week. Even better, choose light tuna instead.

Putting It All Together: A Shopping Strategy

In Chapter 5, I showed you the USDA Food Guide Pyramid for Young Children and talked about the essential importance of balance in the diet, a concept that the pyramid conveys very well. Striking the right balance between carbohydrates, proteins, and fats is one of the key factors of a healthy diet. But I hope you've also come to realize that choosing the best sources of these nutrients is also important, both for children's immediate health and for establishing good habits that they can carry into adulthood.

While I've talked about each of these nutrients separately, many foods contain some combination of all three. When you are actually out in the supermarket choosing what to put in your cart, you'll need to put all this knowledge together. Here are some strategies for making better choices for different kinds of foods:

Grains, Breads, Crackers, Cereals, and Other Baked Goods
- Look for whole grains in the ingredient list. (Whole wheat, rye, or oats are usually the primary ingredient.)
- Check to see if the food contains some fiber.
- Make sure the ingredient list is free of hydrogenated oils, or that the product advertises that it has no trans fats.
- Check the total sugar content and see if there is a comparable product with less sugar.
- Buy whole-wheat pasta or a pasta that is 50/50 whole-wheat and white flour.
- Replace white rice or potatoes with brown rice, or try other whole grains as a side dish, such as barley, quinoa, millet, bulgur, polenta or grits (cornmeal mush), or wheat berries.

Dairy Products and Meats
- Choose leaner cuts of meat, and try occasionally serving fish, which is high in polyunsaturated fats, instead of meat.
- Choose a low-fat option among dairy products. Alternatively, when using dairy products in meals, use just a very small amount of the higher-fat ver-

Carbohydrates, Proteins, and Fats: The Bottom Line

- Children's diets should consist of a balance of carbohydrates, proteins, and fats, amounting to a total caloric intake of about 50 percent carbohydrates, 30 percent fat, and 20 percent proteins.

- Foods that contain larger, more complex carbohydrates and dietary fiber will help smooth out the body's blood sugar and insulin response, provide vitamins and minerals, and have a positive effect on digestion and cholesterol levels. These can be found in whole grains, fruits and vegetables, and generally in foods that are less processed.

- Children's foods are often high in added sugars, which provide calories but little else. When possible, choose whole foods and natural sources of sweetness, like fruit.

- Children need fats in their diets, but certain kinds of fats are better than others. Choosing foods with unsaturated fats will have a positive effect on later health.

- Learn to avoid foods with trans fats by checking the ingredient list for hydrogenated oils.

- Animal products provide higher-quality protein for children's growing bodies, but parents should take steps to avoid meats and dairy products with high amounts of saturated fats.

sion. For instance, many dishes calling for butter, sour cream, or cheese as toppings often taste quite good with just a small amount for flavor.
- Flavored yogurt and milks usually contain a lot of added sugar. Instead, add fruit or a little vanilla flavoring to yogurt or blend into milk for a treat.

Plant Sources of Protein (Nuts, Beans, Seeds, Soy, and so Forth)
- Add nuts and beans to snacks and meals to help boost levels of unsaturated fats.
- Buy "all natural" peanut butter, which contains just peanuts and salt, rather than the standard brands, which add trans fats and sugar.

- When cooking with soy, try plain tofu or shelled soybeans, rather than highly processed soy products, which often contain added sugar and salt.

Jams, Jellies, and Other Fruit Products
- Look for products made with whole fruit rather than just fruit flavorings.
- Check the total sugar content and see if there is an option with less sugar.
- Use sugar-free applesauce, dried fruit, or pieces of whole fruit to add a little sweetness to other foods like yogurt or oatmeal, instead of sugar.

Oils and Fats
- Choose a vegetable oil that is high in polyunsaturated fat, like olive, canola, or safflower oil, for cooking.
- Many baked goods and other dishes can be made with vegetable oils instead of butter or margarine—look for alternative recipes or try substituting ingredients.
- Avoid margarine that is high in trans fats. Look for newer products that advertise no or low trans fats, or simply skip the margarine or butter altogether. (Olive oil on bread is a treat, and one that you may find you prefer to butter!)

For all of these foods, avoiding highly processed foods is almost always the healthiest option. Prepared foods and snacks are always a temptation because they are so convenient, especially for busy parents. See Chapter 12 for some simple but easy alternatives that use whole-food ingredients.

8

Fruits and Vegetables

One piece of nutritional advice is absolutely clear and unchanging: fruits and vegetables are good for you. It is common wisdom that has been passed on by parents everywhere for generations, and it is backed by science. Fruits and vegetables have numerous health benefits, and they deserve a prominent place in every child's diet.

As wonderful as these foods are, three-quarters of Americans fall short of the recommended five servings a day of fruits and vegetables. And Americans are not the only ones missing out on produce. In a study of ten European countries, about 50 percent of the populations surveyed fell short of the three recommended servings of vegetables a day. As modern, industrialized countries opt more and more for processed foods, the prepackaged "convenience foods" of nature—fruits and vegetables—get left by the wayside.

Unfortunately, people are very good at creating foods that tempt us away from the healthier options that nature provides. With all the cookies, french fries, doughnuts, ice cream bars, baked goods, hamburgers, chips, and sweetened beverages available, who wants to reach for a piece of fruit or some carrot sticks? Processed foods make liberal use of added sugars, salt, and fats to appeal to our tastes. When

The Case of the Missing Veggies

Parents are often very conscientious about the health of young infants, and are determined to feed toddlers by the book—introducing lots of vegetables and fruits, limiting sweets, trying to include a balance of different nutrients. But when kids get older, maintaining control of their diet is much more difficult. According to the USDA, most children in the United States have a diet that needs improvement or is poor, and the quality of children's diets tends to worsen as they age. One of the key areas of decline from age two to age nine is in how many fruits and vegetables children eat. Only 25 percent of children aged seven to nine eat the recommended levels of fruits, and only 22 percent eat the recommended number of vegetables. And the situation is probably worse than the numbers show. The USDA counts potatoes as a vegetable—including foods like fries and potato chips—even though potatoes really act more as a starch in the body, and do not provide the health benefits of other vegetables. And juice counts as a fruit, even though it does not contain the fiber of whole fruit. In fact, in the USDA's list of the top foods eaten by children, the first source of fruit appears down at number fourteen—as juice. And no vegetable other than potatoes makes it to the top thirty.

children are exposed to these foods over and over, they develop a taste for these strong flavors, not for the natural and more subtle sweetness, saltiness, and texture of fruits and vegetables. This is why exposing children to fruits and vegetables early to help them develop a taste for natural flavors is one of the best things parents can do for their children's future health. My recommendations for eating fruits and vegetables will echo the advice of *Eat, Drink, and Be Healthy*, and this information can apply to the whole family, not just kids.

Fruits, Vegetables, and Health

Fruits and vegetables are important for children's health for two reasons. First, children's immediate needs for vitamins, minerals, and other nutrients are found abundantly in plants. Without eating fruits and vegetables, children's diets could fall short in nutrients like vitamin C, vitamin A, potassium, and folate, to name a few.

Fruits and vegetables are great sources of many substances children need to grow. Chapter 9 discusses in more detail why vitamins and minerals are needed for growth and health, and why they are best found in foods rather than supplements.

Second, numerous studies show that populations with higher fruit and vegetable consumption have a lower incidence of chronic disease. Young children may not seem to be at risk for these health problems now, but today's eating habits will set the stage for a better diet in adulthood. Some of the health benefits of fruits and vegetables include cancer prevention, cardiovascular benefits, healthy metabolism and digestion, and weight control.

Cancer Prevention

A diet high in fruits and vegetables has been linked to lower incidence of certain cancers. The process of turning a nice, normal cell to an unruly cancer cell begins when something damages a cell's DNA in a particular way. Many kinds of substances can act as carcinogens (cancer causers) in cells, including chemicals in the food we eat and the air we breathe, radiation from the sun, or even by-products of a cell's own metabolism. In fact, carcinogens are always present in a cell. What protects DNA from this ongoing assault is an array of chemicals in cells that can either block carcinogens from reaching DNA, or can keep damaged DNA from causing any real harm.

Antioxidants are an important class of cellular superhero; they actively hunt down and neutralize carcinogens called *free radicals*, which are metabolic by-products of every cell. Fruits and vegetables are a rich source of antioxidants, including vitamins C and A, and it is thought that some of the hundreds of other chemicals in plants might provide similar protection against DNA damage.

The exact relationship between diet and cancer is not completely known, and will take a long time to tease apart. Hundreds of studies have shown a correlation between eating lots of fruits and vegetables and a lower risk of certain cancers. But because people eat lots of different foods in their diet, it is difficult to link any one food with preventing any one disease. Laboratory studies on animals have shown anticancer effects of certain foods, especially leafy green vegetables. While it seems that certain foods offer protection against certain cancers and not others, until more is known, the best strategy is to aim for a wide variety of fruits and vegetables.

Cardiovascular Health

People who eat more fruits and vegetables also have been shown to have a lower risk of developing heart disease and strokes. A large study involving more than eighty thousand men and more than forty thousand women found an inverse association between eating fruits and vegetables—especially those high in vitamin C and green leafy vegetables—and risk of heart disease. And the Women's Health Study, which assessed the diet of nearly forty thousand female health professionals, found an association between eating more fruits and vegetables and a lower risk of cardiovascular disease, especially heart attacks. Fruits and vegetables also seem to have a beneficial effect on cholesterol levels in the blood. It is not yet clear whether this benefit is caused by a direct effect of these foods, or because they are displacing other foods high in saturated fat.

Healthy Metabolism and Digestion

Fruits and vegetables are also important sources of dietary fiber, which, as discussed in Chapter 7, helps to smooth out the rise and fall of blood sugar levels, has a beneficial effect on blood cholesterol levels, and helps prevent constipation. Fiber is found in the stiff walls of plant cells, and is difficult or impossible for humans to digest. As such, it does not provide the body with energy. But globs of dietary fiber in the digestive tract tend to trap bits of partially digested food and slow the rate at which sugars and fats are absorbed on their journey through the intestine. This helps prevent spikes in the level of sugars and fats in the blood that can stress the body's metabolic responses over time. Soluble fiber, found in oats, beans, and fruits, helps trap bile acids that contain a lot of cholesterol, thereby helping to keep the levels of cholesterol in the blood low. Fiber also soaks up water, helping to make bowel movements softer and more regular, relieving constipation and helping to prevent intestinal discomfort.

Weight Control

Eating fruits and vegetables also plays an important role in maintaining a healthy weight. Fruits and vegetables are not calorically dense—meaning they pack fewer calories in a larger space than most foods. In fact, most fruits and vegetables are at least 80 percent water and contain a lot of fiber that is not digested. But fruits and vegetables are also much richer in other nutrients, like vitamins and minerals, than other foods. So they are a great way to provide a lot of nutrition without a lot of extra calories. That also means that you can heap fruits and vegetables into meals and snacks without worrying about portion sizes the way you would with other foods. In other words, go ahead and "supersize" them!

There's No Substitute for the Real Thing

We're used to hearing about the vitamins and minerals in fruits and vegetables, and it's true that plant foods are an important source of these nutrients we need to live (for a detailed discussion of different vitamins and minerals, see Chapter 9). But plants are much more complex, and they contain literally hundreds of different chemicals that may have health benefits for us. Some of these substances, called *phytochemicals* (*phyto* means "plant"), are currently under investigation for their roles in warding off cancer, promoting healthy vision and immunity, preventing memory loss, and combating cardiovascular disease.

Think about it: all the fruits and vegetables we eat were once living, functional parts of plants. We tend to forget this and think of fruits and vegetables like the manufactured foods we eat, as if they are made of a simple list of ingredients. We are told that citrus fruits have vitamin C, carrots have vitamin A, and so on. But the vitamins, minerals, and other phytochemicals in fruits and vegetables exist in a complex package, often working together in ways that we don't fully understand.

As far as we know, the best way to reap the benefits of plants is by eating them in their natural forms. When new research demonstrates a benefit of eating particular fruits and vegetables, many people are quick to attribute that benefit to one particular ingredient. For instance, studies have shown that consuming fruits and vegetables high in carotenoids lowers the risk of developing several kinds of cancer. This finding created a lot of interest in beta-carotene (vitamin A) and led many people to start taking vitamin A supplements to lower their risk of cancer. But fruits and vegetables contain at least forty different carotenoids, sometimes at higher levels than beta-carotene. We simply can't assume that one ingredient will do the same thing in isolation as it will when it is part of a complex package like a plant. It's not just a matter of isolating one component and packaging it in a pill at high doses.

Some Choices Are Better than Others

In general, the message on fruits and vegetables is the more the merrier. Any chance you have to introduce a fruit or vegetable is a good one. But as with other kinds of foods we've discussed, some choices are better than others. The USDA and the American Cancer Society urge all of us, including children, to eat at least five servings a day of fruits and vegetables. Like a student who is only looking for a passing grade, you can cover these requirements by serving your child lots of juice, french fries and mashed potatoes, spaghetti sauce, canned corn, and the occasional apple. Or you could go for the A-plus and serve fresh fruit with breakfast, carrots and celery at snacks, a sandwich with vegetables at lunch, and a salad and vegetable side dish with dinner. The number of servings is not the only important factor—quality counts.

Whole Is Better

Whole fruits and vegetables are by far the healthiest choices. By *whole* I do not mean that it can't be sliced, diced, or pureed. I mean that the whole fruit or vegetable is present in the food. Fruit and vegetable juices, while they contain vitamins and minerals, lack the fiber of the whole form, and often lose important phytochemicals in processing. As we will discuss in more detail in Chapter 10, they also are high in calories and may contain added sugar or salt. Juice, even 100 percent juice, is simply no substitute for whole fruits and vegetables. The same goes for snacks and convenience foods that are made with fruits and vegetables or contain added juice; while they might be a better alternative to similar products, they are rarely as healthful as the real thing. Don't rely on processed foods for the majority of your child's fruit and vegetable sources.

Make (Some of) It Raw

Cooking vegetables can reduce the levels of certain nutrients in them, especially vitamin C, folate, and possibly other phytochemicals. One known exception is lycopene, an antioxidant found in tomatoes and other red vegetables and fruits, which is actually more available to the body in cooked foods since cooking helps release it from the cell walls of the plant. Including some fresh, raw vegetables in your child's meals and snacks, in addition to what you cook in meals, will help you make the most of the goodness of vegetables. Besides, kids often prefer the taste and crunchiness of raw vegetables. (Remember though, that small toddlers shouldn't eat very crunchy foods like raw carrots—these should be cooked slightly to soften them and prevent choking.)

Frozen fruits and vegetables are generally just as nutritious and can be convenient and economical substitutes for fresh produce. Canned versions are also fine, but often contain added sugar and salt. If you often rely on canned and frozen foods for meals, adding a few more fresh vegetables will also help your child learn about the look and texture of the foods in their natural form.

Potatoes Are Veggie Imposters

I won't argue that potatoes can't be a part of a child's diet. They do contain several vitamins and minerals, and can be a fun and filling food. But most of the goodness in potatoes is in the skin. Otherwise, they are basically a simple carbohydrate source and are treated by the body in much the same way a refined grain product like white bread would be. So if you serve potatoes, don't add them into your vegetable tally. The exception is sweet potatoes, which do contain more nutrients, like vitamin A.

 Are Your Fruits and Vegetables Adding Up?

The USDA food pyramid recommends that children eat two to four servings of fruit a day and three to five servings of vegetables a day. But many people are not aware of what counts as a serving. One study found that adults tend to underestimate the amount of grains, fats, and sweets they eat, but often overestimate the amount of healthier foods they eat, including fruits and vegetables. Here are some examples of a serving size of fruits and vegetables for children above age four. Toddlers and younger children will eat smaller portions.

FRUITS	VEGETABLES
½ cup fruit or berries	½ cup chopped vegetables
1 medium piece of fruit	1 cup raw leafy vegetables (side salad)
½ grapefruit	6 to 8 carrot sticks, 3 inches long
¼ cup dried fruit	½ cup cooked or canned beans or peas
12 grapes	¾ cup vegetable juice
¾ cup fruit juice (100 percent juice)	

They are a nice alternative to plain white potatoes, and can be served in all the same ways—mashed, scalloped, cut in wedges, or grilled as home fries.

Variety Is Best

To take full advantage of the goodness of fruits and vegetables, strive for variety in the kinds you choose. It's fine to rely on a few standbys, especially to ensure that a picky eater gets enough fruits and vegetables. But try not to serve only one or two choices, because you may miss out on important nutrients. It's also important to let children try new foods and encourage them to develop broader tastes.

Give Fruits and Vegetables a Leading Role

Fruits and vegetables should be a major part of children's diets. Here are a few tips to help you boost the plant power in your child's diet.

Make It Easy

If serving fruits and vegetables takes too much time, you'll find yourself reaching for ready-made foods instead. Preparing fruits and vegetables doesn't have to be a chore. Salad greens, carrot sticks, watermelon, pineapple, and other fruits and vegetables now come prepared and in convenient packages that kids can take to school. Or you can cut up carrot and celery sticks, bell pepper slices, broccoli and cauliflower florets, and green beans and package them in individual baggies yourself to be used throughout the week. Wash and cut a whole head of lettuce at one time so it's easy to add a side salad to every meal.

Think Small

Kids can find eating a whole fruit or vegetable daunting. There's nothing wrong with eating these foods in smaller pieces, alone or mixed together. Precut pieces of fruit stashed in a small plastic container can be more fun for kids to munch on at school than a whole piece of fruit, and the same goes for raw vegetables for snacking. Chopping or dicing vegetables can help make a big food into a bunch of easy bites.

Mix It In

Instead of cooking a separate side dish of vegetables, you can look for ways to add vegetables to other foods. Just about every dish can be served with some fruit or vegetable added. Here are some examples:

- *Chicken breast:* Top with quickly sautéed mushrooms and tomatoes.
- *Macaroni and cheese:* Mix in green peas or chopped bell peppers.
- *Meatloaf:* Add shredded carrots or chopped tomatoes.
- *Bean burrito:* Add chopped bell peppers or broccoli and canned corn, top with tomato salsa.
- *Spaghetti:* Add chopped bell peppers, broccoli, spinach, mushrooms, or any other veggie to the sauce.
- *Baked dishes and casseroles:* Top with shredded zucchini or carrots for added texture.
- *Peanut butter and jelly sandwich:* Add sliced bananas.
- *Scrambled eggs:* Add diced vegetables or spinach.
- *Macaroni, potato, chicken, or tuna salad:* Defrost and mix in a package of frozen mixed vegetables, or add fresh diced celery and carrots.
- *Rice or other grain side dish:* Add diced vegetables or mushrooms, mix in a can of diced tomatoes, or for a sweeter alternative add raisins and canned mandarin orange slices or chunks of sweet potato or butternut squash (available frozen and precut).
- *Soups and chili:* Homemade soups and chili are easy to make, and can be a flavorful way to introduce new kinds of vegetables. Nutritious green vegetables like kale mellow in flavor in soups, and the spices in chili add zest to zucchini, squash, peppers, okra, and cauliflower.
- *Oatmeal or other hot cereal:* Add raisins or dried apricots, blueberries, canned fruit, unsweetened applesauce, banana slices, apple chunks, or sliced strawberries.
- *Sandwiches:* Always add vegetables to meat or cheese sandwiches; if lettuce and tomato gets boring, try sliced cucumbers, bell peppers, carrots, spinach, cabbage, mushrooms, zucchini, or red onion.
- *Frozen yogurt, ice cream, and other desserts:* If you serve desserts, always look for a way to add fruit to something kids will want to eat anyway: pineapple chunks, strawberries, blueberries, peaches, and mangoes are great toppings for frozen desserts or cakes. Or better yet, skip the ice cream and make a fruit smoothie with frozen fruit pieces blended with orange juice or milk.

Spice It Up

You don't have to drown vegetables and fruits in sugar, salt, or fat to make them palatable. A better alternative is to be creative with flavorings and make liberal use of spices. Try sprinkling cinnamon and nutmeg on sweet potatoes, butternut squash, or sliced warm fruit. Add garlic or lemon juice to vegetables, and use curry powder, chili powder, or cumin to make sautéed vegetables and meats more flavorful.

Simple additions, like chopped nuts, raisins, chives, herbs, or cheese can dress up a bland vegetable dish. Borrowing from different cultures is also one of the best ways to invigorate a bland or monotonous menu. The same vegetables are completely transformed when steeped in an Indian or Thai curry, sautéed in a Chinese sauce, mixed into a Mexican dish, added to a Mediterranean salad, or simmered in a West African stew. With multicultural recipes easily available in bookstores and on the Internet, we have the world at our fingertips. Whatever your cultural background, borrowing ideas from other people and places will increase the variety of your meals and also expose your child to a wider scope of tastes.

Choose for Color

Confused about how to choose vegetables and fruits that provide a variety of vitamins, minerals, and phytochemicals? One of the easiest ways is to mix colors. The color of a plant is more than cosmetic: many of the phytochemicals that give plants color are also thought to have health benefits. Table 8.1 shows the whole rainbow of fruit and vegetable colors and what those colors mean.

Make Food a Learning Opportunity

Choosing for color is also a great way to help kids learn about fruits and vegetables. Make it into a game: on your next shopping trip, have your child help you pick out a rainbow of fruits and vegetables, one for every color. Then have him remind you of the colors as you eat those foods throughout the week. You can also think about color as a way to make food preparation more fun and interesting. When making a salad, ask your child to pick vegetables to add with color in mind: mixing yellow squash with red peppers, or adding jicama sticks for a splash of white on green lettuce. When your child is coloring with crayons or markers, ask which fruits and vegetables they remind her of. Kids are naturally drawn to color, and it can be a great tool for reinforcing ideas about health and nutrition. Color is another reason to use more raw vegetables, since they are often more colorful than cooked ones, adding to their appeal to kids.

You can also make grocery shopping a game by letting young children hunt for certain fruits and vegetables at the store, helping them learn to recognize different foods. Gardening, even growing a small herb garden or tomato plant, can help children learn about where fruits and vegetables come from and appreciate fresh produce that they grow themselves. Visiting a small farmer's market or local farm is also a great way to expose children to the people and work involved in producing fresh foods.

Table 8.1 The Color Connection

COLOR	BENEFITS	EXAMPLES
Blue/purple	Blue and purple fruits and vegetables contain phytochemicals that act as antioxidants and are thought to play a role in memory and urinary tract health; fresh fruits contain vitamin C.	Blueberries, blackberries, purple grapes, prunes, plums, raisins, purple cabbage, purple eggplant
Green	Green fruits and vegetables contain phytochemicals, such as lutein, thought to play a role in healthy vision and are rich sources of vitamins C and A. Green leafy vegetables are powerhouses of vitamins and minerals.	Spinach, broccoli, avocados, artichokes, kiwi; green grapes, brussels sprouts, limes, green beans, green bell peppers, bok choy, collard greens, green cabbage, okra, peas, zucchini, green apples
Yellow/orange	Orange, yellow, and red pigments are created by carotenoids, including beta-carotene (vitamin A), and many are high in vitamin C, an antioxidant.	Oranges, mangoes, papaya, butternut squash, pumpkin, cantaloupe, yellow corn, peaches, grapefruit, pineapple, yellow bell peppers, sweet potato, summer squash
Red	The carotenoid that makes fruits and vegetables red is lycopene, currently under investigation for its ability to prevent cancers.	Red apples, cherries, strawberries, watermelon, red bell peppers, beets, tomatoes, cranberries, pink grapefruit, raspberries, pomegranate
White	White vegetables also contain vitamins and phytochemicals, including allicin from the onion family, which may have benefits for the immune system.	Onions, leeks, shallots, garlic, cauliflower, ginger, bananas, jicama, white corn, parsnips

Are Organic Foods Better?

Many health-conscious parents wonder whether they should choose organic foods over conventional varieties. Demand for organic foods has been growing, and organic products now represent a multibillion-dollar industry in the United States. But these foods can be quite a bit pricier than regular options—are they worth the money?

Organic foods include plant products that have been grown without the use of synthetic pesticides, herbicides, or fertilizers, only natural fertilizers like humus and compost, and certain natural chemical compounds. Organic meat and dairy products come from animals raised on natural feed that have not been exposed to synthetic hormones, antibiotics, or other drugs. In 2002, the USDA set clearer standards for what can be considered organic. Organic whole foods are often labeled with a green USDA Organic sticker that certifies that the product is 95 percent organic. Packaged products may use the wording "100 percent organic" if all the ingredients were produced organically, "organic" if 95 percent of the ingredients are produced organically, and "contains organic ingredients" if 70 percent of the ingredients are produced organically. Individual ingredients can also be labeled as organic on the nutritional label. Other claims—such as "natural," "free-range," or "hormone-free"—are not definitions that are regulated by the USDA.

When you buy organic foods, you are supporting a process, a particular way of growing foods that is more environmentally friendly. But it's less clear that there is a real difference in the product—whether organic foods differ in any meaningful way from other foods. Organic foods often look a little different, but there is no way to differentiate an organic food from a conventionally grown food based on its composition. One study at University of California at Davis found that some organic foods had higher levels of phytochemicals than conventionally grown varieties. But plant foods naturally vary widely in their nutrient levels, and so far there is no evidence to show that organic foods are nutritionally superior in any meaningful way to conventional varieties. A study by the Consumers Union found that organic produce had lower pesticide residues than conventionally grown produce, and many people feel that the more we can reduce our exposure to pesticides, the better. But it's not clear whether the level of pesticide residues found on conventional produce—which fall within the limits of safety set by the Environmental Protection Agency—could pose any threat to health. And organic farmers are allowed to use certain "natural" pesticides, like sulfur and copper compounds. These substances generally break down faster in the environment and are thought to be less toxic, but they introduce another layer of uncertainty about the relative safety of the foods.

In sum, there are many worthwhile reasons to buy organic foods. But in terms of nutrition and health, there is currently no reason to believe that organic foods offer a distinct advantage, or that buying conventional foods is somehow putting children's health or nutrition at risk. It's simply a matter of personal choice.

Fruits and Vegetables: The Bottom Line

- Fruits and vegetables have numerous health benefits and have been linked to lower rates of chronic disease.

- Most children don't eat enough fruits and vegetables, especially after infancy. Boosting the amount they eat is important for their nutrition now and their health later in life.

- Five-a-day is just the first step. You can make the most out of the vegetables children eat by serving a wide variety of whole, nutrient-rich vegetables, rather than relying on potatoes, juice, processed foods, or a very limited set of choices.

- Children learn from what their parents do as well as what they say. By eating more fruits and vegetables yourself, you'll be doing yourself a favor and serving as a role model.

- By teaching children about the foods they eat—such as playing a color game with fruits and vegetables—you can get them involved in their own nutrition.

Be a Role Model

With very few adults in the United States eating enough fruits and vegetables, parents may need to take a look at their own eating habits and make some changes. Not only will adding more fruits and vegetables to family meals help improve your child's diet, but you will be modeling a healthy approach to eating that will make a lasting impression. Your attitudes will come across, whether you see eating healthy foods as a chore or as a pleasure. By being aware of your own eating habits, you can send more positive messages to your child. And of course, making food choices that decrease your risk of developing cancer, heart disease, and other chronic diseases is the best thing you can do for your own health and for your family.

9

Vitamins, Minerals, and Dietary Supplements

Countless kids have grown up munching a daily chewable multivitamin, or chewable vitamin C supplements when they catch colds. It is estimated that about half of all children receive some form of vitamin or mineral supplement. Other than the fruity flavor, what exactly are these vitamin pills providing for kids? And what about all the herbal products, zinc lozenges, and so-called natural remedies for kids that are starting to show up in supermarkets and health-food stores? It's hard for parents to know what role these supplements might play in their child's health, or whether they are even necessary. With a few exceptions, these additional supplements are not necessary if a child has a healthy diet—and they can't take the place of foods rich in vitamins and minerals. While vitamin and mineral supplements have historically been quite useful in treating dietary shortcomings, the idea that extra doses of them can make us even healthier is in most cases suspect.

What Is a Supplement?

When we talk about dietary supplements, we mean something that is added to the diet and is not found in the same quantity naturally in the foods we eat. Sometimes a supplement is clearly separate from our normal food, like a vitamin pill. But lots of things we eat every day also contain supplements or fortifications of natural foods, whether we realize it or not. An example is the iodine usually added to salt, or the extra dose of vitamins and minerals added to flour and breakfast cereal. You may have wondered why the nutrition information on your box of Cheerios reads a bit like a vitamin label; it's part of a concerted effort to ensure that people get the vitamins they need by adding these nutrients to everyday items that are eaten widely. These food supplement and fortification programs have been highly successful for public health, because they deliver nutrients to a majority of the population without trying to force people to adopt a new behavior, like taking vitamins.

Whatever form they take, supplements and fortifications contain nutrients that are taken out of their natural source and added to the diet. It is the difference between popping an antioxidant pill and eating a serving of blueberries that are naturally high in several antioxidants. For infants, manufactured formulas are also a kind of supplement, because the added iron, zinc, and special fats in them are not found naturally in cow's milk or soy but are purified from other sources and added to the formula.

Why Use Supplements?

Supplements have traditionally offered a cheap, efficient way to supply a vital nutrient that is not found at high enough levels in the diet. Sometimes supplements are used to treat malnourished or chronically sick children, or to provide quick, concentrated treatment to a patient suffering from a disease caused by a vitamin or mineral deficiency. But they have also been used proactively—as in the case of fortified foods—to combat dietary shortcomings in a large number of people. An example of this is the use of folic acid supplements in women of childbearing age to prevent birth defects in their babies. Multivitamins, whether for adults or children, are also taken by many people as a dietary safety net, providing many of the vitamins and minerals that people need just in case the diet does not.

What Supplements Can't Do

In the past couple of decades, the definition of a supplement has grown; rather than making up for scarcities in the diet, supplements such as herbals and high-dose megavitamins purport to add something to the diet that will boost health, ease symptoms of disease, change mood, or substitute for normal medications.

The supplement business is booming. The 1990s brought a rapid rise in the number of people using supplements (one survey found a 180 percent increase in the use of herbal supplements, and a 380 percent increase in the use of high-dose megavitamins between 1990 and 1997). Because these supplements are paid for out-of-pocket and aren't regulated by the FDA like medications, they represent a growing market and a great opportunity for companies to sell nonregulated foods and pills with health claims that don't need to be supported with scientific evidence. The health-food approach to marketing supplements, boasting natural, herbal, or

An Industry Unfettered

Amazingly, dietary supplements do not currently have to be manufactured according to any set standards, and their manufacturers don't have to prove they are safe. That's because dietary supplements are regulated as foods, not as drugs. The FDA must investigate and prove a supplement is unsafe before it is taken off the market. And with the supplement business as large as it is, strict regulation is impossible. Several independent studies of herbal supplements have shown that the actual dosages can be much lower—or even much higher—than what is listed on the label.

Supplement manufacturers also can get away with making health claims about their products that aren't true. While they can't say that a certain product "lowers cholesterol," they can say that it "promotes a healthy cholesterol level," a difference that most buyers don't even notice. For children, these products may claim to cure anything from common colds to attention deficit/hyperactivity disorder (ADHD). Many parents who have children with chronic illnesses or difficult psychological disorders like ADHD are understandably attracted to the idea of a natural alternative to medication. But don't be fooled. Giving these supplements to children is gambling with their health. There is no safer option to normal prescription and over-the-counter medications that have been thoroughly tested, both of which should be taken under the guidance of a physician in recommended doses for children.

The FDA, recognizing that something has to be done to rein in this runaway industry, proposed some manufacturing standards for supplement makers in March 2003. Until better oversight exists, it's best to stick with run-of-the-mill vitamin and mineral supplements by known manufacturers that have levels expressed as percentages of the recommended daily value.

organic ingredients, has been so successful for adults that companies are now turning to selling supplements for kids. Very few herbal supplements have been studied for their efficacy or for their potential harmful effects on adults, much less children.

Specific vitamins, minerals, certain fats, and other compounds found in foods have also been touted as having health benefits at concentrated doses. We certainly do need a certain level of these substances, and supplements are a way to bring levels up to normal. But consuming more than what we need is not always a good thing. Just because the body needs a certain amount of zinc, for instance, doesn't mean that taking a high dose of zinc will somehow make the body function better than normal.

For better or worse, our bodies like to exist in a balance, taking in all the things they need but never too much of a good thing. At best, extra doses are simply excreted in the urine. At worst, they can interfere with the absorption of another substance (for instance, high doses of zinc can prevent iron absorption), or they build up in our bodies and cause toxicity. Ongoing research is trying to determine whether consuming higher levels of certain antioxidants—for instance, vitamins C and E, selenium, and carotenoids—can help prevent chronic disease. So far, these associations are unclear, and even if high dietary levels are found to be protective, it doesn't necessarily mean that a high-dose pill is warranted.

Should My Child Take a Vitamin and Mineral Supplement?

That question has posed a conundrum for pediatricians and nutritionists who would like to agree on a broad recommendation that fits all children. On one hand, several surveys have suggested that today's kids are not eating enough of certain key vitamins and minerals like vitamins A and E, iron, zinc, and calcium. But when we look at the use of vitamin and mineral supplements, we find that the kids who have the least healthy diets—and might benefit from supplements—are also the least likely to be given a multivitamin-multimineral supplement. And the kids who are given vitamins often have better diets to begin with and probably don't need them.

If you follow some of the basic suggestions in this book, chances are you will already provide your child with foods that have enough of all necessary nutrients for a healthy diet, and will have no need for extra vitamins.

In fact, a multivitamin is a poor substitute for nutrients in healthy foods. Why can't kids just eat anything they like, and take a multivitamin to make up for a poor diet? Unfortunately for kids who would rather eat cookies and chips than fruits and vegetables, supplements can't take the place of nutrients in food. Organic material like fruits and vegetables is complex, and can't be boiled down to a simple list of ingredients that can be put in a pill.

Most of the nutrients we know to be important for health have been studied in the diets of people who eat them in food. We're not always sure whether the purified substances from pills really do all the same things that food does, although supplement manufacturers are quick to suggest that they're the same. For instance, several studies have shown that eating lots of tomato-based foods may help lower rates of prostate cancer in men. Many supplement manufacturers are now sporting lycopene, an antioxidant that also gives tomatoes and other fruits their red color, in their products. But it's a leap to say that the lycopene found in a pill will have the same benefits as eating tomatoes, which contain several nutrients that may work together to keep the body healthy.

Find It in Foods First, Supplements Second

Wander through a health-food store and you might be left with the impression that the key to good health lies in popping pills and eating sugary snacks fortified with vitamins. It's true that vitamin and mineral supplements can be important for children's health during times of rapid growth, as in the first two years of life and during adolescence. They also can provide a safety net for children who eat restricted diets, such as vegetarians and vegans, or children who are extremely picky eaters.

But for the majority of children, a better strategy for parents to take is to know their nutrients, learn where they lie in foods, and choose foods that will give their children a variety of these substances. This is the truly natural way to provide vitamins and minerals. This chapter offers a brief primer on all the micronutrients—vitamins, minerals, and other substances called *trace elements*—and where you can find them in food. We'll look at some of the foods that already act as supplements, like fortified cereal. Once you know your nutrients, you'll have a better sense of which ones are already in your child's diet, and whether a dietary supplement is needed.

Vitamins, Minerals, Trace Elements: A Primer

People have long known about the basic components of food—carbohydrates, fats, and proteins—but it wasn't until the beginning of the twentieth century that scientists became aware that other compounds in food were necessary for the basic functions of life in animals and humans. The substances are often called *micronu-*

trients because, with the exception of some minerals like calcium, phosphorus, and sodium, most of them are present only in very small amounts in the body. But they pull much more than their weight in keeping our bodies running.

Most micronutrients were initially discovered for their role in certain vital functions of the body, often because a lack of a vitamin led to a specific disease. Vitamins are often grouped into two classes: fat-soluble (vitamins A, D, E, and K) and water-soluble (vitamin C, thiamin [B_1], riboflavin [B_2], niacin [B_3], choline, pantothenic acid [B_5], vitamin B_6, folate, vitamin B_{12}, and biotin). The main difference between the two is that fat-soluble vitamins can accumulate in the body, while water-soluble ones are usually excreted and must be replaced more regularly. Because of their longer staying power, fat-soluble vitamins can become toxic in high doses.

Minerals are considered *inorganic* compounds because they contain no carbon, but are used in many capacities in the body, from building bones to keeping the immune system functioning. Lately, there has been a lot of research accumulating that certain *trace elements*—so called because together they make up less than 0.01 percent of our body weight—have functions in the body that make them an important part of our diet.

Here are a few of the vitamins and minerals that are frequently low in kids' diets. Also see Table 9.1 for a list of all vitamins, minerals, and trace elements that we know are important for health, and where to find them in foods.

Vitamin A

The first vitamin of the alphabet was also the first vitamin discovered, when scientists isolated the fat-soluble factor from foods that was given the name *vitamin A* in 1920. Later it was found that certain vegetable pigments, called carotenoids, are converted into vitamin A in the body. Vitamin A has a role in vision, enabling us to see in dim light. It also keeps the immune system strong, and for this reason is often given as supplements to children in developing countries who are at risk for infections. It also has a role in growth and helps promote the absorption of iron—only one example of how adequate supplies of one nutrient can have an effect on another. Natural sources of vitamin A and carotenoids are liver, fish liver oils, eggs, dairy products, deep orange fruits and vegetables, and dark leafy vegetables.

Table 9.1 Micronutrients and Their Food Sources

MICRONUTRIENT	BIOLOGICAL FUNCTIONS	FOOD SOURCES
Fat-Soluble Vitamins		
Vitamin A	Necessary for normal vision, development, and immune function	Preformed vitamin A can be found in liver, fish liver oils, fish, eggs, and dairy products. You'll find carotenoids (provitamin A) in dark leafy green vegetables and deep orange fruits and vegetables.
Vitamin D	Helps build bones by regulating calcium and phosphorus	Sunlight (through the skin), some fatty fish and fish liver oils, fortified cereals, fortified milk or margarine, and vitamin D supplements
Vitamin E	Antioxidant defense	Vegetable oils, wheat germ, nuts, green leafy vegetables, and whole grains
Vitamin K	Component of many blood proteins; needed for blood clotting	Green leafy vegetables, brussels sprouts, cabbage, milk, eggs, and margarine
Water-Soluble Vitamins		
Thiamin (vitamin B_1)	Used to metabolize carbohydrates and some proteins	Whole and fortified grains and cereals, pork, nuts, seeds, tuna, salmon, beans, tofu, and vegetables including peas, asparagus, and okra
Riboflavin (vitamin B_2)	Component of several chemical reactions in cells; regulates some hormones	Fortified grains and cereals, dairy products, eggs, meat, almonds, tofu, beet greens, and spinach

MICRONUTRIENT	BIOLOGICAL FUNCTIONS	FOOD SOURCES
Niacin (vitamin B_3)	Required for turning foods into energy and maintenance of skin, blood cells, and nervous system	Meat, fish, poultry, whole and fortified grains, and fortified cereals
Choline	Needed to create signals in brain and nervous system	Liver, milk, eggs, and peanuts
Pantothenic acid (vitamin B_5)	Helps convert food to energy; helps produce lipids, neurotransmitters, and hemoglobin	Widespread in foods, including chicken, beef, oats, cereals, tomato products, organ meats, yeast, egg yolks, broccoli, and whole grains
Vitamin B_6	Helps metabolize fats and proteins	Poultry, fish, liver, eggs, whole grains, tofu and other soy products, legumes, oats, and fortified cereals
Folate (folic acid)	Needed for making DNA in new cells and creating the spinal cord and brain in embryos; disposes of homocysteine, a substance that may lead to heart disease	Fortified cereals, dark green leafy vegetables, whole-grain and fortified bread products, legumes, and orange juice
Vitamin B_{12}	Needed to make new cells and prevents anemia	Meat, fish, poultry, milk, cheese, eggs, and fortified cereals

(continued)

Table 9.1 Micronutrients and Their Food Sources (continued)

MICRONUTRIENT	BIOLOGICAL FUNCTIONS	FOOD SOURCES
Biotin	Helps convert food to energy and break down fats	Egg yolks, organ meats, fish, and soybeans
Vitamin C	Antioxidant; helps produce collagen; aids in iron absorption	Citrus fruits, broccoli, bell peppers, tomatoes, brussels sprouts, potatoes, strawberries, cauliflower, and spinach
Minerals and Trace Elements		
Calcium	Formation of bones and teeth; also blood clotting, muscle contraction, and nerve cell communication	Milk, cheese, yogurt, corn tortillas, some tofu, cabbage, kale, and broccoli
Chromium	Helps regulate blood sugar levels	Some cereals, meats, poultry, and fish
Copper	Helps metabolize iron	Organ meats, seafood, nuts, seeds, wheat bran, whole grains, cereals, and cocoa
Fluoride	Prevents cavities and stimulates bone formation	Fluoridated water, dental products, teas, and marine fish
Iodine	Component of thyroid hormone	Iodized salt and some processed foods

MICRONUTRIENT	BIOLOGICAL FUNCTIONS	FOOD SOURCES
Iron	Part of hemoglobin in blood and other enzymes	Most available form (called *heme* form) found in meats and poultry. Non-heme form found in legumes, beet greens, artichokes, tofu, dried fruits, and fortified cereals.
Magnesium	Needed ingredient for some chemical reactions in cells	Green leafy vegetables, unpolished rice and grains, nuts, meat, starches, and milk
Manganese	Aids bone formation and metabolism of proteins, carbohydrates, and cholesterol	Nuts, legumes, whole grains, and teas
Molybdenum	Factor in metabolism of some proteins	Legumes, grain products, and nuts
Phosphorus	Used throughout the body to maintain pH levels, store and transfer energy in cells, and make DNA	Dairy products, peas, meat, eggs, and some bread products and cereals
Selenium	Antioxidant; regulates thyroid hormone	Organ meats, seafood, and leafy parts of plants (if selenium is found in soil)
Zinc	Component of many enzymes and proteins	Red meats, animal products, whole grains, legumes, and whole-grain and fortified cereals

Vitamin D

Vitamin D is a bit of an oddball among vitamins, because it's not really part of the diet at all. Humans absorb little vitamin D from food; instead, we synthesize the vast majority of our vitamin D in our skin when we are exposed to sunlight. Vitamin D helps us absorb calcium and phosphorus, the two minerals that build bones, and for this reason is often added to milk products and calcium supplements. Vitamin D deficiency can lead to a disease called *rickets*, which is rare in the United States and other industrialized countries today but used to be widespread among poorer children. Because vitamin D can be scarce for babies and toddlers who do not have prolonged sun exposure (which carries the risk of causing skin cancer later in life), vitamin D is the one nutrient that the American Academy of Pediatrics recommends supplementing all children with, from birth through adolescence.

Vitamin E

Vitamin E is one of several antioxidants, a class of substances that act as vigilantes in our cells. Just as the energy production in cars and factories leaves behind waste products that can potentially build up and harm our environment, the energy production that fuels cells is constantly creating molecules called *oxygen free radicals* that can cause damage to cells over time. We often think of oxygen as a necessity for life, but when it is attached to various chemicals in our bodies, it can be quite dangerous. Antioxidants scavenge out these extra oxygen molecules and keep them from wreaking havoc in our cells. Vitamin E, one of our primary antioxidant defenders, is found in vegetable oils, wheat germ, nuts, and green leafy vegetables.

Vitamin C

Our dependence on vitamin C was classically demonstrated on ship voyages where sailors often fell ill with scurvy, a painful disease that causes gum bleeding, bruised skin, and difficulty healing. It was finally discovered that stocking up on citrus fruits—or, on many German and Dutch expeditions, sauerkraut—could prevent the disease. Vitamin C contributes to the production of collagen in our tissues, which explains the symptoms of scurvy. It is also a powerful antioxidant and has several functions in the immune system. This vitamin gained a long-standing popularity in American culture when Nobel laureate Linus Pauling proclaimed that megadoses of vitamin C could ward off the common cold. Though a large body of research has thoroughly debunked that hypothesis, vitamin C is still one of the most popular supplements for children, and the myth is still strong. Unfortunately, vitamin C will do little for your child's cold. High doses of it are useless anyway, because vitamin C is water-soluble, and the tissues in your body quickly get overloaded with it and dump any extra out in the urine. However, vitamin C is still necessary for health, and it's important to include foods high in vitamin C in your child's diet. Vitamin C is found in citrus fruits and fruit juices, broccoli, bell peppers, tomatoes, brussels sprouts, and many berries.

Vitamin B$_6$

Vitamin B$_6$ is one of the eight water-soluble B vitamins—thiamin, riboflavin, niacin, pantothenic acid, biotin, B$_6$, B$_{12}$, and folic acid—which all help turn the

Weaning to Age Three: Special Needs for Growing Bodies

Children triple in size the first three years of life. All of that new bulk doesn't come from thin air—like a building under construction, children's growing bodies need a steady stream of raw materials, in this case energy and nutrients in the diet. Because the growth is so rapid, children at this age are particularly vulnerable to dietary deficiencies in vitamins and minerals. And because their bodies are laying a foundation for their adult selves, these shortages have repercussions that are greater than they would be in adults.

Two of the most important nutrients during this time are iron and zinc. Without iron, infants can develop anemia, and a paucity of zinc can lead to a weak immune system or delayed cognitive development.

Fortunately, breast milk usually provides all the necessary nutrients infants need, and infant formulas are supplemented with iron and zinc to prevent deficiencies. Weaning, with the introduction of a wider variety of foods into the diet, can potentially lead to shortfalls if the new food sources aren't very rich in nutrients. It's especially important to choose foods during this time that are high in iron, zinc, and other vitamins, and to feed your infant fortified cereals. See Chapter 3 for more hints on nutrition during weaning.

food we eat into energy and take part in chemical reactions that power the cells of our body. They are often added to fortified cereals and flour, so you probably see them on nutrition labels regularly. B vitamins are found naturally in lots of foods, especially those high in protein. Vitamin B_6 helps metabolize fats and proteins in our bodies. It is one of the most common B vitamin deficiencies in kids. Nursing moms should also make sure they are eating enough foods with vitamin B_6, because the levels of this and other water-soluble vitamins found in breast milk vary depending on a mother's diet. You can find this vitamin in meats, eggs, whole-grain products, some fortified cereals, bananas, watermelon, prunes, and many vegetables.

Calcium

Children need to consume adequate calcium to build bones and prevent osteoporosis later in life. (We will discuss this further in Chapter 10.) Calcium is important during infancy and also later in childhood, because puberty is the time when the body is working most actively to accumulate calcium in bones. Our ability to use calcium in foods also depends on adequate levels of vitamins D and K, and many calcium supplements now include these vitamins. In addition to dairy products, calcium is found in dark green leafy vegetables, tofu, dried figs, legumes, oats, and fortified orange juice, and soy milk.

Iron

Iron is used to make hemoglobin, the substance in red blood cells that carries oxygen to all the body's cells and tissues. A lack of iron results in anemia, an insufficiency of oxygen in the blood. Babies who are brought to full term are born with a reservoir of iron from their mothers, but these stores run out in a few months if they are not replaced. Around the time of weaning, babies need to start getting iron from their diet through iron-rich foods and iron-fortified infant cereals. Finding iron in foods can be tricky because it is not always in a form that we can absorb. The most usable form of iron is found in meats, especially red meat (just like red blood cells, the color red is a sign of iron in animals). Plant foods may be high in iron but in a form that it is harder to absorb. Eating foods that are high in vitamin

Sodium: The Mineral You Don't Need More Of

In Table 9.1, there is one major mineral I left out: sodium. That's because sodium is easy to find in foods, and most of us eat much more of it than we need. Most of this extra sodium is simply excreted from the body, but it also pulls water out of the body's cells, raising blood pressure. It's not yet clear what effect a salty diet has on children's long-term health, but over time, high blood pressure can stress the heart and lead to damage of the arteries. A study by the National Heart, Lung, and Blood Institute in adults found that some people who have abnormally high blood pressure can reduce it to normal levels by lowering salt intake—and those who are in the normal range can lower it even further.

The sodium content of natural plant and animal foods is actually quite low, but just about every processed food we eat has salt slipped in somewhere. Processed foods account for most of the sodium that Americans eat. It's tricky to avoid high-salt foods these days, because many manufacturers know that people on the lookout for sugar, fat, or cholesterol won't mind if their foods are full of salt. The best way to avoid salt is to limit the processed foods you eat. Avoid cured meats and choose canned foods that say "no salt added," unsalted nuts, and low- or reduced-sodium versions of condiments and other foods. Use natural spices in cooking instead of salt. And check labels for sodium content before you choose a product.

C helps with iron absorption; try pairing iron-rich foods with vitamin C–rich foods at snacks and meals. Foods high in iron are meats, legumes, beet greens, artichokes, tofu, dried fruits, and fortified cereals.

Zinc

Many studies conducted in developing countries have documented the need for zinc in the diet. Even a mild zinc shortfall can lead to slower growth in infants and children, and more severe deficiencies can lead to diarrhea, decreased appetite, frequent infections, irritability, and possibly even impaired cognitive development. Zinc is used throughout the body in creating DNA and proteins, and in several components of the immune system. It is crucial that infants have enough zinc for

Enlisting Good Bacteria for Better Health

One kind of supplement that is used worldwide but still has yet to hit it big in the United States is probiotics, or the use of "good" bacteria in the diet to promote a healthy digestive and immune system. It may sound a little exotic but it's not—you're actually using probiotics every time you eat yogurt with live, active cultures. The health benefits of bacteria have been noted since ancient times, but research is finally accumulating to back up the anecdotal evidence.

Think of your digestive system as a vast metropolis teeming with bacteria, and you are a landlord who owns the space they rent. Most of these bacteria are great tenants, and actually help you out in many ways. But others are destructive; they invade and wreak havoc on your property. Getting the right balance of bacteria in your digestive system is crucial to good health. Antibiotics can help destroy an infestation of infectious bacteria, but they leave a lot of collateral damage to the good ones as well. Another tactic is to supply a steady stream of good tenants to crowd out the bad ones and prevent an infection in the first place. This is the basic principle of probiotics: used preventively, they can help ward off potential infections, or used in conjunction with antibiotics during an illness, they can help push the bad bacteria out and establish a healthier balance in your digestive system.

Because the bacteria in probiotics already exist inside us, they are completely benign. Doctors have used probiotics safely on newborns and infants as a medical treatment many times. Though the jury's still out on the exact benefits, probiotics have been shown to be helpful in several situations. For one, almost all infants at some time or another are hit with a gastrointestinal infection that leads to diarrhea, usually caused by a rotavirus. Many studies on children hospitalized with this illness have found that supplementing them with probiotics decreases the average duration and severity of their diarrhea. Good bacteria have also shown promise in preventing diarrhea that can sometimes crop up in children being treated with antibiotics for common infections. And studies have begun to look at how probiotics

their overall health; fortunately, breast-fed babies almost always get what they need from their mother's milk, and formulas are generally supplemented with zinc. During weaning, infants should be fed fortified infant cereals and other foods high in zinc. Zinc is most concentrated in animal products, especially red meat, and also in whole grains, nuts, and legumes, and fortified breakfast cereals and infant cere-

given to newborns or to pregnant or lactating mothers could prevent or lessen allergies and asthma in children, though the evidence is not yet clear.

As a preventive strategy, it makes sense to use probiotics in situations where your child could be exposed to infections, such as during hospital stays or while attending day care. Parents in the United States who are interested in giving their children probiotics currently face some challenges. Supplements are your best bet because yogurts, with the exception of those made by Stonyfield Farm, do not carry enough live organisms to be considered true probiotics. And probiotics supplements are afflicted with all the problems of the supplement industry—a lack of regulation and no guarantee that the product contains what it says it does. Still, you can find some reputable brands in drugstores and health-food stores. Though they often carry a hefty price tag, the best brands guarantee that each pill packs about a billion bacteria (you need to ingest a lot of bacteria to guarantee that enough will survive the trip through your stomach and intestines to have some effect).

While a few different kinds of bacteria are found in probiotics, the type that has been best studied as a supplement is *Lactobacillus casei GG*. As with any supplement, let your doctor know about any probiotics you intend to use, and keep in mind that they cannot substitute for medical treatment of illness or infection.

European infant formulas now often carry probiotics to mimic the health benefits of live breast milk, and it's only a matter of time before U.S. versions follow suit. Americans tend to be a little queasier about the idea of ingesting bacteria, though, so companies are focusing for now on a related strategy called *prebiotics*. While not bacteria themselves, these substances are not fully digested in the stomach and small intestine, so they end up in the colon where they serve as food for good bacteria. An example of natural prebiotics is oligosaccharides, a type of carbohydrate in breast milk. These are now added to some infant formulas as fructose oligosaccharides or inulin. Though studies have not yet shown prebiotics to have the same impact as ingesting live bacteria, they certainly can't hurt and may be helpful.

als. Zinc is one of the micronutrients you don't want to get too much of, because extra doses can actually slow the immune system and interfere with iron absorption. Those zinc lozenges you may have seen advertised to treat colds have failed to lessen the length of colds in clinical studies, so they are most likely useless and may even be harmful to children if the dose is too high.

Building a Multivitamin Diet

As you can see, most vitamins, minerals, and trace elements are lurking in many foods we eat. The key to getting the right balance of them is variety. Kids who eat the same few foods over and over run the risk of missing an important nutrient or two.

One helpful exercise is to make a rough list of all the foods your child will eat in a week. Take a look at the food sources listed next to each nutrient in Table 9.1— is there something in each section that makes its way regularly into your child's diet? See if you can represent each one several times over the course of the week. You may notice some foods on the list come up again and again, like legumes, whole grains, dairy products, and leafy green vegetables. These foods are an efficient way to cover a lot of nutritional bases when eaten regularly. If you include them in your sample week you'll quickly find that most necessary vitamins and minerals will be a daily part of your child's diet. If you notice, however, that any category is lacking, try to find some way to work a food from that list into a few meals or snacks. You may find that building a multivitamin diet adds some variety to the foods your family eats.

This exercise also illustrates why regularly eating sweets and other empty calories can cause double damage; not only do these foods have a potential negative impact on health, they also take the place of something else that could provide essential vitamins or minerals. When kids get too many of their calories from sodas, candy, chips, and the like, it may be hard for them to find all the nutrients they need in other foods without overeating.

When to Seek Supplements

With a healthy diet, children generally don't need extra vitamin or mineral supplements. But there are a few exceptions, and now that you have a good sense of where to find micronutrients in food, you can better assess your child's needs.

Vitamin D for All Children

The universal exception to the "foods first" rule is vitamin D. This is the only vitamin that we're not able to find in our diets alone—we produce it in our skin when exposed to sunlight. A lack of vitamin D can lead to a softening of the bones and rickets. Babies do not always spend much time in the sun, and too much sun exposure without adequate skin protection is dangerous for infants and children, because it can lead to skin cancer later in life. The sunlight in northern latitudes is too scant to provide enough vitamin D to many children and adults, and it's hard for parents to gauge whether their children see enough sun. Dark-skinned children are at a higher risk for a deficiency because their skin pigmentation interferes with vitamin D production.

Bottle-fed babies usually get enough vitamin D in their formula, but breast-fed babies should be given 200 international units (IU) of vitamin D a day, in the form of drops. This same dose should be continued for all kids throughout childhood and adolescence, either as pills or drops.

Vegetarians

As more people adopt a vegetarian lifestyle, or greatly limit the amount of meat they eat, their kids' diets will reflect these choices. As you can see from Table 9.1, meat is an efficient source of many vitamins and minerals, as well as protein. A healthy vegetarian diet, especially for children, is not simply a normal diet minus meat. The nutrients found in meat must be replaced with other food sources, like dairy products, beans, nuts, seeds, tofu, and whole grains. These foods should figure prominently into any diet that is low in meat sources. Children who eat a vegetarian diet may also be at risk for a B_{12} deficiency, especially if they do not eat many eggs or dairy products. Zinc can also be lacking in children who consume few animal products. Zinc and B_{12} supplements at a children's dosage, or a children's multivitamin-multimineral supplement, can help prevent any negative effects on the health of vegetarian or vegan children.

Poor or Monotonous Diets

If your child is an overly picky eater, or for some other reason must have a very monotonous diet without a lot of variety in foods, taking a regular multivitamin is a way to ward off any potential micronutrient deficiencies.

A multivitamin may also be wise if you are concerned about aspects of your child's diet that are out of your control. In today's world, most parents don't have the luxury of making sure that every meal their child eats is nutritious. One recent study of children in day care found that many of the lunches these kids were given were relatively poor in nutrients because there were too many bread products and not enough fruits and vegetables. The bottom line is that a healthy diet is the best way to get needed nutrients, but multivitamins can be an important safeguard against the potential health consequences of an incomplete diet.

Doses and Daily Intake

In light of new knowledge about micronutrients and health, the Institute of Medicine, which advises the government on health policy issues, has developed new rec-

 The Bottom Line: Dietary Supplements Are a Second Line of Defense in a Healthy Diet

- Children need adequate levels of vitamins and minerals in their diet in order for their bodies to grow and thrive.

- Vitamins and minerals can be found naturally in foods (and sunlight in the case of vitamin D). But getting enough of all these nutrients naturally requires choosing a variety of foods, including fruits, vegetables, whole grains, and animal and plant sources of protein. Whole food sources of nutrients are the most complete, and should play the leading part in a nutritious diet.

- Because it can be difficult for every child to eat enough vitamins and minerals from natural food sources alone, many commonly eaten foods are already fortified with extra vitamins and minerals, and these foods can help boost their daily tally.

- Additional vitamin and mineral supplements can serve as a second line of defense against dietary deficiencies when a child's diet is not adequate, especially during key periods of growth in infancy and adolescence. Vitamin D is recommended as a supplement for all infants and children.

- Parents should be cautious to give vitamin and mineral supplements only at recommended doses for children, and avoid any herbal supplements and remedies that have not been tested for efficacy and safety in children.

ommended levels for nutrients called *dietary reference intakes (DRIs)*. These will replace the old recommended daily allowances (RDAs) that you're used to. Not only do the DRIs update the RDA levels based on current scientific evidence, they also now include a tolerable upper intake level (UL) for some nutrients, given the public's penchant for higher and higher doses of vitamins. The UL is defined as the highest amount of a nutrient likely to have no harmful effects on most people. DRIs also include a figure called *adequate intake (AI)* for some nutrients when there is not enough information to establish an RDA.

The DRIs are a little more useful than the old RDAs because, rather than a one-number-fits-all approach, they take into account the different needs people have according to gender, age, and circumstances like pregnancy and lactation. Unfortunately, food and supplement labels, which are controlled by the FDA, use a completely different scale, called a *daily value (DV)*. DVs are based on more broad recommended levels for the general population. In the next few years, DVs will also be updated to include the new information in the DRIs.

Parents need to keep in mind that children generally need less of most nutrients than adults, so any supplement you give your child should be at a dosage specific for children. Never give your child an extra vitamin beyond the recommended dose, even if you suspect a dietary deficiency. In terms of food intake, it's probably not necessary to try to calculate the exact levels of different nutrients in your child's diet. Glancing at DVs on labels or the new DRIs will give you a sense of which nutrients are in your child's diet and whether the levels are adequate. Visit the website iom.edu/board.asp?id=3788 for a table that lists DRIs for children.

10

Milk, Juice, Soda, and Other Beverages

We've talked a lot about what kids should eat. But what should they be drinking? The original beverage was water, and water is the reason our bodies need to drink at all. But most of us drink beverages for more than hydration; we like the taste, or we want refreshment, or we think they will benefit our health. Never before have we had so many choices for something to sip: new products are constantly emerging, from sodas to fruit drinks to flavored waters to milkshakes. The array of choices can be overwhelming for a parent. Many of these products come with colorful labels and fun names specifically aimed at kids, but are these drinks appropriate for children?

Making better choices about what children drink is just as important as choosing the right foods. As with all the foods we've discussed, beverages are not all the same, and some are healthier than others. And it's not just what children drink, but how much: the ever-growing portion sizes of drinks is an enormous problem in children's nutrition today, one that has not gotten the full attention it deserves.

Beverages Are Foods, Too

With the exception of water and diet beverages, just about everything kids drink contains calories and therefore can be considered a food that is part of their diets. But we often think of the beverages we drink as something extra. Most of us simply aren't aware of all the calories we consume as liquids, and we apply different standards of nutrition to beverages than we do to solid foods.

This oversight creates two important problems that threaten kids' health. First, parents are simply unaware of how many calories lurk in the beverages their children drink. And the growing portion sizes of beverages in stores and restaurants don't help. A sixteen-ounce bottle of juice, soda, or a sweetened fruit drink can pack 200 to 300 calories, about the same as a glazed donut, a small peanut butter sandwich, or a candy bar. But many parents don't blink an eye when their children guzzle a large glass of soda or lemonade in a restaurant, and then get a free refill. Instead, children are allowed to drink these beverages as if they were water, not liquid foods. Children and adolescents currently consume about 10 percent of their daily calories as juice or soft drinks.

Furthermore, because parents don't always count the calories in liquids, they don't set the same limits on unhealthy beverages as they do with foods. A twelve-ounce can of soda contains up to the equivalent of seven to nine teaspoons of sugar. Many parents would never dream of letting their children eat that much sugar at a time, but don't pay attention when that sugar is in liquid form. Not only are kids today getting more and more of their calories from beverages, they are not choosing the healthiest ones. National survey data have shown that, by age five, children in the United States consume more sweetened fruit drinks and carbonated soft drinks than 100 percent juice. By age thirteen, their consumption of sweetened fruit drinks and soda surpasses both juice and milk. The nutrition (or lack of it) in children's beverages is a major blind spot for many parents who otherwise encourage good eating habits.

Because the calories in beverages are every bit as important as those from solid foods, parents need to get in the habit of watching what their children drink as well as what they eat. As you think about the foods your child eats and imagine how they fit into a balanced diet such as one illustrated by the food pyramid, include beverages as well. It might surprise you how beverages can alter or skew the balance of an otherwise healthy diet.

Water and Hydration

Next to the air we breathe, water is our most primary necessity for life. Fluids fill each of our cells and bathe our tissues. They carry oxygen and nutrients throughout the body and remove wastes. Water must be constantly replaced in order to keep our bodies functioning properly. If children lose more water than they take in, they can wind up dehydrated, a condition that can range from minor headaches and listlessness to potentially life-threatening illness.

 How Many Calories Are You Drinking?

Quenching your thirst with a beverage other than water can add a lot of hidden calories. Here are calorie contents of an eight-ounce serving of various beverages; keep in mind that many drinks come in larger serving sizes, like twelve-ounce cans, sixteen-ounce bottles, or twenty-ounce bottles and cups.

BEVERAGE	CALORIES PER 8-OUNCE SERVING
100 percent grape juice	170
100 percent orange juice	110
Cranberry-apple juice drink	161
Coca-Cola	100
Nantucket Nectars Squeezed Nectar Lemonade	130
Hi-C Pink Lemonade	120
Snapple Kiwi Strawberry Juice Drink	110
Kool-Aid Bursts Tropical Punch	100 (per 6.6-ounce bottle)
Odwalla Blackberry Fruitshake	140
Gatorade Sports Drink	50
Milk: whole/2% reduced-fat milk/ 1% low-fat milk/skim milk	156/142/127/90
Chocolate milk: whole milk/2% reduced-fat/ 1% low-fat	230/190/170
Hershey's Cookies 'n' Cream Milk Shake	260

Tap or Bottled?

Bottled water has become surprisingly trendy in recent years. The water industry is booming, and bottled water has become the most consumed drink in America behind soft drinks.
Who would have thought that the world's oldest beverage could become so profitable? Bottled water is marketed to sound pure and pristine. But in reality, most bottled water comes
from the ground, just like tap water does, not from bubbling springs in the Alps. The water
is filtered to get rid of any impurities or bad tastes, but the main advantage of bottled water
is convenience. Because it's sold in all the places where sweetened beverages are, parents
can opt for water instead of a soda or fruit drink when they are out running errands with their
children or stopping at a convenience store for a quick snack.

While individual bottles of water are convenient, you don't have to turn to expensive
sources of water if you don't want to. Municipal tap water is regulated by the U.S. Environmental Protection Agency (EPA), and is required by law to adhere to standards for contami-
nants. However, the quality and taste of tap water can vary widely from location to location.
Filtration systems can help remove some of the tap water taste. If you are concerned about
your water quality, you can check the EPA's website for information about your local water
(epa.gov/safewater/dwhealth.html).

Tap water does provide one important benefit to health: fluoride added to tap water can
help prevent tooth decay and possibly osteoporosis. Fluoride is especially important for children's dental health. There are several brands of bottled water that contain fluoride, which
should be noted on the label. Children who rely on bottled water without fluoride may need
to get fluoride supplements from their dentist or doctor.

While children do need water to stay hydrated, they don't just get it from drinking beverages. Water is in the foods we eat every day. Fruits and vegetables are the
most watery of all foods—many are somewhere between 80 and 95 percent water.
But liquid even lurks in unlikely places—up to one-third of the weight of a chewy
bagel and about half the weight of a juicy steak are water. So the amount of water
that children must drink to stay hydrated depends partly on the foods they eat.

For most children, drinking a glass of water or other beverage with every meal
and snack and eating lots of fruits and vegetables will provide them with plenty of
hydration, along with extra water when they are playing outside or engaged in a

physical activity. They will also need extra fluids on hot days when their bodies lose water through perspiration. Unless children are drinking abnormally large quantities of liquids, it's very difficult to overhydrate. A good barometer of hydration is the color of urine. It should be pale yellow; dark yellow is an indicator of dehydration. Certain vitamin supplements can make the urine look darker, while caffeine acts as a diuretic and can make the urine look light when in fact the body is losing fluids.

Water is the best option to provide daily hydration for children without clogging their diet with a lot of sweeteners that come in other drinks. With all the beverage options available to us these days, plain and simple water is often an unsung hero in a healthy diet. Water provides pure hydration without any extra sugar or added calories; it's easy to find and free when you get it from the tap. Drinking small glasses of water (about four ounces at a time) throughout the day can help children keep thirst at bay and discourage the urge to snack, since thirst can be mistaken for hunger.

Milk

Milk has traditionally been a big part of children's diets in the United States and other Western countries. Most people associate milk with strong bones and teeth and a healthy body. But some research is calling into question the benefits of drinking milk. In his book *Eat, Drink, and Be Healthy*, my colleague Walter C. Willett presents compelling evidence that drinking a lot of milk, at least for adults, is not especially beneficial and may carry some negative health consequences, such as added saturated fat in the diet and a potential increase in the risk of developing certain cancers. The evidence that milk may be harmful to children is much less clear, and so far the potential harms are outweighed by the known benefits. While I welcome the results of ongoing research on how milk affects our health, I believe that milk should still be a big part of most children's diets.

Children Need Calcium

When we think of milk, we think of calcium. Calcium plays several roles in the body, but its best known action is to serve as a structural component of bones. It combines with phosphorus to form the glue that holds bones together and makes them dense. Over time, the loss of bone mass can lead to osteoporosis, a condition that afflicts about 10 million Americans and can lead to painful fractures and debilitation.

Several studies have called into question the mantra that high calcium consumption prevents osteoporosis in adults. If calcium is so important for keeping bones strong, why are some of the countries with the highest calcium consumption, such as Scandinavian countries, also those with the highest rates of fractures in the elderly? It is also unclear how much extra calcium in adulthood is actually stored in bones to make them stronger. And no one knows the degree to which calcium consumption is responsible for maintaining strong bones compared with other factors. For instance, exercise helps strengthen bones, especially activities that put body weight on bones, like walking, running, and hiking. And vitamins D and K are needed to regulate calcium and form bones, so they may be just as important as calcium itself.

But there is no question about the role of calcium in children's growth and development. Two factors are known to influence the development of osteoporosis: how much bone you build early on and how much bone you later lose. Osteoporosis has been called a pediatric disease with geriatric consequences. That's because the vast majority of the calcium that is collected into bone is in place by the time a person is seventeen years old, so building bone early on in childhood and adolescence can affect a person's later health.

Most of the research on calcium needs has focused on older children and adolescents aged nine to eighteen. Puberty is the time when bone construction kicks into high gear, and calcium is thought to be more critical during this time of rapid growth. But young children also need calcium, and getting them in the habit of drinking milk or eating other calcium-rich foods now will help get them ready for later years when calcium is more critical.

Milk Is an Efficient Source of Calcium

A lot of the efforts to boost the calcium intake of children has focused on milk—propelled in no small way by the powerful dairy industry in the United States. Despite the clear influence of private interests in a lot of these campaigns, they do have a point. Milk is a very efficient source of calcium. The best estimate for calcium needs of young children aged two to eight is 800 milligrams of calcium per day. With about three cups of milk a day, each containing nearly 300 milligrams of calcium, children eight and under can meet their recommended daily calcium requirement.

A child does not have to drink milk to get calcium. Other dairy products like cheese and yogurt are also great sources. Children who are lactose intolerant—unable to digest the sugar lactose that is present in milk—can often eat yogurt, aged cheeses, or special milk that is low in lactose. Some brands of orange juice and breakfast cereals are now fortified with calcium. Tofu, beans, oranges, and leafy green vegetables like kale, collard greens, spinach, and broccoli also contain a significant amount of calcium. The problem is that it takes a lot of vegetables—several cups a day—to equal the recommended levels of calcium for children, and there are few children I've met who would willingly eat that much kale every day! That's why serving a lot of kid-friendly dairy products in addition to some of these plant sources is generally the best approach for ensuring that most kids consume enough calcium.

Other Benefits of Milk

Milk and other dairy products are also good sources of protein, because they contain proteins that are easily absorbed and closely match the needs of humans (see Chapter 7 for a discussion on protein in foods).

A lot of nutritionists encourage children to drink milk not only out of an appreciation of its benefits but out of fear of the alternatives. As children get older, they tend to drink more sugary sodas and sweetened fruit drinks and less juice and milk. And over the past few decades there has been a gradual increase in the amount of soft drinks that children consume, and a decrease in milk consumption. Milk contains protein, calcium, and other vitamins and minerals. Replace it with a soft drink and you've just removed all those important nutrients from a child's diet without adding anything back except calories from sugar. One of the goals in building a healthy diet is to eliminate sources of empty calories that don't provide the body with other things it needs. By drinking more milk, children are letting their beverage intake benefit their health.

In fact, some nutritionists welcome chocolate milk and other flavored milks that are being offered in stores and in vending machines in some schools. After all, they reason, if children are going to drink sweetened beverages anyway, why not let it be a calcium-rich sweetened milk instead of soda? I'm a little more cautious about embracing flavored milk. Milk is already a fairly high-calorie beverage with lots of natural sugars in the form of lactose. Add even more sugar and you're creating a very high-calorie drink. Some sweetened milk products, like Hershey's Milk Shakes, can pack 600 calories in one bottle! Children who don't like the taste of plain milk can eat other low-fat or fat-free dairy products or calcium-fortified foods instead of relying on flavored milk. At home, you can liven up plain milk without adding a lot of sweetness by mixing in vanilla or cinnamon, or blending milk with fruit as a smoothie. Even homemade chocolate milk, made with a dollop of chocolate syrup or powder, is generally much less sweet than the commercial varieties.

Trim the Fat and Calories

Milk, especially whole milk, does contain a lot of saturated fat, which can raise cholesterol levels and increase a person's risk of developing heart disease. After about two years of age, children should start drinking skim or low-fat milk instead of whole milk, to help reduce the amount of saturated fat in their diets. Skim and low-fat milk also have fewer calories than whole milk but just as much calcium, making it easier for kids to drink enough to fulfill calcium needs without heaping on extra calories. As with any beverage, don't let children drink large amounts of milk as if it were water. Aim for enough milk to cover their calcium needs, but no more.

Juice

Fruit juice is a much better option for children to drink than sweetened beverages and fruit drinks, because it provides vitamins and minerals and because it does not contain sweeteners like high fructose corn syrup that crowd out better foods in their diet. In moderation, juice can be part of a healthy diet, especially as a substitute for sugary beverages or as a way to introduce some added nutrients to breakfasts and snacks of children who do not eat enough fruits and vegetables.

Fruit juice is often marketed as a wholesome, healthy food for children and a source of vitamin C and sometimes calcium. Other food products take advantage of the "halo effect" of juice, advertising that they are sweetened with fruit juice or contain real juice. While it's true that juice does provide some nutrients and is much healthier than sugar-sweetened beverages, it has some serious drawbacks.

Juice Is Not All It's Cracked Up to Be

Juice is very high in calories, most of them in the form of fruit sugars. Drinking large amounts of juice, like any caloric beverage, can add a lot of unnecessary calories to kids' diets. Drinking too much juice can even lead to chronic diarrhea, gas, bloating, and abdominal pain, because the rapid influx of carbohydrates from juice is too much for the small intestine to absorb.

Perhaps the biggest complaint about juice is that it's often seen as a substitute for whole fruits and vegetables. Most juices, unless they are very pulpy, lack the fiber found in whole fruits and vegetables. As mentioned in Chapter 8, dietary fiber includes several kinds of indigestible carbohydrates that may have several benefits for health. Fiber promotes a healthy digestive system, a low cholesterol level, and it smoothes out the response of blood sugar levels to other foods. When you squeeze out an orange for its juice, you are essentially taking the sugars from the fruit and leaving the fiber behind.

While juice retains most of the vitamins and minerals from the original food, there are some components of plants called *phytochemicals* that may be destroyed or reduced in processing. By not eating the fruit or vegetable in its whole form, you could be missing out on some of the health benefits of these substances. And the "juice" that is added to fruit snacks and other foods is very highly processed and may simply contain pure fruit sugars like fructose.

Choose Whole Fruits and Veggies First

Don't think of juice as a substitute for fruits and vegetables. The USDA Food Guide Pyramid states that two servings of a child's daily fruit and vegetable intake can come from juice. But I would urge parents to aim for a full five servings or more of whole fruits and vegetables, and serve a little juice on top of that to children who like it. Only if your child refuses to eat that many fruits and vegetables should you turn to juice as a backup.

Keep Portions Small

Children under twelve are the biggest juice consumers in the United States. Parents don't always set the same limits on juice as they do on soft drinks, because of the

Juices: Reading the Labels

Any beverage containing fruit or vegetable juice is required to label the percentage of the product that is real juice. This statement should appear above the information panel on the juice's label or packaging. Always glance at the ingredient list when you buy juices and other fruit products like fruit spreads, because manufacturers have ways of working around the labeling. Some juices, especially those made of exotic fruits, may actually contain a blend of different fruits with a lot of highly sweet juices like white grape juice. Other juices may add fruit sweeteners or added flavoring while still being advertised as 100 percent fruit juice. Fruit spreads that "contain 100 percent fruit" often contain fruit syrups, pectin, and juice concentrates, all of which help sweeten the product while still technically falling in the category of "fruit." Beverages are not allowed to give the impression they contain juice if they don't—such beverages, such as fruit-flavored waters, must carry a statement saying that they contain no juice.

Children should only drink pasteurized juice, which has been heated to kill any microorganisms that might cause illness. Major brands of juice are generally pasteurized, but some smaller health-food brands offer fresh unpasteurized juice. Companies are required to label unpasteurized juices with a warning, so check the label if you're unsure.

perception that juice is healthy. It's true that 100 percent juice is a more nutritious alternative to sweetened fruit drinks and soft drinks, but it often contains more calories per serving. Juice should only be served as a small glass, the same way you would serve a side of fruit with a meal. The "single-serving" bottles of juice in stores may contain 200 to 300 calories, too much for a refreshing drink. The American Academy of Pediatrics recommends that children aged one to six should drink no more than four to six ounces of juice per day, and children seven to eighteen should drink no more than eight to twelve ounces per day. And there's no reason why a child who already eats a lot of fruits and vegetables needs to drink juice at all.

Beware of "Juice Drinks"

Only drinks that are clearly labeled 100 percent juice count as juices. There are multitudes of other beverages on the market that are "juice drinks," which contain some percentage of juice and often boast their fruit flavors and vitamins and minerals. But look at the ingredient list and you'll see that whatever is not juice is sugar, or another sweetener like high fructose corn syrup. Despite the impression of health and wholesomeness these products project, they are basically soft drinks like soda. In fact, many of them are packaged in larger bottles than soda, making them an especially troubling source of added sugar in children's diets.

Soda and Sweetened Soft Drinks

According to the National Soft Drink Association, Americans guzzled about fifty-two gallons of carbonated soft drinks per person in 2003, an average of a gallon a week. And that doesn't include all the noncarbonated sweetened fruit drinks, lemonades, punches, and powdered drink mixes, many of which are marketed specifically to children. While these various products may have different ingredients and flavors, and some may include a little juice, they are all water with sweetener and can all be considered soft drinks.

Let's take a look at the sweetener used in most soft drinks, high fructose corn syrup. This sweetener was developed about thirty years ago as a cheap alternative to sucrose, or table sugar. It made convenient use of corn, a surplus crop in the United States. High fructose corn syrup is created through a chemical process that turns cornstarch into glucose and then partially to fructose, resulting in a sweetener that is roughly half glucose and half fructose, a ratio similar to table sugar. Sucrose is also made of glucose and fructose, but these two simple sugars are bound together into one molecule, which may affect how the body absorbs it.

Since its introduction, use of high fructose corn syrup has risen more dramatically than any other food product. Along with partially hydrogenated oils, corn syrup has found its way into just about every kind of premade food you can imagine. It is cheap to make, tastes sweeter than sugar so manufacturers can use less of it, and has found its way into beverages as well as baked goods, snack foods, salad dressings, fruit spreads, dairy products, and energy bars. It is estimated that Americans consume between 100 and 300 calories per day in the form of high fructose corn syrup. The cheapness of high fructose corn syrup has allowed it to infiltrate many foods that would never have contained a lot of sugar before; get in the habit of reading food labels and you'll see what I mean. Multiply all those foods over days, weeks, and years, and you'll see that sweeteners have become a major part of our diets. All the added calories from sweeteners either displace something healthier

Caffeinated Kids

On top of all those sweeteners, some soft drinks contain caffeine, a mild stimulant that excites the nervous system, elevates mood, and speeds up the metabolism. The 2004 Sleep in America poll found that 28 percent of first- through third-graders and 18 percent of preschoolers drink one or more caffeinated beverages a day.

Is caffeine harmful to children? While caffeine appears to be a rather benign drug for adults, one that may even carry some health benefits if consumed in moderation, it is still a drug, and an addictive one. When regular caffeine users miss their daily dose, they are often plagued by headaches and irritability. Exposing children to addictive stimulants early in life, even mild ones, is unnecessary and potentially harmful. Because children's bodies are smaller, they are more sensitive to the effects of caffeine, and some children may be particularly susceptible to stimulation. One of the biggest immediate impacts caffeine can have is to interfere with children's natural sleep patterns.

Parents should be on the lookout for caffeine in foods and beverages. Unfortunately, manufacturers are not required to label the amount of caffeine in their products. A 2003 study by Consumer Reports found a surprising amount of caffeine in foods and beverages—for instance, a half-cup of Häagen-Dazs coffee ice cream had as much caffeine as eight ounces of Coke, and a serving of Dannon low-fat coffee yogurt contained as much caffeine as eight ounces of Mountain Dew, one of the most highly caffeinated sodas. Chocolate also contains a small amount of caffeine. And while coffee has traditionally been an adult drink, the highly sweetened milky concoctions that are available in coffee shops today, complete with whipped cream, candy, or sugary syrup, are increasingly appealing to kids (and a nine-and-a-half-ounce

(like more complex carbohydrates, good fats, or protein) or they simply add extra calories that may over time contribute to weight gain.

In recent years, high fructose corn syrup has come under fire from critics who argue that it may be an instigator in the escalating rates of obesity, type 2 diabetes, and other metabolic conditions in adults and children. Some of the criticism focuses on the fructose in the sweetener, which is floating freely rather than being locked up into pairs with glucose in the form of sucrose. George Bray, an obesity and diabetes expert at Louisiana State University, has led the charge against high fructose corn syrup, pointing to evidence that the surge of fructose in our diets, particularly from soft drinks, has led people to consume more calories and gain weight.

bottle of Starbucks Frappucino has almost as much caffeine as *three* twelve-ounce cans of Coke). Energy drinks, which often contain even more caffeine than soda and plenty of sugar, increasingly find their way into soft drink shelves and have bright packaging that may appeal to children.

ITEM	TYPICAL MILLIGRAMS OF CAFFEINE
Coffee (8 ounces, brewed, drip method)	85
Decaffeinated coffee (8 ounces, brewed)	3
Iced tea (8 ounces)	25
Coke (8 ounces)	24
Pepsi (8 ounces)	27
Barq's Root Beer (8 ounces)	15
AMP energy drink (8 ounces)	77
SoBe Energy Citrus Flavored Beverage (8 ounces)	25
Snapple Lemon Iced Tea (8 ounces)	19
Hot cocoa (8 ounces)	6
Chocolate milk (8 ounces)	5
Milk chocolate (1 ounce)	6
M&Ms, plain (¼ cup)	8
Dark semisweet chocolate (1 ounce)	20
Chocolate syrup (1 ounce)	4

It's still unclear whether something about high fructose corn syrup makes it particularly harmful to health. Some people have dismissed these arguments to say that sugar is sugar, no matter what form it takes. But we used to think that fat was just fat, and now we know the picture is more complex—different fats have very different effects on health. But whether high fructose corn syrup acts differently in the body or not, it has already caused a problem in how quickly and completely it has invaded our food supply, allowing sweeteners to become more prevalent than ever before.

About two-thirds of the high fructose corn syrup consumed in the United States is in beverages. Most of these beverages, like soda, contain little more than sweeteners, carbonated water, and flavoring. Other drinks, like Snapple, SoBe, or Fruitopia, contain some fruit juice but also a hefty dose of high fructose corn syrup. These fruit drinks are perceived as healthier, but they are a major source of added sugars and calories in children's diets. For that reason, I would urge parents to put the same limits on these drinks as they would on candy and other sweet foods. If you allow children to drink them occasionally as a treat, you can limit the portion size by not giving them the entire bottle (one bottle of Snapple Mango Madness juice drink contains about the same number of calories as a bar of Hershey's chocolate, and more grams of sugars).

Artificially sweetened diet sodas and fruit drinks can be a good low- or no-calorie alternative to sugary beverages, and can help children who are used to sweetened beverages cut back on calories. Ideally, though, it's best not to get kids hooked on sweet flavors by offering them a lot of diet beverages from the start. The purpose of artificial sweeteners is to fool you into thinking they are sugar, so from the standpoint of establishing healthy tastes and habits, they are one and the same. Later in this chapter, I'll offer some soda alternatives that don't rely on ultrasweet flavors.

Sports Drinks, Fruit-Flavored Waters, and the Rest

Peruse the aisles at your local supermarket and you'll see that beverages are big business. It's no longer a matter of Coke versus Pepsi; today's shopper can choose between several kinds of sweetened fruit drinks, fancy iced teas, imported fruit sodas, sports drinks, flavored waters (sparkling or plain), and energy drinks. While not all of these drinks are marketed to kids, many of them are appealing because they are sweet and refreshing and seem like a good alternative to soda. But it's important to realize that any drink that is not 100 percent juice, milk, or a diet drink almost certainly contains sweeteners, usually in the form of high fructose corn syrup. It may have 10 or 20 percent juice, but it still has a lot of sugar and a lot of calories. Some of these drinks have fewer calories than soda, but they often come in larger bottles.

What about sports drinks? Drinks like Gatorade were developed specifically for athletes to drink during games or bouts of exercise. In addition to water, they contain sugars and salts (often denoted with the fancy term *electrolytes*) that improve the taste and help speed hydration. Sports drinks can help keep children from dehydrating when they are engaged in intense physical activity, especially an activity that gets them sweating and lasts an hour or more. And an active kid who doesn't like to drink a lot of water may find the taste of a sports drink more appealing. But for everyday use, the added ingredients in sports drinks are not necessary for hydration and are simply adding extra calories through sugar, just like any soft drink. Plain old water works fine, and is less expensive.

A few brands of flavored waters are calorie-free. Some sparkling waters have only a hint of flavor and, while they may be too subtle for many kids' tastes, they are a good alternative to sugary soda. Other drinks use artificial sweeteners along with fruit flavor. These might be good alternatives for children who are used to drinking sweetened soft drinks, but as mentioned earlier, there may be a downside to letting children get hooked on the sweet taste of artificially sweetened foods and drinks.

Choosing Beverages for Health

People have a surprisingly accurate ability to regulate the amount of food they eat day to day. If we eat a very large meal, for instance, we tend to make up for it by eating a little less at the next meal. But sweetened beverages seem to throw this natural ability out of whack. Different mechanisms control thirst and hunger in the brain; we are wired to think of solids as food and liquids as water. When we take in a liquid that's full of calories, we don't seem to register those calories in the same way as if they were solid food. Instead, many people can easily guzzle twenty-four ounces of a sweetened beverage as if it were water.

The frightening rise in obesity among children stems from a lot of different factors. But one of the likely culprits is the trend toward drinking larger and larger quantities of beverages, especially sweetened ones. In a study of over five hundred adolescents in Boston as part of the Planet Health project at Children's Hospital, those kids who drank more sugar-sweetened beverages at the outset of the study weighed more for their height, and those who drank more such beverages throughout the study gained more weight. And a 1999 analysis of national dietary survey data found that children who drank more soft drinks ended up taking in more calories overall.

Many parents allow their kids to drink sweetened beverages throughout the day as a substitute for water or as a way to pacify them with something sweet-tasting. When you start to think of caloric beverages as food, you realize how allowing a child to idly sip on a beverage throughout the day can really throw an otherwise healthy diet out of balance, loading it with extra sugars and unneeded calories.

Children do need water to hydrate them throughout the day. Make water the beverage of choice to quench a child's thirst. Other beverages should contribute to

Beverages: The Bottom Line

- A dizzying array of beverages exists to quench our thirst, but nothing beats water for daily hydration. Children should get their liquids by drinking plain and simple water throughout the day.

- Caloric beverages are foods and should be considered a part of the diet like any other food. Avoid the tendency to let children drink caloric beverages as if they were water.

- Even healthier beverages, like fruit juice and milk, should be served in portions that are reasonable for the number of calories they contain.

- Sweetened beverages add nothing but excess calories to a child's diet, and they may be a contributing factor in the rise of obesity and metabolic disorders in children.

- Drinking 100 percent juice in moderation can help add vitamins and minerals to a child's diet. But juice shouldn't substitute for eating fruits and vegetables. Children aged one to six should drink no more than six ounces a day, and older children no more than twelve ounces a day. Diluting juice is a good way to reduce its calorie content and provide a healthier soft drink substitute.

- Milk is an important source of protein and calcium for children. Children over two years of age should drink low-fat or skim milk, to avoid excess saturated fat. Kids who don't like milk should be sure to eat other dairy products and foods rich in calcium.

- Limit soft drinks, fruit drinks, lemonades, and other sweetened beverages. Sports drinks are only beneficial during intense physical activity, otherwise water is fine.

a child's overall diet by providing nutrients—a small glass of 100 percent juice will add vitamins and minerals, while a glass of milk with meals or in cereal will help ensure that your child is consuming enough protein and calcium. Add these drinks to help balance other foods in the diet, but not simply as a thirst-quencher. In general, the more you can avoid sweetened beverages, the better. And when your child does drink them, pay careful attention to portion size. Think of a sweet drink as any treat, such as candy, cookies, or ice cream, and put a limit on how much a child can have at one time. Beware of free refills at restaurants, huge cups of soda, and oversized bottled drinks.

If your child is a big fan of drinking lots of juice or sweet beverages, consider these natural lower-calorie alternatives:

• *Dilute your juice.* There's no reason juice has to be served full strength. By mixing it with water, or making it from concentrate with an extra can or two of water, you can create a beverage that tastes just as good with fewer calories. Try diluting it gradually if your child is already used to full-strength juice. Adding lots of ice can also help water it down.

• *Make your own juice soda.* Instead of plain water, add sparkling water or soda water to juice to make a healthier soda alternative. It's a great refreshment for kids who like the taste and feel of carbonation.

• *Spritz up your water.* Adding a slice of lemon, lime, or orange to plain water can make a leap forward in flavor, adding a nice tinge of citrus while cutting out any tap water taste.

• *Look for soda alternatives.* There are several brands of calorie-free flavored sparkling water on the market. Sometimes the flavors are too subtle for kids' tastes, but it's worth a try as an alternative to soda. There are also newer fruit-flavored waters that have no calories, using artificial sweeteners instead of corn syrup. However, again, relying on too many artificial sweeteners can undermine your efforts to establish healthy tastes.

11

How to Recognize a Healthy (and Unhealthy) School Lunch

So far, I've talked about how parents can learn to choose the best foods for children. But what about the foods you can't choose? Though it would be nice to think that you have complete control over your child's diet, let's get real. As soon as children enter day care or school, they will be exposed to foods that are outside your control. Even if you carefully pack lunches yourself, your children are entering an environment where other food options can tempt them. And most children rely in some form or another on food provided directly at school.

Of course, this can come as a real relief. The National School Lunch Act was passed in 1946, "as a measure of national security, to safeguard the health and well-being of the Nation's children and to encourage the domestic consumption of nutritious agricultural commodities and other food." By recognizing that it is in the nation's interest to provide children with nutritious food at relatively low or no cost, this legislation took an important step toward alleviating hunger and malnutrition among children and taking some of the financial burden off of parents. The program now provides lunch to over twenty-six million children in the country each day. Nearly 88 percent of schools participate in it.

The aims of the School Lunch Program may be admirable, but the nutrition environment of many schools today is deeply flawed. Lunches served at schools can be unhealthy or unpalatable, while candy, soda, and other junk foods are increasingly infiltrating campuses, tempting kids away from lunches served in the cafeteria.

Decades after it first began, the School Lunch Program has become a large, bureaucratic institution we generally take for granted. But even though it is a federal program, it is managed at a local level, so there is a wide variation in how each school district controls its food service. For instance, the Brewster-Pierce Memorial School in Vermont has attracted attention for using organic ingredients and fresh, homemade foods while still participating in the federal lunch program. Food-service director Allison Forest makes foods from scratch, uses whole-wheat pastry flour in baked goods, won't serve processed meats, and is always introducing new fruits and vegetables. And countless other schools are also taking innovative approaches to better nutrition. Parents don't always realize the capacity they have to shape and guide the nutritional policies of their children's schools. All over the country, programs initiated at a local level have helped to create a better environment for nutrition at certain schools. Several states have created laws that build upon the existing federal guidelines, and individual schools have also made their own rules and improvements. Getting to know your school lunch program is an important part of ensuring your child's nutrition. Even if your child attends a school that does not participate in the federal program, this information can help you evaluate how well a school is doing compared with national standards, so you can advocate for changes where needed.

How the School Lunch Program Works

The School Lunch Program is a federal assistance program in which the government gives participating schools cash subsidies and agricultural products for each meal they serve. Schools can select from a list of more than one hundred foods called *entitlement foods* that are distributed by the federal government. Additional "bonus" foods are made available periodically depending on surpluses. And there are special measures in place to make sure that children in need have access to food. Children from families whose incomes fall at or below 130 percent of the poverty level qualify for free meals, while those whose incomes are between 130 and 185 percent of the poverty level can get meals at a reduced price.

In exchange for federal support, the schools must serve meals that adhere to certain nutritional guidelines. Since 1995, the USDA has been working toward improving the nutrition of meals by reducing the fat, saturated fat, cholesterol, and sodium content of foods, while providing more fruits, vegetables, and grains. Meals should contain no more than 30 percent of calories from fat, and less than 10 percent from saturated fat. School lunches should provide one-third of the recommended dietary allowances (RDAs) of protein, vitamin A, vitamin C, iron, calcium, and total calories.

Over the years, schools have gotten better and better at changing the way they cook, using lean meats and avoiding sauces that are high in saturated fat, while adding a variety of vegetables and fruits into meals. School meal planners now have the option of designing meals according to traditional food groupings (fruits and vegetables, meat or meat alternate, grains and breads, and milk), or they can design them based on a computer analysis of the nutrient content of different foods. The quality of school lunches varies widely between different schools and school districts—the healthier programs are often those in wealthier school districts that can afford to be innovative.

And How It Can Fail

Though the School Lunch Program is improving, the current system cheats your child out of the most nutritious food in two important ways. The first relates to how it operates. It is governed by the United States Department of Agriculture—the same folks who gave you the Food Guide Pyramid. And as Walter Willett pointed out in his critique of the food pyramid, the USDA is always serving two masters. On one hand, the organization has a commitment to the nutrition and health of Americans. On the other, its mandate is to promote the big business of American agriculture, including the powerful meat and dairy industries. Read the food nutrition materials created by the USDA, and you will rarely hear anything about the downsides of any food that is an agricultural product of the United States. Why should it be critical of something it's trying to promote?

In the School Lunch Program, the competing interests of the USDA are even more apparent, because foods are provided directly to schools as they become available through agricultural surplus. To put it more bluntly, a lot of the foods that are given to children are leftovers. The federal government buys surplus farm products and sends them to schools to use in their lunches. This plan sounded like a win-win situation; farmers would receive subsidies for their products, children would be fed, and food wouldn't go to waste. Under this system, children become a mass market for industries that often rely on government support for their financial security. This practice means that food choices are made not based simply on nutrition and taste, but on industry pressure. When the beef industry was hurting after September 11, 2001, the USDA responded with a bonus purchase of extra beef for schools. And when cans of salmon were sitting around in Alaska, a request by the state's governor resulted in an influx of salmon into the nation's school lunches. Perhaps the best-known example of politics coming before nutrition was in the 1980s, when ketchup was reclassified as a vegetable as part of several changes made in response to budget cuts. But more recently, the USDA in 2004 approved classifying french fries as a "fresh vegetable," a move that carries financial rewards for companies that process and sell frozen potatoes.

Not only are food choices subject to the whims of political and market forces, but the overall emphasis of food purchases is lopsided. The federal government spends far more money on beef and dairy products than on fruits and vegetables. That's why many school lunch menus are stuffed with beef enchiladas, hamburgers, cheese pizzas, and quesadillas. Meat and dairy products aren't bad for kids; as we discussed in Chapter 7, they are important sources of protein and other nutrients. But loading them into meals, especially if they are not lean or low-fat products, can create a diet that is high in saturated fat and bad for health.

Ideally, the nutritional guidelines set by the federal government would prevent any nutritional imbalances. But these standards are difficult to enforce. A study conducted in 2001 found that, while school lunches have moved toward serving more meals that are lower in fat and saturated fat, the vast majority of schools still fall short of meeting the standards set for them. And the standards are very simplistic, focusing exclusively on fat while ignoring the importance of better carbohydrate sources like whole grains. There is nothing to limit a school from serving lots of refined carbohydrates like white bread, white rice, potatoes, and pasta—in fact, overloading on these foods helps reduce the fat content and makes the meals look better to the USDA.

The system not only creates problems for nutrition, but also for how the meals taste. Salmon is a great, healthy food, for instance, but how are menu planners supposed to devise multiple meals that appeal to kids and also happen to use a lot of salmon? The end result can be uninspired lunches that children hate. And that means they will opt for candy and snacks from vending machines instead.

In the past several years, the School Lunch Program has made significant improvements. It has increased the kinds of foods it provides to schools, offered more fresh fruits and vegetables, and offered schools flexibility in planning meals while better standardizing the nutritional value of those meals. While most schools do depend on food products from the USDA, they have the ability to choose or refuse foods as they see fit. If a school has a motivated food-service director, it can work within the system to design healthy and appealing meals. For instance, Needham High School in Massachusetts has made a point of forgoing french fries and other fried foods in favor of baked snacks and fresh fruits and vegetables.

Despite my criticisms, the federal program does ensure that children receive reasonably nutritious meals, and it is constantly getting better at improving the healthfulness of the foods it provides. It is in many ways an admirable program, given its flaws. But the benefit of these foods depends on children actually eating them. And in more and more schools, vending machines and snack bars tempt children away from the healthier options in the cafeteria. Would you encourage your kid to eat only the healthiest foods and then leave large piles of sweets around the house? That would be crazy. And yet that's the exact result of setting nutritional standards for school lunches while vending machines full of candy and soda sit right outside the lunchroom door. I could not imagine a better way to undermine good nutrition.

Know the Competition

The federal lunch program has only minimal control over other foods that are sold at school, often called "competitive foods" because they compete with the federal lunches for children's money and attention. The USDA prohibits any foods to be sold in the same area and at the same times as school meals if the foods are deemed to be "of minimal nutritional value." This includes foods that fail to provide at least 5 percent of the recommended daily allowance of key nutrients—complete junk foods like soda, chewing gum, and certain candies. But those foods can be sold anywhere outside the lunchroom or during other times of the day. And relatively unhealthy foods such as ice cream, which contains a lot of sugar and saturated fat but does provide at least 5 percent of the RDA of calcium and protein, can be sold right alongside the federal lunches. That's why it's particularly important to check out the policies for competitive foods at your child's school.

For many schools, that translates into a lot of vending machines filled with candy bars and soda in the halls. It means that desserts or other extra foods might be sold in an à la carte line next to the regular lunches. It means that snack bars and stores in the school can sell treats as well, as can school fundraisers. In other words, all those carefully designed, nutritionally sound lunches are looking pretty unappealing in an atmosphere of snacks and sweets. According to a study by the Centers for Disease Control and Prevention, 43 percent of elementary, 74 percent of middle/junior high, and 98 percent of senior high schools have either a vending machine or a school store, canteen, or snack bar. Most of these sell soft drinks, sports drinks, or fruit juices that are not 100 percent juice; salty snacks; and cookies and other baked goods.

Sometimes, private companies can even compete with the lunches themselves. About one in five schools offers brand-name fast foods to students. Some make deals with fast-food companies like Burger King or Taco Bell for exclusive rights to sell food at their school. Usually fast food comes in at the high school level, but it can appear in lower grades as well. Not only are these meals usually high in calories, salt, saturated fat, and sugar, but they create a double threat to the healthier school lunches. Many kids see these brand-name lunches as status symbols, and the children at the school who receive free or reduced-price lunches through the federal program end up feeling stigmatized because they can't afford the flashier foods.

Why, you might ask, are schools willing to undermine the health of their students by making junk food available to them? The answer, in most cases, is money. School administrators have argued that they depend on the money from vending machines and other food sales to support the functions of the school. And school bands, sports teams, parent-teacher groups, and other organizations all see the sales of foods, especially junk food, as a prime source of financial support.

We all would like our schools to have more money available to provide better educational opportunities for children. But remember that the money the school makes from food sales is coming from the children themselves. And in exchange for their money, the school is giving kids foods high in sugar, fat, and excess calories, all while promoting unhealthy eating habits. Is it right to profit on the poor diets of children, even in the name of their own education? If schools depend finan-

To Pack or Not to Pack?

With all this concern over school lunches, should parents just pack all their kid's lunches if they can? The quality of school lunches varies from school to school, so first check out the lunch program at your child's school. Packing lunches offers parents the most control over what their children eat. But many parents simply don't have the time to pack each lunch, and they shouldn't feel that they are giving their children short shrift by relying on school lunches. That said, if you have concerns about the quality of your school's foods, packing may be the best option, or alternating between lunches from home and lunches at school.

The trick to packing lunches is making the healthy foods we've talked about convenient and fun for kids to eat. Unhealthy prepackaged foods are everywhere to tempt you with their convenience—like individual-sized bags of cookies and chips, sweetened drinks in fun colors, and chocolate-covered snack bars. Products like Lunchables offer a conveniently packaged meal but often with a candy bar and sweetened drink along with it, and come at a hefty price. Instead of relying on these convenience foods, it's usually healthier and more economical to buy the foods you choose and package them yourself in individual baggies and small plastic containers. Try preparing them in bulk—a week's worth of carrot sticks in individual servings, for instance. Many stores now offer healthier foods packaged for kids—like sugar-free applesauce, whole wheat crackers, trail mix, carrot sticks with ranch dressing, and low-fat string cheese. Chapter 12 includes some ideas for quick and healthy snacks to pack in lunches.

The goal of feeding kids healthy foods is not to drive them to seek out sweets on their own. After all, your child will be eating that lunch in the midst of all her peers, all with their own lunches packed by parents with different ideas about nutrition. If she feels her lunches are too boring or bland, she may seek out treats in vending machines or from friends. If trying to fill lunches with only the healthiest foods is backfiring, talk to your child to find a compromise that works. For instance, you can offer foods that have some sweetness but still offer something of nutritional value, like fruit-flavored yogurt, trail mix with chocolate chips, chocolate milk, or cookies or snack bars made with whole grains. All kids need treats once in a while; it's just a matter of finding the treats that satisfy them but fit into a healthy diet.

cially on children eating junk foods, how can they have an interest in promoting the health and nutrition of their students? As you can see, this is a difficult problem to solve.

How Do You Create a Healthier Food Environment?

If we were to create a reasonably healthy environment for children at school, what would it look like? Well, we might say that the lunches prepared at school should meet nutritional guidelines but still appeal to kids. We might even improve upon the USDA standards by including more whole grains and fresh fruits and vegetables. We might ask that children not always have to eat whatever surplus food is offered to them if that food is unappealing or unhealthy. We might ask that children be given enough time to eat and fully digest their meals; currently, about 20 percent of schools give children twenty minutes or less to eat their food. (When kids eat too quickly, they outpace the time it takes for the body to feel full and satisfied after a meal; eating meals too fast or on the run can lead to overeating.) We might set limits on the competitive foods that can be sold outside of lunches, asking that foods high in sugar or fat, especially processed foods that contain added sweeteners and trans fats, not be sold at school. We might instead stock vending machines with fruit, whole-grain snacks, low-fat dairy products, 100 percent juices, and bottled waters. We could oppose any deals with private companies for exclusive rights to sell fast food or soda to our children and tempt them away from healthier options.

These are just some of the ways that the food situation at schools could be improved, and these are all strategies that are being piloted and promoted in school districts all over the country. Over the past few years, there has been a burgeoning movement to innovate and improve the nutrition at schools. The growing problem of childhood obesity has spurred many school officials and dietitians to make positive changes at a local level. For example:

- Farm-to-school programs are helping to bring locally grown produce into schools. A school district in California created a "farmer's market salad bar," along with trips to farmer's markets, a school garden project, and education about produce.
- A school in the District of Columbia has banned soda and candy from school—the school doesn't sell them, and students aren't allowed to bring these foods to campus.
- In Maine, a school decided to replace the soda and candy in its vending machines with water, juice, and healthier snack foods like granola bars. At the students' request, fruit and yogurt were later added.
- A pilot program in Nevada will set limits for the fat and sugar content of foods and beverages sold in fundraisers, vending machines, school stores, and à la carte lines in participating schools.

- The New York City School System, the nation's largest school district, is setting nutritional standards for all of the vending machines in its schools, as part of a program to improve all of the foods served on campuses.
- Boston public schools have a new policy that bans the sale of all sodas, sports drinks, and high-fat, high-sugar snack foods that compete with the USDA's National School Breakfast and Lunch Program. Students can choose from healthier foods such as low- and nonfat milks, small servings of fruit juices, and bottled water, as well as smaller serving sizes of chips, granola bars, and trail mixes.

Many other programs are getting in gear, all with the aim of making schools into places that support health, not places that profit from unhealthy eating. One of the biggest excuses not to change the system is fear that the schools will lose money by promoting health. But in many cases, school leaders have found that offering healthy foods isn't a losing prospect. In fact, some students, like the ones in Maine, prefer to eat more varied, healthier foods in vending machines. When kids are raised in health-conscious homes, they learn to expect nutritious foods outside the home. As long as students are offered some real choices that taste good, they won't necessarily choose to eat junk all day.

Do a Little Sleuthing

When your child enters a new day care or school, check out the food environment at the institution. Consider the lunch program itself, but also the foods available on the campus, both inside and outside the lunchroom. Most schools provide a menu to children that details the kinds of entrees served there. But simply looking at the menu won't always tell you about the details. Are the rolls whole-grain or white? Does the school serve low-fat or whole milk? Are the vegetables cooked in a light sauce or steeped in butter? How lean is the beef? In other words, all those choices we've talked about in the preceding chapters can mean the difference between a healthy lunch and a questionable one. And all of this information should be accessible by contacting the school food service or the administration. In addition to looking at the school lunches, find out who decides what foods and drinks are served in vending machines, and whether the school has any policies about the nutritional content of foods, where the machines are located, and when kids can access them. You can also find out whether your state has any special policies restricting competitive foods in schools at fns.usda.gov/cnd/lunch/competitivefoods/state_policies _2002.htm.

If the system at your institution doesn't match up to your nutritional standards, you can help make changes by contacting school officials directly or by working through the PTA or other groups at the school. Your requests will be most productive if they address specific goals and choices about foods. Here are some possible requests:

- All meals should comply with USDA regulations for fat, saturated fat, cholesterol, and nutrient content.
- Fruits and vegetables should be served at every meal, with fresh fruits and vegetables offered regularly.
- Beverages served anywhere at school should include only nonsweetened fruit juice, milk, bottled water or seltzer waters, low-fat or fat-free milk, or milk substitute (like calcium-fortified rice or soy milk).
- Any vending machines on campus should offer healthy beverages and snacks (limit or eliminate candy, sweetened foods, and baked goods and chips containing trans fats; offer healthier foods like whole-grain crackers, trail mix, fresh fruit, yogurt, and low-fat string cheese).
- The school should create a policy for offering healthier treats at school functions and fundraisers.
- The school should not offer brand-name fast foods or enter into contracts with private companies that require the school to serve soft drinks or unhealthy snacks in vending machines.
- When possible, beverages and foods should come in kid-sized portions—for instance, juice boxes instead of large sixteen- or twenty-ounce bottles.
- Children should have enough time to sit down and eat lunch, as well as recess time before or after lunch.

It takes pressure to change any system, and schools will only alter their nutritional policies if parents insist on a healthy environment for their children.

Other Nutrition Programs for Kids and Families

The School Lunch Program is the most widespread federally funded program that relates to children's nutrition. But there are a few other federal programs that pro-

School Lunch Resources

You can make a difference in improving the healthfulness of foods served at schools. Following are resources available for parents who want to promote good school nutrition at the local, state, or national level.

Local Level

- Contact your local school food-service director, principal, or superintendent for information on the lunch program and competitive foods at your school.

- To make changes, work with school officials as well as school groups like the PTA, school board, or city council.

State Level

- Find contact information for state agencies administering the federal child nutrition programs at fns.usda.gov/cnd/contacts/statedirectory.htm.

- Find out if your state has policies for restricting competitive foods in schools at fns.usda.gov/cnd/lunch/competitivefoods/state_policies_2002.htm.

- Contact state legislators or the governor's office to advocate for legislation to improve school foods. The Center for Science in the Public Interest provides examples of proposed and current legislation, as well as a tool kit for improving school foods at cspinet.org/schoolfoods.

National Level

- Find more information on the National School Lunch Program at fns.usda.gov/cnd/lunch.

vide nutritional support to children and parents. Some of these offer special help to kids and families who are economically disadvantaged and who otherwise might have trouble affording healthy foods. For more information about these programs, see the Selected Resources section of this book for a list of websites.

The School Breakfast Program

About 57 percent of schools participate in the School Breakfast Program, which was established in 1966 to ensure that nutritionally needy children would have the opportunity to eat a good breakfast. Like the School Lunch Program, it offers free and reduced-price meals to children who qualify. Breakfasts are supposed to follow the same restrictions in fat, saturated fat, and cholesterol as the lunches, and they must provide one-fourth of a child's needed calories, protein, iron, calcium, vitamin A, and vitamin C. Breakfasts must include milk; a fruit, vegetable, or juice; bread or other grain product; and meat or a meat substitute.

Breakfast is an important meal for children, and several studies have shown that kids who regularly skip breakfast tend to have a lower overall intake of important nutrients. Breakfast foods tend to include milk, juice or fruit, and fortified cereals, so they have traditionally been a good source of vitamins and minerals. Some studies have found that kids who skip breakfast are more likely to be overweight. A study of three schools in Baltimore and Philadelphia found that implementing a school breakfast program can improve academic performance while reducing the rates of tardiness and absenteeism among students. The Breakfast Program can suffer from the same problems as the School Lunch Program—foods that are unappealing or not as healthy as they could be. But it can make a real difference for kids who might otherwise not receive a full, nutritious breakfast at home.

The Special Milk Program

This program from the USDA provides milk to children who don't receive it through the School Lunch or Breakfast programs, often through day-care programs, summer camps, and schools that don't participate in federal lunch programs. The milk served in this program is often whole or 2 percent reduced-fat milk, which are both high in saturated fat and calories. Parents whose children get milk at school through this program can advocate for serving skim or 1 percent low-fat milk, both of which provide the same protein and calcium and are healthier options for children.

The Special Supplemental Nutrition Program for Women, Infants, and Children (WIC)

The WIC program is a large, federally run program that provides free nutritional support and education to low-income pregnant or lactating women and their children up to five years old. About 47 percent of all babies born in the United States participate in WIC, and more than seven million people receive benefits every month. Rather than being part of the educational system, WIC is closely linked to health-care services. WIC participants can get vouchers to buy specific foods that are needed during pregnancy, breast-feeding, infancy, and early childhood. Physicians and other health-care workers can also give WIC participants prescriptions for special infant formulas and foods for specific medical conditions.

WIC is a unique program in its broad approach to child health that includes the health of mothers. A woman's health during pregnancy can affect the health of her child, and many mothers need nutritional support for themselves while they are breast-feeding and caring for infants. Foods offered through WIC are high in protein, calcium, iron, vitamin A, and vitamin C, and might include milk, fruit or vegetable juice, beans, carrots, tuna fish, eggs, and iron-fortified infant or adult cereal. Eligibility for WIC is determined by income and by recommendation by a health professional, usually based on an inadequate diet or medical condition that requires special nutrition. WIC also offers a Farmers Market Nutritional Program, which helps make fresh, locally grown produce available to WIC participants.

Food Stamp Program

This program, run by the USDA's Food and Nutrition Services, is the main source of nutritional assistance for low-income people in the United States. It is an entitlement program, meaning that anyone who meets certain economic criteria is qualified to receive assistance. As unhealthy foods seem to get cheaper and cheaper, the Food Stamp Program can really help families afford the foods that make up a healthy diet. The name is a bit of a relic from the past; participants no longer receive stamps or coupons, but instead use an electronic benefits transfer card that you can often swipe at the checkout counter yourself as you would any debit or credit card. You can contact your state or local welfare office for an application.

12

Recipes and Meal Planning Tips

In this chapter, you'll find nutritious meals for infants and young children. Some of them are easier, some might take a little time, but they all provide delicious options for feeding your kids. Most ingredients can be found in a regular supermarket, and substitutions are noted for items that might be harder to come by.

Foods for Weaning

Infants should start on single-ingredient foods for a few months and gradually work up to mixed-food recipes.

Single-Ingredient Foods for Weaning Four- to Six-Month-Olds

Blended Fruit

Blend fresh or frozen or canned (packed in own juice or light syrup) fruit with water to desired consistency (very smooth and thinner consistency for younger infants and thicker with more texture for the older infant). Strain if seeds, skins, or chunks are present.

You can pour leftovers into ice cube trays and freeze. Then put the cubes into freezer bags and keep in freezer. When ready to use, defrost and heat up the desired number of cubes. Avoid adding sugar, salt, or other spices.

Rice Cereal   *Makes two ½-cup servings.*

    3 tablespoons finely ground brown rice (ground fine in blender or coffee
        grinder)
    1 cup boiling water

Sprinkle ground rice over the boiling water, lower heat to a low simmer, and stir for 8 to 10 minutes. Thin to desired consistency with breast milk or formula. Cool and serve.

 ### The Pros of Store-Bought Cereal

Cereal you find in the supermarket is usually fortified with zinc and iron. These nutrients are especially important for infants four to six months old who can't eat meat. So at this age, store-bought cereals that are unsweetened are superior to the homemade ones you'll see listed for older infants.

Multi-Ingredient Foods for Weaning Six- to Eight-Month-Olds

Barley Cereal

Makes two ½-cup servings.

¼ cup finely ground barley (ground in blender or coffee grinder)
1 cup boiling water

Sprinkle ground barley over boiling water, lower heat to a low simmer, and stir for 8 to 10 minutes. Thin to desired consistency with breast milk or formula. Cool and serve.

Yogurt Cheese

Makes approximately 1 cup.

This recipe condenses the nutrients of the yogurt by reducing the water content. Note that some yogurts have more live, active cultures than others—the brand cited in this recipe provides a lot of cultures.

1 pint Stonyfield Farm plain yogurt
Coffee filter and metal strainer

Place yogurt in coffee filter in strainer and place in a plastic container leaving at least 1 inch between the strainer and the bottom of the container. Cover and refrigerate 1 hour or more (overnight is fine); the longer it sits, the firmer it will become. Mix into cereals or mashed sweet potatoes as desired.

Avocado Mash

Makes approximately three ½-cup servings.

1 ripe avocado
½ cup Yogurt Cheese (see recipe)

Puree avocado in blender or food processor, mix in yogurt cheese, and serve.

Sesame Sweet Potatoes
Makes two ½-cup servings.

1 medium sweet potato
1 tablespoon tahini (sesame seed paste)

Preheat oven to 350°F. Wash sweet potato and poke with a fork several times. Bake until soft, approximately 1 hour. Let cool slightly, cut in half lengthwise, and scoop flesh out of potato. Puree and mix in tahini.

Cottage Cheese and Peaches
Makes approximately three ½-cup servings.

½ cup whole-milk cottage cheese
1 ripe peach (frozen, no sugar, if out of season)

Mash cottage cheese and peach together to a smooth consistency.

Multi-Ingredient Foods for Weaning Eight- to Ten-Month-Olds

Spinach and Beef Mash
Makes two ½-cup servings.

½ pound baby spinach
½ pound 90 percent lean ground beef
2 hard-boiled egg yolks, grated

Wash and dry spinach. Roughly chop or tear into smaller pieces. Place ground beef in sauté pan and cook. Drain fat off and mix spinach and grated egg yolk into warm beef. Puree until smooth in food processor.

What to Do with Leftovers

Many of these recipes make portions much too large for your infant to eat in one sitting, but you can freeze leftovers in ice cube trays or quarter-cup servings and use them for meals later.

Broccoli and Ricotta
Makes four ½-cup servings.

½ pound broccoli
1 cup whole-milk ricotta cheese

Wash broccoli and cut into small pieces. Cook in boiling water for 2 to 3 minutes or until tender when poked with a fork. Drain water. Let broccoli cool a little. Do not run cold water over the broccoli to cool it as this will diminish the nutrients. Puree in food processor, then add ricotta cheese and puree together.

Multi-Ingredient Foods for Weaning Ten- to Twelve-Month-Olds

Brown Rice with Vegetables and Lentils
Makes three 1-cup servings.

1 ½ cups low sodium chicken broth
½ cup brown rice
½ cup lentils (high in protein, iron, and calcium)
½ 10-ounce package mixed frozen chopped vegetables

Bring chicken broth to a boil, add rice and lentils. Lower heat and simmer approximately 45 minutes until rice and lentils are soft. Rinse frozen vegetables under cold water to thaw and add to cooked rice and lentils.

Ground Turkey with Kidney Beans,
Tomato, and Green Beans

Makes five 1-cup servings.

The kidney beans used in this recipe are rich in calcium and iron. This recipe makes quite a lot and you can freeze the leftovers.

    1 pound ground turkey breast
    2 teaspoons dried basil
    1 15-ounce can cooked kidney beans, rinsed and drained
    1 15.5-ounce can diced stewed tomatoes (check label for no sugar)
    1 cup chopped cooked green beans

Sauté ground turkey meat on medium heat until pink color disappears, add dried basil. Drain fat from pan and place turkey in bowl. Add kidney beans, stewed tomatoes (include juice), and chopped green beans. Mix together, heat, and serve.

Foods for Kids One Year and Older

Top Tomato Sauce

Once you make your own delicious and easy tomato sauce you may never buy another canned or bottled sauce. Check labels on canned tomatoes and avoid those that have sugar listed. This family recipe can be doubled or tripled and frozen for later.

    2 peeled carrots, sliced thin
    1 small onion, sliced thin
    2 cloves garlic
    2 tablespoons olive oil
    1 28-ounce can peeled tomatoes
    1 tablespoon dried basil or 2 tablespoons chopped fresh basil

Sauté carrots, onion, and garlic in olive oil for 2 minutes; add tomatoes and basil. Continue cooking for approximately 45 to 60 minutes. Let cool a little and puree in blender or food processor.

Bullwinkle Dip

You may remember your mother or grandmother telling you to "eat that liver on your plate." Well, they were right. Calf's liver contains important nutrients for growing bodies (for example, iron and zinc). The addition of sesame seed paste and mushrooms (also high in zinc) improves the flavor of the liver. Because this recipe is technically calf's liver mousse, we nicknamed it Bullwinkle Dip.

4 ounces calf's liver
¾ cup milk
1 Granny Smith apple, peeled, cored, and sliced
8 ounces cremini or white mushrooms with stems trimmed, washed and
    sliced
1 tablespoon safflower oil
¼ cup orange juice
1 teaspoon ground cinnamon
2 tablespoons sesame tahini
1 tablespoon dried (or 2 tablespoons fresh) chopped parsley

Dice liver into medium to small cubes and cover with milk. Refrigerate 1 hour or more (overnight is fine, too). This reduces bitter taste.

Sauté apple and mushrooms in oil until lightly browned. Remove from pan. Drain milk from the liver and add the liver to the pan. Cook liver until centers of cubes are light pink. Remove liver and add orange juice to the pan. Cook it until the quantity is reduced by half. Add juice to liver and cool. Place liver, mushrooms, and apples in blender or food processor; add cinnamon, tahini, and parsley. Puree until smooth and chill.

This is great alone or on a whole-wheat cracker or apple slice for toddlers. Note that you should be sure that your child has had each of the ingredients separately before introducing this recipe into his or her diet.

Magic Meatballs   *Makes four servings.*

This recipe also makes great hamburgers with more protein and calcium for the little one!

½ pound baby spinach, washed and dried
1 15-ounce container whole-milk ricotta cheese
1½ pounds lean ground beef

Preheat oven to 350°F. Tear spinach leaves (something your child can help with) or roughly chop. Combine ricotta with chopped spinach, add meat, and mix well. Now here comes the magic. Press mixture into a cookie sheet with sides, bake until juices are no longer pink, and cool. Let your child use cookie cutters to create specially shaped "meatballs." Alternatively, you can roll the meat mixture into small meatballs (another thing Junior can do) or use a melon scooper to form. Serve with Top Tomato Sauce (see recipe).

Spaghetti Squash "Spaghetti"   *Makes four servings.*

1 large spaghetti squash
2 red peppers
2 zucchini
2 tablespoons olive oil

Preheat oven to 375°F. Poke squash with a fork several times. Place whole squash in baking dish and put into preheated oven. While squash bakes, dice peppers and zucchini. Toss vegetables in a small bowl with olive oil. After squash has cooked for 1 hour, add diced vegetables to baking dish. Continue cooking for another 30 minutes (or more) until squash is soft to the touch. Remove squash from pan keeping any juices vegetables may have created. Let squash cool so you can handle it. (Tip: Keep a bowl of ice water nearby, so you can quickly dip your hands in it if you try to pick up the squash while it's still too hot.) Cut squash in half from stem to bottom. Use a large fork to strip out the spaghetti-like strands of squash by pulling from top to bottom of squash. Place in a bowl and mix with cooked vegetables and the juices from the pan. Serve with Top Tomato Sauce (see recipe) and any grated cheese.

Banana Jam

Makes 1 cup.

A great alternative to jelly for sandwiches or maple syrup for pancakes.

½ cup pureed ripe bananas
1 teaspoon ground cinnamon
1 teaspoon vanilla extract
½ cup Yogurt Cheese (see recipe)

Mix pureed bananas with cinnamon, vanilla, and Yogurt Cheese. If necessary, thin the mixture with a little extra Yogurt Cheese. For sandwiches, add less yogurt to achieve a thicker consistency.

Pancakes

Makes approximately ten 4-inch pancakes.

½ cup whole-wheat flour
¼ cup soy flour (a great way to sneak in some extra protein!)
½ cup oat bran
¼ cup wheat germ
½ teaspoon ground cinnamon
1 teaspoon baking powder
½ teaspoon baking soda
2 large eggs
1½ cups buttermilk
1 teaspoon vanilla extract
Safflower oil for cooking

In a large bowl combine whole-wheat flour, soy flour, oat bran, wheat germ, cinnamon, baking powder, and baking soda. In another bowl combine eggs, buttermilk, and vanilla. Add liquid to dry ingredients and mix well. Lightly coat bottom of pan with safflower oil. Use 2 tablespoons batter for each pancake. When bubbles appear on pancake, flip and cook on other side until lightly browned.

Colorful Rice and Beef

2 ripe avocados
Juice from 1 lemon
½ cup brown basmati rice
1 pound lean ground beef
1 15.5-ounce can black beans (high in protein, calcium, and iron)
1 28-ounce can diced tomatoes (look for tomatoes with no sugar added)
2 teaspoons chili seasoning
1 teaspoon ground cumin

Cut avocados into ½-inch cubes, toss with lemon juice (to keep the pieces from turning brown), and set aside. Bring 1 cup water to a boil. Add rice, bring back to a simmer, cover and simmer gently for approximately 30 to 40 minutes, or until tender. Cook ground beef in another pan until juices are no longer pink. Drain fat from beef. Mix black beans, tomatoes, chili seasoning, and cumin in a large bowl. Add drained beef and cooked rice. Add avocados to cooked beef and rice mixture before serving.

Spinach Loaf   *Makes 1 loaf.*

2 packages frozen chopped spinach
6 large eggs
1 cup part-skim ricotta cheese
½ cup Parmesan cheese or soy Parmesan cheese

Preheat oven to 375°F. Spray 10″ × 6½″ pan with cooking spray (like Pam). Defrost spinach under cold running water (do not use microwave) or leave in a bowl in refrigerator overnight. Mix eggs with ricotta and Parmesan cheese. Add defrosted spinach and mix until blended. Pour into prepared pan and bake approximately 45 minutes or until firm to touch.

Trail Mix   *Makes 9 cups.*

You needn't include every item on the following list, just those that appeal to you. When shopping for ingredients, look for fruits with no added sugars, and nuts and seeds without added salt. It's okay to have one or two types of salted nuts or seeds, but more than that will add too much sodium. Warning: May be a choking hazard for kids under three years old.

1 cup roasted pepitas (pumpkin seeds)
1 cup roasted peanuts
1 cup roasted green peas
1 cup roasted edamame (soy beans)
1 cup roasted almonds
1 cup dried pears (no sugar added)
1 cup dried cherries (no sugar added)
1 cup dried plums (a.k.a. prunes!)
1 cup dried apricots (no sugar added)
½ cup almond meal
1 tablespoon ground cinnamon

Place all seeds and nuts in a large bowl. Cut dried fruits into bite-size pieces—this is also a good way to check for stray pits. Toss cut fruits with almond meal and cinnamon. Add to nuts and seeds and toss together. Store in airtight containers or portion in small Ziploc bags. Keep extra nuts and seeds in freezer or refrigerator. Extra dried fruits, nuts, and seeds are great in hot breakfast cereals or yogurt!

Snacks for Kids Two and Older

Here are some fun and nutritious snack recipes for children aged two and over.

Bag of Snack

Goldfish crackers

Cheerios

Raisins (Omit raisins for children under three years of age, as they may be a choking hazard.)

Small pretzels

Mix all ingredients and place in small Ziploc bags for a healthful, portable snack.

Edible Candle   *Makes two servings.*

1 banana

2 canned pineapple rings

2 cherries

Cut banana in half; stand into pineapple rings; place cherry on top of each for flame.

Purple Cow

1½ cups milk

3 tablespoons frozen grape juice concentrate

½ cup frozen vanilla yogurt

Mix all ingredients in blender and enjoy.

Popsicles

Pour 100 percent fruit juice into an ice cube tray; put a plastic spoon in each section; freeze and enjoy. (Or use plastic "Popsicle" molds.)

Ants on a Log

Celery

Cream cheese or peanut butter

Raisins (Warning: May be choking hazard for children under three years of age.)

Cut celery into sticks; spread cream cheese or peanut butter onto sticks; place raisins on top.

Orange Banana Flax Bread

Makes 2 loaf pans or 24 muffins.

1½ cups oat bran
1 cup ground flaxseed
1½ cups whole-wheat flour
1 tablespoon baking powder
1 teaspoon ground cinnamon
2 oranges, peeled, seeded, and cut into quarters
4 large ripe bananas
1 teaspoon baking soda
1 teaspoon vanilla extract
2 large eggs
1 cup buttermilk
½ cup safflower oil or olive oil (use olive oil light in color)
1 cup golden raisins

Preheat oven to 375°F. Spray two loaf pans (or two 12-cup muffin tins) with cooking spray. Combine bran, flaxseed, whole-wheat flour, baking powder, and cinnamon in a large bowl. Blend oranges, bananas, baking soda, vanilla, eggs, buttermilk, and oil in blender or food processor until smooth. Add to dry ingredients and mix until blended. Add raisins and pour into prepared pans. Bake 25 to 30 minutes in loaf pans or 12 to 15 minutes for muffins (or until toothpick comes out clean). Cool 5 minutes before turning out of pan.

Green Eggs and Ham

Makes two servings.

2 slices lean ham
2 handfuls baby spinach (washed and dried)
4 large eggs, beaten in a small bowl
½ ripe avocado cut into small pieces (Avocados are ripe when they yield slightly to touch.)

Dice or tear ham into small pieces. Coat pan with cooking spray and place on medium heat. Sauté ham and spinach until spinach wilts and ham is warm. Add beaten eggs. Stir gently until eggs are cooked. Add avocado and serve.

Sample Meal Plan for Two- to Eight-Year-Olds

Breakfast

¼ to ½ cup 100 percent juice

½ to 1 egg (or ¼ to ½ cup low-fat cottage cheese, 1 to 2 tablespoons peanut butter, 1 to
    1½ ounces cheese or meat)

½ to 1 slice whole-grain bread or ¼ cup unsweetened cereal

4 to 8 ounces milk

Morning Snack

½ natural peanut butter and jelly sandwich on whole-wheat bread or 3 to 4 whole-grain
    crackers with ½ to 1 ounce cheese

Lunch

1 to 2 ounces ground beef, poultry, fish, or tofu

¼ to ½ cup vegetable with 1 teaspoon nonhydrogenated margarine

¼ to ½ cup potato, rice, or pasta

¼ to ½ cup fruit or ½ to 1 piece of fruit

4 to 8 ounces skim or 1 percent milk

Afternoon Snack

4 ounces plain yogurt with ¼ to ½ cup fruit or 2 tablespoons hummus with vegetable sticks
    (Warning: May be a choking hazard for children under three years old; cook carrots or
    other vegetables for a short time in the microwave to soften them for younger toddlers.)

Dinner

1 to 2 ounces meat, poultry, fish, or tofu

¼ to ½ cup deep green or yellow vegetable, sprinkled with 1 ounce cheese

¼ to ½ cup whole-grain bread, potato, rice, or pasta

¼ to ½ cup fruit

4 to 8 ounces skim or 1 percent milk

Evening Snack

½ to 1 grilled cheese sandwich on whole-wheat bread or ¼ to ½ cup low-fat pudding or ½
    to 1 cup skim or 1 percent milk

Green Pea Soup
Makes approximately 6 cups.

It doesn't get any easier than this!

2 ripe avocados, peeled, pitted, and cut into pieces
¼ cup lemon juice
20 to 24 ounces low sodium chicken broth
1 16-ounce bag frozen green peas, thawed
1 teaspoon ground cumin
½ teaspoon salt

Toss avocado pieces with lemon juice and set aside. Bring chicken stock and peas to a boil. Remove from heat. Drain broth from pan and save. Place peas and avocados in blender or food processor and puree until smooth. Gradually add chicken broth to desired consistency. Add cumin and salt. This soup can be served hot or cold. Adding a little Whole-Wheat Couscous (see recipe) makes a nonmeat meal with complete protein.

Whole-Wheat Couscous
Makes four ½-cup servings.

Note that whole-wheat couscous may not be available at your corner grocery store. Try specialty stores such as Whole Foods or Trader Joe's.

1 cup whole-wheat couscous
1 cup water
2 tablespoons olive oil

Place couscous in a bowl. Bring water and oil to a boil and pour over couscous. Cover and let stand 5 minutes. Fluff with a fork and serve. Add to Green Pea Soup (see recipe) to make soup a complete protein, or serve as a side dish with vegetables.

Alternatives to Unhealthy Frozen Foods

INSTEAD OF FROZEN . . .	TRY . . .
French fries	Baked potato "fries": Slice potatoes or sweet potatoes, place on pan sprayed with oil, sprinkle with olive oil, and bake.
Pizza	Mini pizza: Use half of a medium whole-grain pita, bagel, or English muffin, add tomato sauce and mozzarella cheese, and bake.
TV dinners	Ready-made broiled chicken with fresh, frozen, or canned vegetables. Or, when you have the time, make a double portion of a dish and freeze for later use.

Broccoli Polenta and Cheese   *Makes four 1-cup servings.*

1 cup water
1 cup low-fat milk
1 teaspoon salt
½ cup quick-cooking polenta
½ to 1 cup part-skim shredded cheese (cheddar, mozzarella, or whatever you like)
1 cup cooked, chopped broccoli

Bring water, milk, and salt to a simmer. Stir in polenta. Lower heat to medium and continue stirring for approximately 6 to 10 minutes. Remove from heat. Stir in cheese and cooked broccoli. Serve plain or with Top Tomato Sauce (see recipe).

Oatmeal Cookies

Makes approximately 5 dozen.

1 cup oatmeal
2 cups whole-wheat flour
1 teaspoon ground cinnamon
1 teaspoon baking powder
½ to ¾ cup raisins
3 ripe bananas
4 large eggs
½ cup safflower or olive oil
1 cup pumpkin seeds (high in essential fatty acids, fiber, and iron)
1 teaspoon vanilla extract

Preheat oven to 350°F. Place oatmeal, flour, cinnamon, baking powder, and raisins in a large bowl. Puree bananas in blender or food processor; add eggs, oil, pumpkin seeds, and vanilla extract. Blend until smooth. Add pureed mixture to dry ingredients and mix. Coat cookie pans with cooking spray. Spoon teaspoonfuls of batter onto pans and bake 8 to 10 minutes.

Crustless Vegetable Quiche

Makes one 10-inch quiche.

6 large eggs
1 cup skim or low-fat milk
Your favorite hot sauce to taste, keeping in mind your child's preferences
2 cups frozen diced mixed vegetables, thawed
1 cup shredded low-fat cheese (your choice)

Preheat oven to 375°F. Beat eggs and milk together; add hot sauce, vegetables, and cheese. Coat 10-inch pie pan with cooking spray. Pour mixture in pan and bake approximately 40 minutes or until top is firm to touch.

Healthy Desserts

Even if you serve desserts, there are ways to make them healthier, including the following:

- Low-fat frozen yogurt (instead of ice cream)

- 100 percent frozen fruit-juice pops

- Low-fat or low-sugar pudding

- Fresh fruit

- Cake without frosting or with low-fat whipped topping

- Cheesecake made with low-fat cream cheese and egg whites

- Graham crackers with peanut butter

- Low-sugar Jell-O

Orange Dip for Fruit   *Makes 2 cups.*

1 16-ounce container low-fat cottage cheese
4 to 6 ounces frozen orange juice concentrate
1 teaspoon vanilla extract

Blend cottage cheese in blender or food processor until smooth. Add orange juice concentrate and vanilla to taste. Chill and serve with fruit for dipping.

Fruit Tofu "Ice Cream"   *Makes four 1-cup servings.*

2 cups frozen strawberries (or blueberries, peaches, or whatever you like)
1 16-ounce container soft tofu
4 tablespoons frozen orange juice concentrate

Place frozen fruit in blender or food processor and mix until broken into small pieces. Add tofu and orange juice concentrate and mix until smooth. Serve immediately.

Tofu "Ice Cream" Popsicles

Place leftover tofu ice cream into "Popsicle" molds, in ice cube trays, or small paper cups with a plastic spoon in each section or cup, and freeze.

Whole-Wheat Couscous Pudding   *Makes 3 cups.*

1¼ cups low-fat milk
½ cup whole-wheat couscous
1 cup Orange Dip for Fruit (see recipe)

Bring milk to a boil and pour over couscous. Cover and let sit 30 minutes or until milk is totally absorbed. Add 1 cup Orange Dip for Fruit. Chill and enjoy.

Tahini (Sesame Seed) Dipping Sauce   *Makes 1 cup.*

Sesame seeds are a great source of zinc.

2 cloves garlic
½ teaspoon salt
½ cup tahini
¼ cup water
¼ cup safflower or olive oil
2 teaspoons dried cilantro or 1 tablespoon chopped fresh cilantro
1 tablespoon chopped flat Italian parsley
½ teaspoon ground cumin

Chop the garlic fine and whisk together with remaining ingredients. Use as a dipping sauce for Crispy Chicken Fingers or on Falafel in Whole-Wheat Pita (see recipes).

Crispy Chicken Fingers
Makes two servings.

1 skinless and boneless chicken breast
1 large egg, beaten
¼ teaspoon ground cumin
¼ teaspoon salt
¼ teaspoon pepper
½ cup almond meal (You can buy this or make your own by grinding almonds in a coffee grinder or blender.)

Preheat oven to 350°F. Spray cookie pan with cooking spray. Rinse and dry chicken breast. Slice into strips. Dip in beaten egg and sprinkle with cumin, salt, and pepper. Roll in almond meal and place on cookie pan. Bake approximately 10 to 15 minutes, or until meat is white in the center. Serve with Creamy Citrus Dressing or Tahini Dipping Sauce (see recipes).

Creamy Citrus Dressing
Makes approximately 3 cups.

This is a great dressing with a lower ratio of oil to citrus than most classic vinaigrettes, and the tofu adds protein.

¾ cup orange juice
2 tablespoons lemon juice
6 to 8 ounces tofu
1 tablespoon dried parsley or 2 tablespoons chopped fresh parsley
1 teaspoon salt
1¼ cups safflower or olive oil

Place orange juice, lemon juice, tofu, parsley, and salt in blender. Blend briefly. Resume blending and slowly add oil. Place in covered container and store in the refrigerator.

Falafel in Whole-Wheat Pita

Makes 4 sandwiches.

Chickpeas (garbanzo beans) are a good source of protein, calcium, and iron.

1 small onion
1 15.5-ounce can chickpeas
½ cup flat Italian parsley leaves with stems removed, washed and dried
1 large egg
1 teaspoon dried cilantro or 2 teaspoons chopped fresh cilantro
1 tablespoon tahini (sesame paste; optional)
Olive oil or safflower oil for cooking
Whole-wheat pita, lettuce, tomato, avocado, and Tahini Dipping Sauce (see
    recipe) for sandwich

Peel onion and cut into small pieces. Rinse and drain chickpeas and set aside. Place onion and parsley in food processor or blender. Blend until smooth. Drain off excess liquid. Transfer to a small bowl and set aside. Place rinsed chickpeas in food processor or blender and blend until smooth. Add egg. Then add onion and parsley mixture, cilantro, and tahini and blend until smooth. Lightly coat bottom of a frying pan with a thin layer of oil and heat on medium heat. Carefully place one tablespoon of batter at a time in pan and press with the back of a spoon to flatten slightly. Sauté until golden brown on one side and turn and do the same on the other.

You can also bake these in a 375°F oven. Lightly coat a sheet pan with oil and using a tablespoon, place mixture onto pan, using back of spoon to flatten slightly. Bake for 15 to 20 minutes or until set.

Serve in a whole-wheat pita with lettuce, tomato, avocado, and Tahini Dipping Sauce (see recipe). You can also serve falafel over a salad or by itself.

Chicken Salad with Granny Smith Apples, Toasted Walnuts, and Creamy Citrus Dressing

Makes two servings.

3 to 4 ounces walnuts, broken into small pieces
8 ounces cooked chicken, cut into bite-size pieces
8 ounces mixed salad greens, chopped (The darker the color the better!)
2 Granny Smith apples, seeded and cut into bite-size pieces
Creamy Citrus Dressing (see recipe)

Place walnuts in pan on medium heat and stir for 2 to 3 minutes to toast. Remove and cool. Mix chicken, greens, apples, and walnuts together and toss with Creamy Citrus Dressing. Serve alone, place in whole-wheat pita, or roll in a whole-grain tortilla shell or sandwich wrap.

Bean Dip for Veggies

Makes approximately 3 cups.

Pinto beans and navy beans are good sources of calcium, iron, and protein.

1 large tomato, or 1 15.5-ounce can diced tomatoes, drained (no sugar added)
1 15-ounce can pinto beans
1 15-ounce can navy beans
7 ounces tofu
2 teaspoons ground cumin
1 teaspoon dried cilantro or 2 teaspoons chopped fresh cilantro
1 tablespoon dried parsley or 1 tablespoon chopped fresh parsley

Cut tomato in half horizontally and squeeze out seeds. Cut tomato into small pieces and set aside. Rinse and drain pinto and navy beans. In food processor or blender, puree beans and add tofu, cumin, cilantro, and parsley and puree until smooth. Place in bowl and mix in tomato pieces, cover and refrigerate for at least one hour before serving. Use as a dip for vegetables (slightly cooked vegetables for children under three) or as a sandwich spread.

Broccoli Slaw or Cole Slaw with
Balsamic Vinaigrette

Makes four 1-cup servings.

½ cup balsamic vinegar
1 teaspoon dried basil or 2 teaspoons chopped fresh basil
½ teaspoon salt
2 teaspoons Dijon mustard (or any mustard)
1 cup olive, safflower, or canola oil
1 10-ounce bag shredded cabbage or broccoli slaw

To make the vinaigrette, mix the balsamic vinegar, basil, salt, and mustard in a blender. While blending, slowly add oil. Place shredded cabbage or broccoli slaw in a bowl and toss with vinaigrette. Chill and serve.

Carrot Salad with Crushed Pineapple
and Creamy Citrus Dressing

Makes approximately four ½-cup servings.

½ to 1 cup crushed pineapple (no sugar added)
1 pound carrots, peeled and grated
½ to 1 cup Creamy Citrus Dressing (see recipe)

Squeeze juice from pineapple (save juice for drinking or discard). Mix pineapple together with carrots and Creamy Citrus Dressing. Chill and serve. You could also add this to a pita pocket sandwich or roll in a soft whole-grain tortilla or sandwich wrap.

Mashed Sweet Potatoes with Green Beans
and Balsamic Syrup   *Makes four 1-cup servings.*

4 medium sweet potatoes
8 ounces frozen green beans, thawed
1 cup balsamic vinegar
½ cup Creamy Citrus Dressing (see recipe)

Preheat oven to 375°F. Wash sweet potatoes and pierce several times with a fork. Place in pan or on cookie sheet and bake approximately 45 minutes or until soft. While potatoes are cooking, cut green beans into very small pieces. Set aside. Put balsamic vinegar in a saucepan on low heat and simmer until reduced by half the volume and vinegar becomes syrupy. When potatoes are cooked, remove from oven and let cool for approximately 10 minutes. Cut potatoes in half and scoop out centers. Mash with a fork and add green bean pieces and Creamy Citrus Dressing; mix well. Place on serving dish and drizzle with balsamic syrup.

Watermelon, Spinach, and Ham Salad   *Makes three servings.*

8 ounces spinach, washed, dried, stems removed
1 1-inch-thick slice of watermelon, cut into bite-size pieces (½-inch cubes),
    with seeds removed
6 ounces lean ham, cut into bite-size pieces
Creamy Citrus Dressing (see recipe)

Chop spinach into bite-size pieces. Mix watermelon, spinach, and ham pieces together. Toss with Creamy Citrus Dressing.

Easy Packed Lunches

Try these ideas for packing healthy but appealing lunches for school-age children:

- Use a small thermos or insulated coffee cup to pack soups (such as the Green Pea Soup in this group of recipes), leftover pastas, or casseroles.
- Freeze a small bottle of water, individual carton of low-fat milk, or 100 percent juice box to put in the lunch for a cold drink.
- Use an insulated lunch bag with an ice pack to pack perishable foods like Crustless Vegetable Quiche (see recipe); a tuna salad sandwich made with lettuce, pickles, celery, and green peas; a lean ham, turkey bologna, or turkey sandwich with lettuce, tomato, and low-fat cheese; or chicken salad with celery, cut-up grapes, green peas, and lettuce.
- Add a piece of fresh fruit or individual fruit cups packed in juice (not syrup).
- Withholding treats from lunches can backfire if kids are tempted with sweet foods at school. Serve a healthier treat, like Oatmeal Cookies (see recipe).
- Opt for low-fat chips, pretzels, and crackers. Graham crackers can be a good choice. Many snack foods now advertise whole grains and no trans fats (hydrogenated or partially hydrogenated oils), so look for these at your local store. Whole-grain breakfast cereals also make good snack foods when eaten plain.
- Serve snack-size portions of raw vegetables with packets of low-fat salad dressing.
- The most convenient foods are often the least healthy. Plastic containers now come in extra-small sizes for packing healthful dips and dressings, like the ones in this chapter.
- Fill a small container with plain yogurt, unsweetened applesauce, and berries or granola for an alternative to high-sugar yogurt and puddings.
- Low-fat string cheese or nuts make good high-protein snacks. Nuts are calorie-dense and should be served in small portions.
- Whole-wheat pita bread or tortillas make a fun substitute for bread to make sandwiches.

Selected Resources

T his section provides resources for additional reading on various topics that you might find helpful.

Growth Charts

The following six figures are the growth charts referred to in Chapters 3, 4, and 6.

Websites

cdc.gov/growthcharts

Growth charts from the U.S. Centers for Disease Control and Prevention can be viewed or downloaded at this website of the CDC's National Center for Health Statistics.

CDC Growth Charts: United States

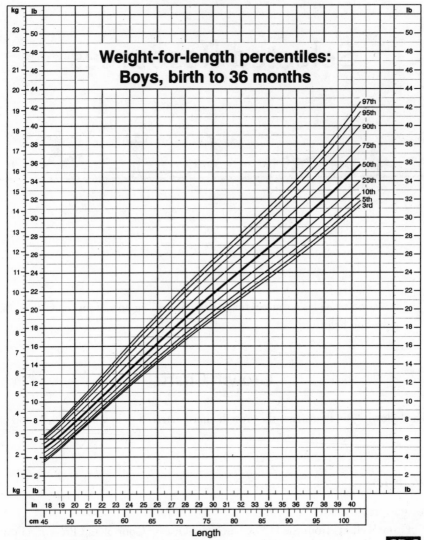

Weight-for-length percentiles: Boys, birth to 36 months

Length

Published May 30, 2000 (modified 6/8/00).
SOURCE: Developed by the National Center for Health Statistics in collaboration with
the National Center for Chronic Disease Prevention and Health Promotion (2000).

SAFER · HEALTHIER · PEOPLE™

CDC Growth Charts: United States

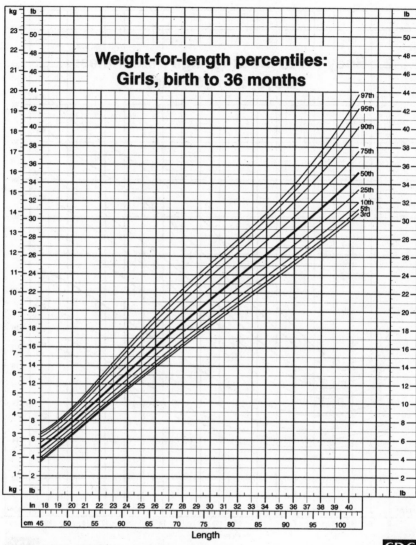

Weight-for-length percentiles: Girls, birth to 36 months

Published May 30, 2000 (modified 6/8/00).
SOURCE: Developed by the National Center for Health Statistics in collaboration with
the National Center for Chronic Disease Prevention and Health Promotion (2000).

SAFER·HEALTHIER·PEOPLE™

CDC Growth Charts: United States

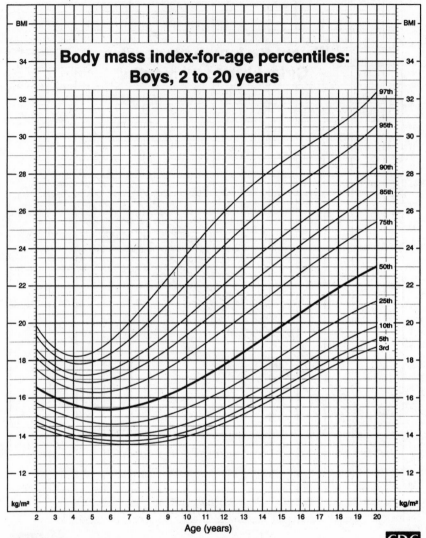

Body mass index-for-age percentiles:
Boys, 2 to 20 years

Published May 30, 2000.
SOURCE: Developed by the National Center for Health Statistics in collaboration with
the National Center for Chronic Disease Prevention and Health Promotion (2000).

CDC
SAFER·HEALTHIER·PEOPLE™

CDC Growth Charts: United States

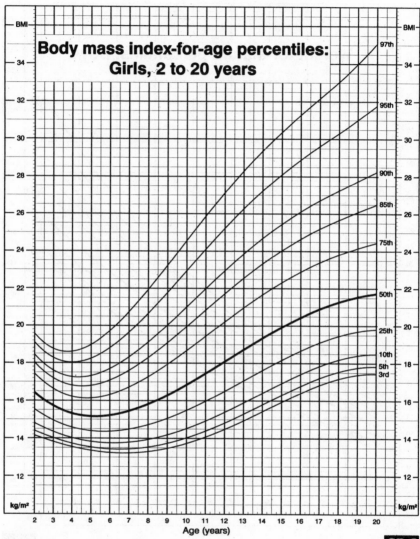

Body mass index-for-age percentiles:
Girls, 2 to 20 years

Published May 30, 2000.
SOURCE: Developed by the National Center for Health Statistics in collaboration with
the National Center for Chronic Disease Prevention and Health Promotion (2000).

CDC

SAFER · HEALTHIER · PEOPLE™

CDC Growth Charts: United States

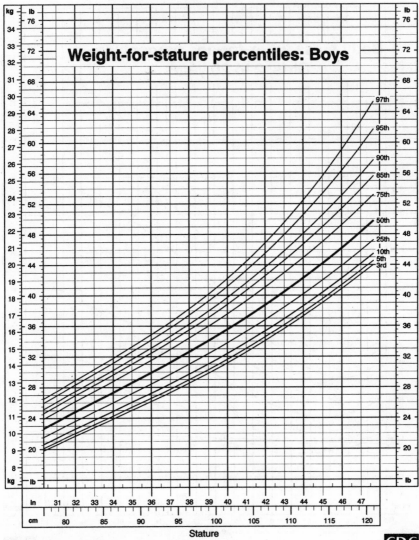

Weight-for-stature percentiles: Boys

Published May 30, 2000 (modified 11/21/00).
SOURCE: Developed by the National Center for Health Statistics in collaboration with
the National Center for Chronic Disease Prevention and Health Promotion (2000).

CDC
SAFER • HEALTHIER • PEOPLE™

CDC Growth Charts: United States

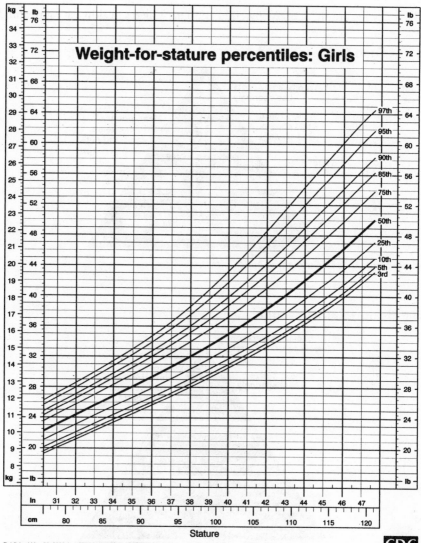

Weight-for-stature percentiles: Girls

Stature

Published May 30, 2000 (modified 11/21/00).
SOURCE: Developed by the National Center for Health Statistics in collaboration with
the National Center for Chronic Disease Prevention and Health Promotion (2000).

CDC

SAFER·HEALTHIER·PEOPLE™

Food Guide Pyramids

The following are the USDA's pyramid and Dr. Willett's healthy eating pyramid.

USDA Food Guide Pyramid

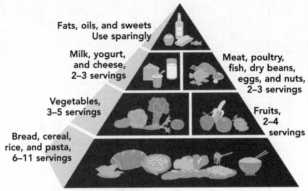

Fats, oils, and sweets
Use sparingly

Milk, yogurt,
and cheese,
2–3 servings

Meat, poultry,
fish, dry beans,
eggs, and nuts,
2–3 servings

Vegetables,
3–5 servings

Fruits,
2–4
servings

Bread, cereal,
rice, and pasta,
6–11 servings

Adapted from U.S. Department of Agriculture

The Healthy Eating Pyramid

Alcohol in moderation
(unless contraindicated)

Use
sparingly

Sweets,
potatoes,
white rice,
white bread,
and pasta

Red
meat,
butter

Dairy or calcium sup-
plement, 1–2 times a day

Fish, poultry, and
eggs, 0–2 times a day

Nuts and legumes,
1–3 times a day

Vegetables,
in abundance

Fruits,
2–3 times
a day

Whole grains,
at most meals

Plant oils, including
olive, canola, and corn

Daily exercise and weight control
Multiple vitamins for most

Adapted from *Eat, Drink, and Be Healthy; The Harvard Medical School Guide to Healthy Eating* by Walter C. Willett, M.D. (Simon & Schuster, 2001)

General References

Books

Kleinman, Ronald, ed. *Pediatric Nutrition Handbook*, 5th ed. Dallas: American Academy of Pediatrics, 2002.

Sears, William, et al. *Dr. Sears' Lean Kids*. New York: New American Library, 2003.

Walker, W. Allan, John B. Watkins, and Christopher Duggan, eds. *Nutrition in Pediatrics: Basic Science and Clinical Application*, 3rd ed. Hamilton, Ontario: B. C. Decker, Inc., 2001.

Willett, W. C., and P. J. Skerrett. *Eat, Drink, and Be Healthy: The Harvard Medical School Guide to Healthy Eating*. New York: Simon and Schuster Source, 2001.

Websites

brightfutures.org

Bright Futures at Georgetown University is an initiative whose mission is to promote the health and well-being of children by improving relationships between them and their families, health-care professionals, and the general community. Its website has links for educational resources and training tools.

cdc.gov/nccdphp/dnpa/tips/index.htm

The Centers for Disease Control and Prevention (CDC) is an agency of the Department of Health and Human Services committed to protecting and improving the health of the general population. Their website contains tips and resources for healthy eating.

usda.gov/cnpp/kidspyra

The Center for Nutrition Policy and Promotion (CNPP) is a part of the U.S. Department of Agriculture. The CNPP researches and develops nutrition policy within the USDA and publishes materials for dietary guidance. Their website contains a Food Guide Pyramid for Young Children.

Breast-Feeding

Books

Lawrence, R., and R. M. Lawrence. "Approach to Breastfeeding." In *Nutrition in Pediatrics: Basic Science and Clinical Application*, 3rd ed., edited by W. Allan Walker, John Watkins, and Christopher Duggan, 562–79. Hamilton, Ontario: B. C. Decker, Inc., 2001.

Journal Articles

Bernt, K., and W. Walker. "Human Milk as a Carrier of Biochemical Messages." *Acta Paediatrica Supplement* 88 (1999): 27–41.

Committee on Drugs. "The Transfer of Drugs and Other Chemicals in Human Breast Milk." *American Academy of Pediatrics* 93 (1994): 137–50.

Websites

lalecheleague.org

The mission of La Leche League International is to promote breast-feeding and provide support and education for mothers who wish to breast-feed. The website contains general information as well as links to product catalogs and to other resources.

4woman.gov/breastfeeding

The National Women's Health Information Center is a project of the U.S. Department of Health and Human Services. Its website provides information and educational resources about breast-feeding. This site contains guidelines for breast-feeding, a section of commonly asked questions, and a hotline number for mothers to call.

Weaning

Journal Articles

Briend, A., et al. "Linear Programming: A Mathematical Tool for Analyzing and Optimizing Children's Diets During the Complementary Feeding Period." *Journal of Pediatric Gastroenterological Nutrition*, January 2003, 12–22.

Hallberg, Leif, et al. "The Role of Meat to Improve the Critical Iron Balance During Weaning." *Pediatrics* 111 (2003): 864–70.

Mehta, K. C., et al. "Trial on Timing and Introduction to Solids and Food Type on Infant Growth." *Pediatrics* 102 (1998): 569–73.

WHO Working Group on the Growth Reference Protocol. "Growth of Healthy Infants and the Timing, Type, and Frequency of Complementary Foods." *American Journal of Clinical Nutrition* 76 (2002): 620–27.

Nutrition After Weaning

Journal Articles

Garza, Cutberto, and Edward Frongillo. "Infant Feeding Recommendations." *American Journal of Clinical Nutrition* 67 (1998): 815–16.

Smith, M. M., et al. "Carbohydrate Absorption from Fruit Juice in Young Children." *Pediatrics* 95 (1995): 340–44.

Sutphen, J. L. "Growth as a Measure of Nutritional Status." *Journal of Pediatric Gastroenterological Nutrition*, April 1985, 169–81.

Weight Control and Physical Activity

Journal Articles

Bowman, Shanthy, et al. "Effects of Fast-Food Consumption on Energy Intake and Diet Quality Among Children in a National Household Survey." *Pediatrics* 113 (2004): 112–118.

Bray, G. A. "Predicting Obesity in Adults from Childhood and Adolescent Weight." *American Journal of Clinical Nutrition* 76 (2002): 497–98.

Committee on Nutrition of the American Academy of Pediatrics. "Prevention of Pediatric Overweight and Obesity." *Pediatrics* 112 (2003): 424–30.

Dietz, W. H. "Critical Periods in Childhood for the Development of Obesity." *American Journal of Clinical Nutrition* 59 (1994): 955–59.

Rolls, B. J. "The Supersizing of America: Portion Size and the Obesity Epidemic." *Nutrition Today*, March 2003, 42–53.

Rolls, B. J., D. Engell, and L. L. Birch. "Serving Portion Size Influences 5 Year Old but Not 3 Year Old Children's Food Intakes." *Journal of the American Dietetic Association*, February 2000, 232–34.

Websites

niddk.nih.gov/health/nutrit/nutrit.htm

The National Institute of Diabetes and Digestive and Kidney Diseases (NIDDK) is a part of the National Institutes of Health that researches these diseases and is also involved with treatment and prevention. Its website provides information about weight loss and control.

Fruits and Vegetables

Websites

hsph.harvard.edu/nutritionsource/fruits.html

This website from the Department of Nutrition at the Harvard School of Public Health contains information about the health benefits of eating fruits and vegetables, especially their role in lowering the risk of certain diseases.

ams.usda.gov/nop/indexie.htm

The National Organic Food Program is a part of the U.S. Department of Agriculture. It is the source of certification standards for organic food. The website outlines the standards organic products must meet and the process of becoming certified.

Vitamins, Minerals, and Dietary Supplements

Journal Articles

Committee on Nutrition of the American Academy of Pediatrics. "American Academy of Pediatrics: Calcium Requirements of Infants, Children, and Adolescents." *Pediatrics* 104 (1999): 1152–57.

Websites

supplementinfo.org

This website for the Dietary Supplement Information Bureau contains information about dietary supplements, including details about their regulation by the government. There is also an alphabetical list of supplements with explanations about their origins and uses.

http://vm.cfsan.fda.gov/label.html

This part of the U.S. Food and Drug Administration's website contains explanations about the claims on food labels, as well as other nutritional information and resources.

nichd.nih.gov/milk/whycal/food_pyramids.cfm

The National Institute of Child Health and Human Development is part of the National Institutes of Health. The mission of this organization is to keep children healthy, both before and after they are born. This website provides information about the benefits of calcium for children.

nal.usda.gov/fnic/foodcomp

Part of the U.S. Department of Agriculture, the Nutrient Data Laboratory found at this website is a database of information about the nutritional value of foods.

Beverages

Books

Zeisel, S. H., et al. "Dietary Supplements (Nutraceuticals)." *Nutrition in Pediatrics: Basic Science and Clinical Application*, 3rd ed., edited by W. Allan Walker, John Watkins, and Christopher Duggan, 986–96. Hamilton, Ontario: B. C. Decker, Inc., 2001.

Journal Articles

Ludwig, D. S., K. E. Peterson, and S. L. Gortmaker. "Relation Between Consumption of Sugar-Sweetened Drinks and Childhood Obesity: A Prospective, Observational Analysis." *Lancet*, February 2001, 505–8.

Websites

epa.gov/safewater/dwhealth.html

This website provides information from the U.S. Environmental Protection Agency about the United States water supply, its safety, and the standards that it is held to.

School Lunch and Other Food Programs

Websites

cspinet.org/schoolfoods

Center for Science in the Public Interest is an advocacy organization whose goal is to conduct research and operate as an educational resource about general health for consumers. This website is a guide and instructional tool kit for improving foods and beverages in schools.

The mission of the Food and Nutrition Service, which is part of the U.S. Department of Agriculture, is to provide the public with education about nutrition and better access to food and a more healthful diet. The following websites are all from the FNS.

fns.usda.gov/fsp

This website contains information on the Food Stamp Program, the main source of nutritional assistance for low-income people in the United States.

fns.usda.gov/cnd/lunch

The National School Lunch Program is run by the FNS to provide healthy, low-cost or free lunches to children who need them. This website provides information about the program, as well as links to other resources.

fns.usda.gov/cnd/breakfast

This website has information on the School Breakfast Program, which provides breakfast before school to children and offers free and reduced-price meals to those who qualify.

fns.usda.gov/cnd/contacts/statedirectory.htm

This website provides contact information for the state agencies that oversee federal child nutrition programs.

fns.usda.gov/cnd/lunch/competitivefoods/state_policies_2002.htm

This website outlines the guidelines for the school meals programs of each state. It also outlines state policies for restricting the sale of foods that compete against the school lunch.

fns.usda.gov/cnd/milk

The Special Milk Program provides milk to children who don't receive it through the School Lunch or Breakfast programs.

fns.usda.gov/wic

Special Supplemental Nutrition Program for Women, Infants, and Children (also called the WIC Program) provides free nutritional support and education to low-income pregnant or lactating women and their children.

Index